T0214668

Post-Human Futures

This volume engages with post-humanist and transhumanist approaches to present an original exploration of the question of how humankind will fare in the face of artificial intelligence. With emerging technologies now widely assumed to be calling into question assumptions about human beings and their place within the world, and computational innovations of machine learning leading some to claim we are coming ever closer to the long-sought artificial general intelligence, it defends humanity with the argument that technological 'advances' introduced artificially into some humans do not annul their fundamental human qualities. Against the challenge presented by the possibility that advanced artificial intelligence will be fully capable of original thinking, creative self-development and moral judgement and therefore have claims to legal rights, the authors advance a form of 'essentialism' that justifies providing a 'decent minimum life' for all persons. As such, while the future of the human is in question, the authors show how dispensing with either the category itself or the underlying reality is a less plausible solution than is often assumed.

Mark Carrigan is Postdoctoral Research Associate in the Faculty of Education at the University of Cambridge, UK.

Douglas V. Porpora is Professor of Sociology in the Department of Communication at Drexel University, USA.

The Future of the Human
Series Editor

Margaret Archer, University of Warwick, UK

Until the most recent decades, natural and social science could regard the 'human being' as their unproblematic point of reference, with monsters, clones and drones were acknowledged as fantasies dreamed up for the purposes of fiction or academic argument. In future, this common, taken for granted benchmark will be replaced by various amalgams of human biology supplemented by technology – a fact that has direct implications for democracy, social governance and human rights, owing to questions surrounding standards for social inclusion, participation and legal protection. Considering the question of who or what counts as a human being and the challenges posed by anti-humanism, the implications for the global social order of the technological ability of some regions of the world to 'enhance' human biology, and the defence of humankind in the face of artificial intelligence, the books in this series examine the challenges posed to the universalism of humankind by various forms of anti-humanism, and seek to defend 'human essentialism' by accentuating the liabilities and capacities particular to human beings alone.

Titles in this series

Realist Responses to Post-Human Society: Ex Machina
Edited by Ismael Al-Amoudi and Jamie Morgan

Post-Human Institutions and Organizations
Confronting The Matrix
Edited by Ismael Al-Amoudi and Emmanuel Lazega

Post-Human Futures
Human Enhancement, Artificial Intelligence and Social Theory
Edited by Mark Carrigan and Douglas V. Porpora

For more information about this series, please visit: www.routledge.com/The-Future-of-the-Human/book-series/FH

Post-Human Futures

Human Enhancement, Artificial Intelligence
and Social Theory

**Edited by Mark Carrigan
and Douglas V. Porpora**

Routledge
Taylor & Francis Group

LONDON AND NEW YORK

First published 2021
by Routledge
2 Park Square, Milton Park, Abingdon, Oxon OX14 4RN

and by Routledge
52 Vanderbilt Avenue, New York, NY 10017

Routledge is an imprint of the Taylor & Francis Group, an informa business

British Library Cataloguing-in-Publication Data
A catalogue record for this book is available from the British Library

Library of Congress Cataloging-in-Publication Data
Names: Carrigan, Mark (Mark Alexander), editor. | Porpora, Douglas V., editor.
Title: Post-human futures : human enhancement, artificial intelligence and social theory / edited by Mark Carrigan and Douglas V. Porpora.
Description: Abingdon, Oxon ; New York, NY : Routledge, 2021. | Series: The future of the human | Includes bibliographical references and index.
Identifiers: LCCN 2020049911 (print) | LCCN 2020049912 (ebook) | ISBN 9780815392781 (hardback) | ISBN 9781351189958 (ebook)
Subjects: LCSH: Technological innovations—Social aspects. | Artificial intelligence—Social aspects. | Humanity.
Classification: LCC HM846 .P67 2021 (print) | LCC HM846 (ebook) | DDC 303.48/3—dc23
LC record available at https://lccn.loc.gov/2020049911
LC ebook record available at https://lccn.loc.gov/2020049912

ISBN: 978-0-815-39278-1 (hbk)
ISBN: 978-0-367-76143-1 (pbk)
ISBN: 978-1-351-18995-8 (ebk)

Typeset in Times New Roman
by Apex CoVantage, LLC

Contents

Illustrations

Figures

Tables

Contributors

Ismael Al-Amoudi is Professor of Social and Organisational Theory and Director of the Centre for Social Ontology at Grenoble Ecole de Management, Université Grenoble Alpes (Communauté Université Grenoble Alpes, France). His work borrows from anthropology, management studies, political philosophy, social theory and sociology. One recurring theme in his research concerns the nature of social norms and the basic processes through which they are legitimated and contested. Another theme concerns the contribution of ontology to the human and social sciences. He is a member of the editorial boards of *Organization* and of the *Journal for the Theory of Social Behaviour*. Recent publications include articles in the *Academy of Management Learning and Education, British Journal of Sociology, Business Ethics Quarterly, Cambridge Journal of Economics, Human Relations, Journal for the Theory of Social Behaviour, Organization,* and *Organization Studies*.

Margaret S. Archer founded the Centre for Social Ontology at the Ecole Polytechnique Fédérale de Lausanne in 2011, where she was professor of social theory. Currently she is Visiting Professor at the Arctic University of Norway, Tromsø; the University of Navarra (Pamplona); and the Uniwersytet Kardinała Stefana Wyszńskiego in Warsaw. Pope Francis appointed her as President of the Pontifical Academy of Social Sciences in 2014. Previous to that, she was elected as the first woman president of the International Sociological Association at the 12th World Congress of Sociology (1986). She was a founding member of both the Pontifical Academy of Social Sciences and the Academy of Learned Societies in the Social Sciences and is a trustee of the Centre for Critical Realism. She has published many well-known works on social theory including *Culture and Agency: The Place of Culture in Social Theory* (1988), *Realist Social Theory: The Morphogenic Approach* (1995), *Being Human: The Problem of Agency* (2001), *Structure Agency and the Internal Conversation* (2003), *Making Our Way through the World: Human Reflexivity and Social Mobility* (2007), and *The Reflexive Imperative in Late Modernity* (2012).

Mark Carrigan is a sociologist in the Faculty of Education at the University of Cambridge. His research explores how the proliferation of digital platforms is reshaping education systems, with a particular focus on knowledge production within universities. He is a fellow of the RSA, co-convenor of the SRHE's Digital University Network, co-convenor of the BSA's Digital Sociology group, co-convenor of the Accelerated Academy, a member of the Centre for Social Ontology, an associate member of CHERE at Lancaster University and a research associate in the Public Policy Group at LSE. His current research looks at questions of digital platforms through the lens of the structure and agency debate.

Pierpaolo Donati is Alma Mater Professor (PAM) of Sociology at the University of Bologna. Past president of the Italian Sociological Association, he has served as an executive committee member of the IIS and director of the National Observatory on the Family of the Italian Government. He is currently a member of the Pontifical Academy of Social Sciences (since 1997) and of the Academy of Sciences of the University of Bologna (since 1998). He has published more than 800 works. He is known as the founder of an original 'relational sociology' or 'relational theory of society'. Among his more recent publications are *Relational Sociology: A New Paradigm for the Social Sciences* (2011); *The Relational Subject* (with Margaret S. Archer; 2015); *Discovering the Relational Goods* (2019); *Life as Relation: A Dialogue between Theology, Philosophy, and Social Science* (with A. Malo and G. Maspero; 2019); and *Sociología relacional de lo humano* (2019).

Gazi Islam is Professor of People, Organizations and Society at Grenoble Ecole de Management and member of the research laboratory IREGE (Research Institute for Management and Economics). He has served as faculty at Insper, Tulane University, and the University of New Orleans. He is editor for the Psychology and Business Ethics section at the *Journal of Business Ethics*. His current research interests revolve around the contemporary meanings of work and the relations between identity, group dynamics and the production of group and organizational cultures.

Emmanuel Lazega is Professor of Sociology at the Institut d'Etudes Politiques de Paris (Sciences Po), a member of the Centre de Sociologie des Organisations (CNRS) and a senior member of the Institut Universitaire de France. His current research projects focus on social network modelling of generic social processes such as solidarity, control, regulation and learning. His publications can be downloaded from www.elazega.fr.

Andrea M. Maccarini is Professor of Sociology and Associate Chair in the Department of Political Science, Law and International Studies, University of Padova. He is Head of the Class of Social Sciences in the Galilean School of Higher Studies. He has been Chair of the Italian Sociological Association (AIS) section of Education and has served as Italian representative at the governing board of OECD-CERI (Centre for Educational Reform and Innovation). His main research interests lie in social theory, cultural change and the sociology of education. He is the author or editor of several books and articles, including *Deep Change and Emergent Structures in Global Society;*

Explorations in Social Morphogenesis (2019) and *Sociological Realism* (edited with E. Morandi and R. Prandini, 2011).

Jamie Morgan is Professor of Economic Sociology at Leeds Beckett University. He co-edits the *Real-World Economics Review* with Edward Fullbrook. He has published widely in the fields of economics, political economy, philosophy, sociology and international politics. His recent books include *Trumponomics: Causes and Consequences* (edited with E. Fullbrook, 2017), *What Is Neoclassical Economics?* (2015), and *Piketty's Capital in the Twenty-First Century* (edited with E. Fullbrook, 2014).

Douglas V. Porpora is Professor of Sociology in the Department of Communication, Drexel University, and co-editor of the *Journal for the Theory of Social Behaviour*. He has published widely on social theory. Among his books are *Reconstructing Sociology: The Critical Realist Approach* (2015), *Landscapes of the Soul: The Loss of Moral Meaning in American Life* (2001), *How Holocausts Happen: The United States in Central America* (1992) and *The Concept of Social Structure* (1987).

Introduction

Conceptualizing post-human futures

Mark Carrigan and Douglas V. Porpora

This is the third volume in a series we began in 2017 after completing a prior project on what we termed 'social morphogenesis'. This speculative notion invited us to consider the viability and character of a social order in which change came to achieve a final victory over stasis, as the possible horizon for what comes after *late modernity, second modernity* and *liquid modernity*, to name the three most influential epochal diagnoses which cast a long shadow over social thought in the 1990s and 2000s (Beck 1992, Giddens 1991, Bauman 2000). While we reached no consensus among our interdisciplinary group of philosophers, sociologists, economists and international relations scholars, it was a productive exercise which led to five volumes that between them analysed a remarkably diverse array of social, cultural and agential changes alongside the meta-theoretical question of what *is* change and how do we come to *know* it (Archer 2013). Two themes stood out among the many that cut through this inquiry: the significance of emerging technology and how, if at all, human beings come to be challenged by their diffusion. There was a certain inevitability, therefore, that our next project would turn to the place, and challenges, of the human in an emerging social order in which some technologies, once emerging (e.g., the smartphone, wearable computing, social networking, machine learning and the internet of things), are rapidly becoming ubiquitous parts of daily life, while other technologies, still emerging, hold out the possibility of yet more radical social change.

In the first volume, *Realist Responses to Post-Human Society*, we sought to examine the ways in which recent advances in technology threaten to blur and displace the boundaries constitutive of our shared humanity. In the second volume, *Post-Human Institutions and Organizations*, we adopted a more sociological focus through analysis of the role of smart machines in driving change within the basic organizations and institutions responsible for social integration. In this volume, we deepen the dialogue between these two clusters of issues, turning our attention to *post-human futures*, with a particular emphasis on the social and cultural significance of artificial intelligence.

Philosophy concerns itself, as Sellers once put it, with understanding how things in the broadest sense of the term hang together. Our project across these volumes could be summarized as understanding where social life, in the broadest sense, is going. The human is our focal point for this concern because these technologies have emerged from our own productive capacities, actuated within organizational contexts and embedded within broader systems of production and exchange. But what becomes of *Homo faber* in an age of intelligent machines? As you will see, we take issue with many of the existent treatments of emerging technologies and human nature while nonetheless taking seriously the possibility that a profound change is, or soon will be, underway. Explaining what we mean by this claim, not to mention the conceptual grammar inherent in making it, entails a brief detour through accounts of the human and their relationship to socio-technical change.

Humanism, post-humanism, transhumanism

The theorist of the post-human Cary Wolfe (2010) begins his book *What Is Post-humanism?* by identifying a discrepancy. At that time, despite the much-heralded demise of humanism, the phrase 'humanism' returned 3,840,000 hits on Google while 'post-humanism' returned only 60,200. Doing similar searches a decade later,[1] we found the returns had reached 11,000,000 and 497,000, respectively. It was inevitable that both would have increased for the simple fact that the internet has grown in the preceding decade while the search engine's indexing of it has become more comprehensive. It is, however, clear that post-humanism has grown *more* in this time. There's a limited amount we can meaningfully infer from this change, but it's a striking example of how the time horizons of scholarly publishing can fail to grasp the pace at which the world publications describe is changing. While searching in this way lacks robustness as a digital method, it does illustrate how the discursive universe of post-humanism has exploded in a period of time that barely registers in scholarly publishing. Ten years is not a long time for academic writing, but it is an eternity when it comes to understanding an emerging philosophical movement with a foundation in rapid social, cultural and technological change. It is for this reason that we will advocate treating *humanism, post-humanism* and *transhumanism* in historical terms, shaped by history while contributing to shaping it. This task first necessitates that we achieve a degree of clarity about what these terms mean, how they relate to each other and the work they do within the world.

Although humanism is widely criticized by post-humanists as defending a white, imperialist, masculinist version of the human, humanism's proponents often understand it as a defence of the qualitative aspects of humanity not capturable by the positivist reduction of the human being to quantitative variable analysis. Our intention at this stage is not to intervene in this debate but rather to point to the contested nature of these terms and the ambiguity they give rise to in debate. As Davies (2008: 2) points out, "Humanism is a word with a very complex history and an unusually wide range of possible meanings and contexts," to an extent which troubles attempts to fix its meaning within what Porpora (2003: 22) calls the critical space of argument and counterargument. It too easily slips into being an elicitation device to encourage the reiteration of pre-established positions as opposed to a deeper exchange about *how* we talk in these terms and *what* we are trying to achieve by doing so. Furthermore, it becomes difficult to retain any purchase on the question of how intellectual doctrines propounded by social scientists and philosophers relate to what's going on 'out there'. Even if most would agree that theoretical debates don't drive cultural change in wider society (at least in any sort of straightforward or consistent manner), we're left with the question of what the causal relation is and how it ought to inform our debating. The same point can be made about post-humanism and transhumanism. However, there's an important sense in which these are anchored by humanism, producing a great chain of ambiguity which lies at the heart of a voluminous literature in the social science and the humanities. For this reason, we don't attempt in this introduction to provide definitive accounts of these terms but rather to elucidate the thrust of these positions, as well as to reconstruct some of the meta-theoretical questions which tend to get lost within a polarized (and polarizing) debate.

Braidotti (2013) usefully distinguish between three forms of post-humanism circulating within the academy: (1) a 'reactive' post-humanism she identifies with thinkers like Martha Nussbaum; (2) the recognition of non-human actors and agents found in actor-network theory; and (3) a concern for the shifting reality of the human condition among speculative post-humanists such as herself. If we assume her first category designates advocates of humanism, with the 'post' simply indicating the contemporary character of their advocacy,[2] this helpfully illustrates how philosophical, methodological and disciplinary factors mix together in establishing the matrix of humanism, post-humanism and transhumanism. Fuller and Lipinska (2014: 3) stress the cultural orientations which drive these differences: the post-humanist inclination "towards 'humbling' human ambitions in the face of nature's manifestly diverse and precarious character"[3] and the transhumanist inclination towards "diagnosing humanism's failure in terms of insufficient follow-through on its own quite reasonable ambitions." By focusing on the thrust of these disagreements, it becomes to easier to get beyond the ambiguity which plagues these debates.

This contrasting reaction to humanism is why Wolfe (2010) emphasizes the importance of distinguishing between transhumanism and post-humanism, "two diametrically opposed responses to the shortfalls of the modern humanist worldview" (Fuller & Lipinska 2014: 3). He sees the former as antithetical to the latter, representing an intensification of humanism rather than a retreat from it. As Whitaker (2017) puts it, transhumanism "takes the central tropes of modernity and injects them with steroids – infinity, progress, the transcendence of bodily confines, control over evolution, belief in the human capacity to remake itself, the limitless capabilities of human intellect." In this sense we can see it as a radicalization of modernity rather than a rejection of it, a belief in the capacity of science and technology to let us act back upon ourselves and leave behind the fleshy inheritance which has constrained our capacity to realize our human potential. In its most dramatic manifestations, transhumanism manifests itself in a focus on the deferral of death, uploading ourselves to the machine, or the consequences of the much-invoked singularity. But these spectacular claims, with their tendency to blur the boundary between philosophical speculation and science fiction, risk obscuring the underlying continuities with humanist thought. Thus, philosopher

Nick Bostrom, founding director of the Future of Humanity Institute, frames transhumanism as a continuation of individualistic humanism but in a way which dispenses with the assumption that "the human condition is and will remain essentially unalterable." He considers technological advances such as super-intelligent machines, recalibration of the brain's pleasure centres, space colonization, vastly extended life spans and reanimation of cryonics patients as real possibilities which ought to inform "how we perceive the world" and "how we spend our time" (Bostrom 2001). As he puts it:

> Transhumanism has roots in secular humanist thinking, yet is more radical in that it promotes not only traditional means of improving human nature, such as education and cultural refinement, but also direct application of medicine and technology to overcome some of our basic biological limits.
>
> (Bostrom 2005)

In a discussion of "the integration of cutting-edge research in nano-, bio-, info- and cognosciences for purposes of extending the power and control of human beings over their own bodies and their environments," Fuller (2011: 102–105) draws attention to the different ways in which this agenda has been conceived and the distinct human future implied by each of them. Each of these comes with distinct moral, political and economic challenges: a 'reflexive evolution' brought about by genetics and an extension of the lifespan in some sense belong in the same category but nonetheless have to be dealt with in their specificity. This is why Fuller and Lipinska (2014) stress the collective and normative implications of these developments in contrast to what they identify as a libertarian tendency preoccupied by morphological freedom. While they share an understanding of transhumanism as "the indefinite promotion of the qualities that have historically distinguished humans from other creatures, which amount to our seemingly endless capacity for self-transcendence," they recognize the profound challenge that follows from this capacity: "What does it meant to act responsibly in a world where we are aiming to increase our power among many dimensions at once?" (Fuller & Lipinska 2014: 1).

Epochal theorizing about post(human) futures

Our concern is less with the specifics of these doctrines as much as what they imply about potential futures and the work they do towards their realization. We can only gesture here to the complexity of the debates that have emerged within the voluminous literature on the question of humanism as well as the shift through which post-humanism came to replace anti-humanism as humanism's fundamental antagonist.[4] In the interests of making a virtue out of this vice, we should stress that treating these positions *as positions*, which is to say as doctrines developed in the context of scholarly exchange, risks obscuring the socio-cultural and socio-technical currents (particularly the groups, organizations and movements with their material and ideational interests) to which these formulations sit in ambiguous relationship. Herbrechter (2013) notes that terms such as 'post-human', 'post-humanist' and 'post-humanism' have a longer history than one might suspect, even if they only began to receive academic attention as the new millennium began to unfold. He observes that the texts that initiated this explosion of academic interest, described by the political commentator Mason (2019) as the 'post-human industry', clustered around the end of the twentieth and the beginning of the twenty-first centuries. The question thus is how much concern with the post-human reflects a fin de siècle experience of social transition and the pathologies that accompany it (Alexander 1995). With the benefit of hindsight, the social panic surrounding the 'millennium bug', the expectation of widespread software failure because of a ubiquitous technical shortcoming, looks something akin to a millenarian panic[5] manifesting from increasing social understanding of our reliance on digital infrastructure. The fact this bug would (theoretically) leave systems unable to distinguish between 1900 and 2000, as a consequence of encoding dates with two rather than four digits, underscores the point: the technology that we expected would take us forward into the new millennium might instead leave us lodged in the century we expected to leave behind.

Alexander (1995: 8) argues that formulations like 'modernity', 'socialism' and 'capitalism' describe "deep shifts in historical sensibility" as well as "competing theoretical positions." The same point holds about the upsurge of writing that identifies itself as post-humanist, and a sense of historical consciousness pervades this literature. For example, Wolfe (2010: xv–xvi) talks in terms of an "historical moment in which the decentering of the human by its imbrication in technical, medical, informatic and economic networks is increasingly impossible to ignore," leading to the necessity of "new theoretical paradigms" and a "new mode of thought that comes after the cultural repressions and fantasies, the philosophical protocols and evasions, of humanism as a historically specific phenomenon." This formulation leaves it rather unclear whether the significant factor is the extent of this immersion[6] (ontological), the unavoidability with which it presents itself as an object of awareness (epistemological) or the combination of both at this particular historical juncture. There is an avant-garde tendency within this literature, valorizing *creation* as a response to *novelty* (we need new ideas, terms and frames to respond adequately to these new times) but doing so in a way which too often leaves the former unmoored from the latter (Ghosh 2018: 220–223). In this introduction, we want to recover this link between our changing circumstances and the intellectual resources through which we seek to make sense of them. We are not denying the reality of changes taking place or their potential significance. However, we are insisting the ontological, epistemological and methodological complexity involved in diagnosing epochal shifts be recognized from the outset, at least if we aspire to do more than simply register the aggregate of empirical changes which can be identified (Archer 2013).

Much post-humanist discourse is an example of what Savage (2009) calls "epochal theorizing": a preoccupation with detecting new kinds of transformation that underscore the uniqueness of the times in which we are living. This point was made in response to concepts of *late modernity, liquid modernity* and *second modernity*, which proliferated within British sociology, constituting

> a kind of sociology which does not seek to define its expertise in terms of its empirical research skills, but in terms of its ability to provide an overview of a kind that is not intended to be tested by empirical research.
>
> (Savage & Burrows 2007)

Once, however, we recognize the influence of these epochal accounts – as well as the de-differentiated character of contemporary social theory identified by Mouzelis (2003), which enables conceptual innovations to circulate across disciplinary boundaries more easily than was previously the case – the apparent differences melt away to disclose an obvious similarity. Epochal theorizing is prone to what is sometimes called 'the shock of new' in ways which can obscure ironic continuities between our present circumstances and their postulated future.

It is worth noting how much the rhetoric of authors like Fuller and Lipinska (2014) echoes that of Giddens (2006) in his pronouncement that we have moved beyond left and right. While the nature of the change understood to be taking place varies significantly between these figures, there is a common structure to the claim they make: sociological and technological developments have brought us to a point where the familiar matrix of left and right can no longer capture the real issues that are at stake. In part this relies on an implausible reading of the left/right distinction as involving little more than the extension or limitation of state power, taking the neoliberal and neoconservative right at their libertarian word in spite of the expanded carceral and security apparatus which has accompanied their hegemony. This is ascribed to the left being "on the defensive" as a result of the "persistence (if not resurgence) of poverty, inequality and ethnic discrimination, despite a succession of well-intentioned, often well-financed and indeed sometimes partly successful welfare programmes" (Fuller & Lipinska 2014: 39).

As a reading of political economy and social policy, this is truly shallow stuff. However, it's interesting in its repetition of the orthodox bromides more likely to be found in opinion columns than scholarly literature: *the welfare state has failed, the left has been discredited, government is the problem rather than the solution.* It's difficult to see how their "proactionary welfare state" which would "provide a relatively secure bio-social environment for the taking of calculated life risks in return for reward, repair or compensation at the personal level" (Fuller & Lipinska 2014: 35–37) is in any way outside the horizons of the mainstream right and (post–social democratic) left of recent decades. This can all be found in Giddens's (2013) foundational text on the *third way* in its discussion of the welfare state: the top-down distribution of benefits which can have perverse consequences, the right's critiques being proven at least partially true by events, the insufficient room granted for personal liberty and the necessity of ensuring psychological outcomes rather than being narrowly preoccupied with material ones. While Fuller and Lipinska's (2014) terminology and concerns appear somewhat idiosyncratic, their account clearly overlaps with Giddens (2006: 381), who worries that "the welfare state isn't geared up to cover new-style risks such as those concerning technological change, social exclusion or the accelerating proportion of one-parent households." Perhaps more importantly, it is entirely in keeping with the dominant thrust of social policy in North America and Europe in recent decades. If we substitute their philosophical terminology for the technocratic language of contemporary politics, what they boldly present as the ethos of the proactionary welfare state begins to look like an unremarkable statement of political orthodoxy:

> We have seen that proactionaries would re-invent the welfare state as a vehicle for fostering securitized risk-taking while precautionaries would aim to protect the planet at levels of security well beyond what the classic welfare state could realistically provide for human beings, let alone the natural environment.
>
> (Fuller & Lipinska 2014: 42)

What would this look like in practice? While Fuller and Lipinska (2014) make some genuinely thought-provoking, if contentious, suggestions about science policy later in the book, the more mundane face of the proactionary state would resemble trends in social policy such as workfare, requiring economic activity from welfare benefits to avoid unsustainable dependence, which have been with us for decades. Seen in this light, there's something almost nostalgic about the forceful pronouncement of a radical approach to the welfare state at precisely the moment when the politico-economic settlement described by Stiglitz (2004) as the Roaring Nineties began to break down as history returned with a vengeance, first with 9/11 and its disruption of the geopolitical order and then with the financial crisis and its disruption of the global economic order (Žižek 2009). The populist insurgencies of left and right, the global rise of authoritarian politics and the Covid-19 crisis have only taken us further down this road. In fact, it's difficult to see a role for the proactionary state in the present pandemic, with the widely rejected strategy of herd immunity being its obvious expression in public health. Regardless of what assessment we might make of their arguments in their own terms, the thrust of what Fuller and Lipinska (2014) are saying seems curiously out of synch with the times, in spite of the concern with the cutting edge of change which runs through the book.

Not only can their proactionary/precautionary distinction be coded in terms of familiar distinctions of left and right, but in European welfare states it *is* the form taken by the left-and-right distinction in its centre left and centre right manifestations until recent years: from New Labour's empowerment of individuals through to Emmanuel Macron's pursuit of a 'start-up nation', the self-professed centre ground of politics has sought to move beyond left and right by reforming the welfare state in a manner that better 'empowers' individuals. The reasons for this reframing are complex and far beyond the scope of our introduction, with vast literatures addressing the policy questions in substantive domains of intervention such as employment policy (Gilbert & Van Voorhis 2001). What is often called 'triangulation' has certainly played an important role in this, with an increasingly professionalized political class seeking to split the difference across the electorate by combining aspects of left and right (Crouch 2004). But these developments are also driven by serious engagements with social, economic and demographic transformation that can too easily be overlooked if we remain fixated on their presentational elements.

The point we are making is not to assess these policies but rather to underscore how what Fuller and Lipinska (2014) present as moving beyond left and right in fact reproduces the 'radical centrism' which has been political orthodoxy for at least a couple of decades. What makes their obliviousness particularly curious is that they offer this reformulation at precisely the point where this centrism is unravelling alongside the global economic order it emerged in relation to (Callinicos 2010, Varoufakis 2011, 2016, Žižek 2009). Far from helping us grasp the complexity of the ensuing political terrain, their up-winger and down-winger politics (effectively a matter of doubling down on technology-driven modernization or seeking to curtail it through the protective state) collapses the political possibilities confronting us into something akin to *techno-liberalism* and *luddite-nationalism*. In practice it reinscribes political coordinates which have been breaking down for years, as opposed to offering a novel outlook on the challenges which confront us in an increasingly uncertain world.

There's a parallel here to Žižek's (1999) observation that claims of the new epoch we are entering[7] often seek to preserve the core elements of classic sociological models, making minor adjustments to the conceptual architecture and fiddling with the presentation in order to adapt them to new realities while avoiding any more significant reappraisal of their underlying axioms. In this sense, we should be cautious about post-humanist and transhumanist political thought, not because they represent a novel intrusion into contemporary politics but rather because they reproduce orthodox elements of it with only a veneer of novelty. This does not mean we should dismiss it, only that we recognize its self-conception and self-presentation might prove immensely misleading. The point we are making is that social theoretical accounts of social, cultural and technological change exist within a tradition of theorizing that responds to and shapes what it purports to describe in a way rarely if ever acknowledged by the theorists concerned. To use Sloterdijk's (2020: 13) phrase, there is no "outside thinking." The context of discovery too often drops out in social thought, making it difficult to track how proliferating conceptions of where we are *going* reflect where we *are* (as well as who 'we' are taken to be) and what their influence might be over unfolding events. Insisting on this context does not imply that nothing has changed and that we should stop talking about transformation; a dogmatic quietism in the fact of accumulating novelty is the inverse of a manic modernism that continually sees the new epoch being born within whatever developments are most exciting this year. We are instead seeking to move beyond these opposing errors in order to facilitate a more cautiously reflective dialogue between *social theory* and *emerging technologies*.

What does it mean to theorize about the future?

In the introduction of her most recent book, Braidotti (2019: 12) talks about the post-human condition in terms of "swinging moods, which alternate between excitement and anxiety." There is "euphoria at the astonishing technological advances that 'we' have accomplished" but also "anxiety in view of the exceedingly high prize that we – both humans and non-humans – are paying for these transformations." It is precisely this oscillation as well as the implicit cultural politics of technology as salvation or curse that we have sought to avoid in this volume and the broader project of which it is a part. If we see what Braidotti (2019) terms the post-human predicament as a response to the exogenous shocks of socio-technical change, exhilarating or anxiety provoking depending on which element we focus on in a particular moment, it becomes difficult to theorize in anything other than a reactive mode.

In parallel to the argument we have made above about Fuller and Lipinska (2014), there are deep similarities between how a thinker like Braidotti (2019) conceptualizes the post-human condition and what Savage (2009) calls the epochal theorizing embodied by theorists like Zygmunt Bauman, Ulrich Beck and Anthony Giddens, which were so influential within social thought in the 1990s and 2000s[8] (Outhwaite 2009). There are profound changes underway driven by the accumulation of social, cultural, technological and environmental novelty, which generates opportunities and challenges for human beings. We are confronted with, as Braidotti (2019: 7) puts it, "a chain of theoretical, social and political effects that is more than the sum of its parts." In her case, the post-human is a theoretical device to sort through these changes, including overcoming the particular dualisms and other conceptual legacies that prevent us from grappling with the complexity of what we confront, as well as identifying convergences across a range of intellectual currents that are in different ways responses to them.[9] There is an implicit admission of the limitations of empiricism at work here: a sense that we must postulate something beyond the chain of empirically identifiable changes in order to grasp the enormity of the broader transformation that is underway. In his final book, Ulrich Beck gestured towards this recognition of a meta-transformation that eludes and exceeds our characterization of particular aspects to it:

> There is no shame in admitting that we social scientists are also at a loss for words in the face of the reality which is overrunning us. The language of sociological theories (as well as that of empirical research) allows us to address the recurring patterns of social change or the exceptional occurrence of crisis, but it does not allow us even to describe, let alone to understand, the social-historical metamorphosis that the world is undergoing at the beginning of the twenty-first century. The word, concept or metaphor that I introduce in this book for this speechlessness as a distinguishing feature of the intellectual situation of the age is that of the metamorphosis of the world.
>
> (Beck 2016: 67–68)

If we approach this text as sympathetic readers, we might hold that the gnomic quality of Beck's language serves a purpose by delineating a trans-empirical horizon of change that is inherently difficult to discern without collapsing it into empirical manifestations of that change.[10] In other words, it is sometimes advantageous to be a bit vague in order to convey a sense of the bigger picture. However this tone shifts as we find ourselves confronted with 'the metamorphosis of traffic' which is understood in terms of straightforward mechanisms such as the creation of new norms which shape consumer habits and the diffusion of technical knowledge which helps shape policy (Beck 2016: 172–174). The ineffable quality of metamorphosis evaporates rather rapidly when the discussion turns to traffic, inviting us to consider what work the language of metamorphosis is *really* doing.

In fact, it is hard not to suspect that it is actively mystifying what would otherwise be an interesting and pertinent claim. The same point can be made about 'the metamorphosis of urban political decision making' that incorporates "cooperation and competition; economy and environment; equality and inequality; solidarity and self-interest; localism and cosmopolitanism" in a blurring of boundaries as prophetic as it is unexplained (Beck 2016: 179). Beck's apparent point in using this language is that "we need new ways of seeing the world, being in the world, and imagining and doing politics" in a way that encompasses the world itself and the practices through which we come to know it (Beck 2016: 180). He frames this is in a proto-Heideggerian manner as coping with

> "the permanency of a metamorphosis when nobody can say where it is heading, a metamorphosis that affects the centre and the periphery, the rich and the poor, Muslims, Christians and seculars alike, a metamorphosis that does not arise from failure, crisis or poverty but that grows and accelerates with the successes of modernization, a metamorphosis that is not halted by non-action but speeded up by."
>
> (Beck 2016: 186)

However, the scope of this ambition seems continually repudiated by the clunky conceptual grammar and clumsy concept work that pervades the book, as new concepts are continually introduced with little explanation as to how they were developed or the purpose they serve.

Burrows (1997) made the useful observations two decades before this final intervention from Beck: "It is not just technology which appears to be accelerating towards meltdown, so are our cultural and sociological understandings of the world." What he termed "sociological passéification," the rendering passé of past neologisms with each successive wave of conceptual (pseudo-)innovation,[11] leaves us further way from the empirical changes we had sought to describe. Instead we see "ever more frantic attempts to provide some sort of sociological frame for a constantly moving target" (Burrows 1997: 235). It would be deeply naive if we fail to recognize the political economy of knowledge production at work here: rewards are accumulated by those who are perceived to innovate and establish frames of reference seen as current and influential (Bacevic 2019). Epochal accounts can be rewarding because they provide an overview that *frames*, without being tested by empirical research (Savage & Burrows 2007, Carrigan 2014). Defining a changing world by what we have left behind (*post*) or what we are moving towards (*neo*) substitutes for a fundamental lack of specificity concerning the change which is postulated to be taking place (Crouch 2011: 2).

Ontological reasoning can play a crucial role in facilitating debate by drawing out these often unspoken assumptions and specifying what is at stake when they clash. Consider, for example, Braidotti's (2019: 129–130) presupposition that extending legal subjectivity from human to non-human actors is inherently progressive. While it's easy to see the virtues of the examples she cites where this is extended to nature,[12] it's even easier to imagine examples in which this might be deeply problematic. For instance, the attribution of subjectivity to manufacturing robots could be used to insulate firms from legal challenge to the much anticipated mass redundancy driven by the rollout of automation technology (Kaplan 2015, Ford 2015). She suggests this move can help us liberate data from market actors, but it could just as readily be used as a legal device to deepen the hold of firms over the data produced through interaction with their proprietary infrastructures (Carrigan 2018). Could claims of consumer sovereignty over personal data really be sustained if the 'data doubles', generated through our digitalized interaction, would be granted a degree of legal autonomy? We should not forget that, as the Republican Mitt Romney put it in the 2012 presidential elections in the United States, "corporations are people too, my friend"; extending personhood to non-human entities has been established in this sense for at least a couple of hundred years, with socio-political consequences that sit uneasily with the politics espoused by Braidotti.

We could likewise imagine how the injunction towards "a kind of ontological pacifism, that is to say, that one cannot blame external circumstances alone, like the bush fire, for one's own misfortune," as Braidotti (2019: 135) describes it, could be leveraged towards undesirable ends. The point Braidotti makes is fundamentally an ontological one, namely that the co-production of events complicates the unilateral attribution of causation to putatively objective factors. It could easily be incorporated into a reactionary politics which stresses individual responsibility when a subject invokes the significance of external circumstances; for example, is a notion akin to ontological pacifism not at work when claims of poverty are dismissed as 'excuses' for criminal behaviour? We shouldn't reject Braidotti's argument because of the uses to which it *could* be put, but recognizing these uses gives us reason for caution in the face of the narrow reasoning which pervades her ethics. It's not obvious that many of these claims are inherently positive in the way she seems to suggest and she doesn't engage, or even recognize, the ambiguity latent within them. The translation of ontological observations[13] into social life is an uncertain process to which Braidotti's work, as well as the broader post-humanist oeuvre, seems somewhat tone deaf. It might be that "apportioning blame" is "not only ineffectual but also unjust," but this possibility needs to be established rather than simply asserted as Braidotti (2019: 145) does.

We can see something like what Bhaskar (2010), in a deeply thoughtful critique of Richard Rorty, called a 'free-wheeling' conception of freedom' at work here. It fails to hook on to concrete states of affairs in the world in a manner liable to exercise an influence over them. The point is not that the cultural politics advocated by Braidotti are inherently regressive. It is rather that this style of analysis sits uneasily with the imperative to be specific about the condition under which one outcome is more likely than the other, with the a priori valorization of conceptual decisions providing no basis to discern where those concepts might lead us later.[14] It is a curiously self-involved approach to conceptualization, preoccupied by its own generative capacity while perversely devoid of methodological reflexivity about *how* and *why* this is being undertaken as an intellectual exercise.

This is why the recovery of ontology is so important. While Braidotti (2019) would certainly claim to be working in an ontological mode, it is striking how rarely she identifies the changing reality that drives her post-human project as opposed to reflecting on the conceptual architecture of that project itself. There's a curious circularity running through her work, such that "the collective project of seeking a more adequate understanding of the complexity of factors that structure the post-human subject: the new proximity to animals, the planetary dimension and the high level of technological mediation" (Braidotti 2013: 94) comes to be nearly exhausted by concept work that makes only passing reference to these changing realities.

To take an example, Braidotti (2019: 95) writes that emerging forms of materialism "are supported by and intersect with changing understandings of the conceptual structure of matter itself." In what sense does *matter* have a conceptual structure? Our understanding (something epistemic) may have a conceptual structure orientated towards matter (something ontologically independent of our understanding), but matter itself does not have a conceptual structure in any easily discernible sense. Braidotti's point is that "contemporary bio-genetics and information technologies" are leading us to understand matter in new ways (a plausible but unsupported claim) and that the resurgence of materialism as a philosophical position[15] is consistent with it. Braidotti fails, however, to untangle the relationship between epistemology and ontology, so that a conceptual shift becomes indistinguishable from a shift in the objects being conceptualized, leaving her with a position functionally indistinguishable from the constructionism she disavows, even though it is expressed in a radically different conceptual vocabulary. It could be objected that we have seized upon an isolated example here in which the author was merely loose with language, but this conceptual laxity pervades her text. The point we're making is less to criticize Braidotti as much as to use this work as an example, illustrating the conceptual and methodological complexity involved in addressing post-human futures.

How do we theorize post-human subjects?

What nonetheless leaves Braidotti (2013, 2019) someone with whom to productively engage is her focus on agency and change throughout her analysis. Still, it is far from clear what is the intended locus of the putative changes she cites. At times, it seems as if it is a matter of personal[16] adaptation to our present moment, our finding tools "to resist nihilism, escape consumerist individualism and get immunized against xenophobia" (Braidotti 2019: 19). The post-human in this sense is a project of overturning "a set of familiar formulae, a compilation of motifs and mental habits 'we' had embroidered around the notion of the human" which have become exhausted and inhabit our capacity to turn the risks we confront into opportunities for change, growth and resistance (Braidotti 2019: 17). At other times, it reads as if this is a matter of adapting our conceptual tools to the changing nature of the reality we apply to them, as when Braidotti criticizes contemporary leftist thought for remaining wedded to "the modernist and constructivist vision of the social space as defined essentially by anthropomorphic conflicts and resistance, vigilance and solidarity" (Braidotti 2019: 31).

We recognize Braidotti's (2019) repeated affirmations that her work is 'empirically grounded,' but the issue is the nature of this grounding rather than the presence of the empirical as such. There are recurrent sketches of interesting issues but these are invariably brief, as if Braidotti assumes the substance of the matter can be taken for granted and the reader would immediately prefer her to return to more abstract terrain. For example, Braidotti considers the potential value of technological innovation, describing herself as "rather technophilic" such that "I will always side firmly with the liberatory and even transgressive potential of these technologies, against those who attempt to index them to either a predictable conservative profile, or to a profit-oriented system that fosters and inflates individualism." She describes the tendency of liberal thinkers to "panic" in the face of these changes and "blame" our technology for them (Braidotti 2013: 65) This recognition of the range of potentials inherent in technological developments leads her to stress the significance of "finding new and alternative modes of political and ethical agency for our technologically mediated world and the inertia of established mental habits on the other" (Braidotti 2013: 57). If one were to read Braidotti (2013, 2019) uncharitably, it could be suggested that the former becomes the latter, particularly in the later book. Even though she recognizes there's more to 'political and ethical agency' than the framing of our choices and responses to them, the conceptual structure of this framing is what she remains focused on in practice.

There's a sense in which Braidotti (2019) is atypical of post-humanists in her affirmation that the human subject as such should not be discarded. In fact her arguments for this are the most compelling feature of her account. It could be suggested this means she is far from indicative of post-human thought, insofar as she offers an account of the subject, but our claim is that this is why it is so important to engage with her (i.e., she theorizes rather than refuses to theorize the subject). Who are Braidotti's nomads? Consider what she describes as "the capacity of transversal subjects to detach themselves from the historically sedimented determinations of power, aims at releasing transversal lines of resistance and not integral lines of power" (Braidotti 2019: 171). That description could easily be recast in critical realist terms as a statement about the reflexive modalities of agency in

Archer's (2003, 2007, 2012) sense. It is an affirmation of the latent reflexivity, the capacity to *do* and *be* otherwise, possessed by *all* subjects, even if this potential remains unrealized under constraining conditions in which people live dominated lives. A critic such as King (2010) might suggest this equation misses the relationality of Braidotti's position, but his was always a profound misreading of Archer's work, which is relational to the core[17] (see Donati & Archer 2015).

In this sense, Braidotti's (2019) affirmative ethics is preoccupied with how to stress the *realizability* of these capacities: affirming how interdependence helps us achieve things, recognizing how negative affect can lead us to self-limit and how suffering can be an opportunity for change and so forth. The problem is that it primarily rhetorical, providing us with an encouraging and optimistic way to *speak* about these possibilities while providing little to help us *understand* what they are or how we might be able to bring them about. Braidotti's affirmative ethics is a form of self-work concerned with how subjects can realize their potential under post-human conditions. It's surely correct to argue that subjects will need to change if it's going to be possible to have widespread "pragmatic engagement with the present (as both actual and virtual), in order to collectively construct conditions that transform and empower our capacity to act ethically and produce social horizons of hope, or sustainable futures" (Braidotti 2019: 172). It's surely correct to argue that a "transmutation of values" could help us embrace "generative encounters with others" which we might miss in our present condition (Braidotti 2019: 175). However Braidotti remains at a purely formal invocation that 'if people can change, things can change' without providing any clarity about the conditions which shape the former, the latter or the relationship between them.

Exactly what 'transmutation of values' is necessary to embrace which 'generative encounters'? Braidotti is only able or willing to answer this question at such a high level of abstraction that it remains a celebration of agency's capacity to make things otherwise, interrupting the habitual reproduction of social life and introducing new possibilities to it. What Braidotti offers is at root an ethos for responding in a creative way to a world that many experience as difficult. Leaving aside the question of how this differs from the more esoteric end of productivity culture,[18] it's difficult to see what exactly it helps us understand about how we can realize this potential. In fact the potential itself is mythologized as a great creative force latent within the world.[19]

For a fair appraisal of post-humanist thought, it's crucial to recognize the use that has been made of it within empirical research.[20] For example, Lupton (2019) writes about the "more-than-human assemblages" through which data comes to play a role in our lives. As she puts it, such assemblages "generate agential capacities that shape people's embodied responses and actions, their sense of selfhood and their relationships with other people and with other things" (Lupton 2019: 98–99). This could be read as a post-humanist statement par excellence, in that it affirms a transhuman category (in the sense of an analytic category that doesn't take the human as a starting point, as opposed to affirming transhumanism as a doctrine) and frames human characteristics as outcomes of transhuman processes (e.g., their personal identity or their embodied habits). However, when it comes to empirical claims, much of what Lupton (2016, 2019) is interested in is a matter of how people relate to the data that is generated by personal devices, as well as the meaning that it holds for them. Her affirmation of a "more-than-human" approach is a conceptual device used to highlight the affective and meaningful orientation that users have to their use: the data matters to people (Sayer 2011). Lupton (2019: 82) stresses the empirical finding that "biographical disruptions or ruptures" play a significant role in people turning to self-tracking to help them during transitions such as milestone birthdays, having children or being diagnosed with a serious health problem. This behaviour is important because a growing body of work shows that while people understand that surveillance is taking place through digital technology, they tend to be much less sure about who is doing it, how it is being conducted and how their data is being shared (Lupton 2019).

To grasp the causality of this can be a difficult undertaking, not least of all when it comes to the novelty and intimacy of smart objects (speakers, wristbands, phones, tablets, etc.) which *intervene* in everyday life while nonetheless fading into the background. In this sense the philosophical interest in the "things themselves and how they are dependent on and connected with other things rather than solely what purpose they serve for humans" serves an obvious methodological purpose (Lupton 2019: 39). The implied focus on 'entanglement' can be a useful way of sensitizing ourselves to the interconnections within an emerging field site filled with unfamiliar objects of research. This is particularly useful when established concepts are unhelpfully rigid with regards to which aspects of a phenomenon they recognize. Lupton (2019: 75) observes how the dominance of the analogy of literacy serves to exclude "the interplay between the human senses and the digital sensors that work to document the body." Her more-than-human approach helps cut through this conceptual clutter in order to sustain a focus on how people are "making sense of the information, deciding how valid or valuable it is, and what to do with these details." The obvious retort from a critical realist perspective is that these are mundane issues of human reflexivity (Archer 2000, 2003). However, simply making this observation provides no methodological support for those who are examining this capacity as embodied in novel engagements with novel objects.

Post-human futures: an overview

In contrast to the self-conscious oscillation between excitement and anxiety which characterizes a thinker like Braidotti (2019), the contributors to this volume adopt a much more sober approach while agreeing we cannot avoid a confrontation with the socio-technical novelty which pervades our increasingly post-human world. The reason for our extensive detour through issues of social change and epochalism in this introduction, as well as a detailed examination of Braidotti's recent works rather than a more shallow analysis of a wider corpus of thinkers, is because the conceptual grammar with which the post-human has tended to be treated militates against the sobriety we've sought to embody here, instead leading to breathless invocations that utopia or dystopia are on the horizon. This deprives us of many things but foremost among them is the capacity to be clear about *what changes* and *what doesn't*. There's a parallel here to what Taylor (2009: 22) calls a "subtraction story" in which social changes are explained in terms of human beings "having lost, or sloughed off, or liberated themselves from certain earlier, confining horizons, or illusions, or limitations of knowledge." The valence of the story varies among commentators on these issues, from transhumanists celebrating liberation from constraints on morphological freedom through to gloomy humanists mourning the loss of what makes us who we are, but there is a certain convergence to their poetics which can be seen beneath the surface.

In this introduction, we made a modest attempt to recover the conceptual grammar of theorizing about post-human futures in order to illustrate their complexity across a number of dimensions: the dilemmas of epochal theorizing, the risk of reproducing contemporary orthodoxy, the perennial challenge of conceptualizing the subject and its relationship to empirical research. In the chapters that follow, there is far from a common orientation to these questions but there is a shared *style* of theorizing which is alive to their complexity, developed as an intellectual collective which has engaged in a form of what Archer (2007) describes as "thought and talk" for almost a decade. We offer no final answers or definitive statements for the obvious reason that nothing can be final and definitive about these matters. But through careful conceptual engagement with the socio-technical novelty emerging around us, we have provided ontological foundations for a confrontation with the post-human futures incipient within our present conditions.

In the opening chapter, Pierpaolo Donati explores what he calls the digital technological matrix (DTM), "defined as the globalized symbolic code that governs the creation of digital technologies designed to enhance or replace human action, radically changing social identities and relationships." Donati speculates that in a world where a DTM environment becomes dominant, human relationality will tend to become a "a 'mental relation' populated by disembodied minds." The relationality through which we become who we are will fade away as a casual force, being replaced by its spectral representation through technological means. This leaves us with the challenge of either considering humanism dead or redefining the human for our new digital environment.

A similar challenges runs though Andrea M. Maccarini's chapter on being human as an option. What worries Maccarini is how in question it now is that humans have a unique ontological status that is our duty to preserve. He accordingly turns his attention to the potential of human enhancement's transhumanizing effects to elide the normative aspects of what it means to be a human person inhabiting a human body. Should that potential be realized, then, Maccarini concludes, being – or staying – human becomes but an option. Unfortunately, the deep change of human enhancement outstrips the governing capacity of the lib/lab dialectic of freedom and control. This risks leaving us with a situation in which inequality is "engraved in personal ontology" in a way that would make "obstacles to social mobility eventually insurmountable."

Emmanuel Lazega's contribution explores the difference between online advice-seeking from an AI and advice-seeking in a collegial workplace defined by its own structural and cultural constraints on interactional and relational activity. His worry is that the "perplexity logs," his coinage for the records of all queries an AI receives from any person/citizen, "are likely to be used for epistemic domination and algorithmic regulation in society." In pursuing the likely consequences of this algorithmic regulation, Lazega presents us with a bleak vision of a militarily bureaucratized world characterized by an epistemic control incompatible with the core axioms of liberal democracy.

In the following chapter, Jamie Morgan analyses the potential roles that artificial intelligence (AI), robotics and such might play in social care in the future and the impacts that this may have on who we are and how we relate to each other. Technologies such as social robotics and machine learning are emerging as the pool of paid and unpaid caregivers is shrinking, creating a confluence with radical implications for the social care sector. He argues we increasingly need to ask "what will care for us?" rather than "who will care for us?" – a transition with the potential to disrupt seemingly long-settled assumptions about the semantics of care in human society.

This reflection on care continues in Ismael Al-Amoudi and Gazi Islam's chapter on care relations between enhanced and unenhanced humans. It foresees a world in which many (though not everyone) are enhanced with powers beyond those of current humans, leading them to consider the temptations to withdraw care and solidarity under these circumstances. These influences are likely to operate reciprocally, with both groups facing influences inclining them to withdraw care from the other. Their argument, however, is that even under this hypermodern condition of inequality, social solidarity need not be lost. There are still reasons, they argue, for enhanced and unenhanced humans to care for each other.

Our penultimate chapter from Margaret S. Archer takes a slightly different approach, exploring the robotic personhood that might emerge from relational interaction with a human collaborator. Building on her contributions to the previous volumes in this series, Archer argues that artificial beings can in principle attain personhood contrary to those critics who restrict this status to human beings. She makes the case that humans and AI robots can be friends, grounded in a thought experiment exploring the relational consequences of synergy when the two work together. It is offered as an optimistic scenario, rather than a prediction, but one which calls into question the orthodox assumption of what Archer calls 'robophobia' and takes issue with the ontological premises underpinning it.

In the final chapter, Douglas V. Porpora speculates about post-human persons at humanity's end, casting his gaze much further into the future than the other contributors to the volume. He wonders whether in a million years we will have made self-conscious robots our heirs and whether self-conscious robots are likely to be the form of any extraterrestrial intelligence we encounter. If they remain in their biological form when a million years or more ahead of us, it would give us reason to suspect that should humanity endure as long, then we will as well.

This is not the final volume in this series. While it was initially intended to be the third of three, the debates it raised within our group revolved around a fundamental question: "does the human being have an essence which is exclusive to our species?" In these chapters we have explored the challenge of post-human futures across a range of issues, mapping out a terrain of where these developments might be leading in the broadest sense. In the final volume we will address the philosophical question we have all continually encountered in these explorations, even if we each have different answers to it. Aiming towards a conclusion about post-human futures would be a self-defeating exercise given we are, at best, pointing towards a horizon of change and the proximate challenges we see as we orientate ourselves to it. However unless we can be clear about the *human*, finding a way through the thickets of discursive ambiguity we reflected on earlier in this introduction, discussions of the 'post' cannot meaningfully be brought to a close.

Notes

1 On 1 March 2020.
2 It's otherwise mystifying why Braidotti (2013) would describe Nussbaum as a post-humanist when her own discussion acknowledges the explicitly humanist character of Nussbaum's arguments. Therefore, to read charitability, we might see this category as neo-humanism (i.e., contemporary formulations of humanism responding directly or indirectly to post-humanist and transhumanist critiques).
3 This doesn't do justice to twentieth-century anti-humanism's more obviously radical character. As Badmington (2000: 7) puts it, the claim that "'we' are naturally inclined to think, organise and act in certain ways" makes it "difficult to believe that human society and behaviour could ever be other than they are now." However it's beyond our capacity to account for the complex relationship between *anti-humanism* and *post-humanism* in this introduction.
4 Wolfe (2010: xii) suggests two competing genealogies in the literature. One goes back to the 1960s and was typified by Foucault's famous image of the face drawn in sand being washed away at the edge of the sea. The other goes back to the Macy conferences (1946–1953) which initiated the field of cybernetics. Turner (2010) provides the definitive account of how such an apparent mismatch of counterculture and technoscience can be more congruous in practice than one might imagine.
5 It should be stressed there was an engineering problem which required precautionary action on the part of organizations responsible for maintaining computer systems. Our point is simply to ask why this technical difficulty captured the public imagination to the extent which it did.
6 Can one really be imbricated within such networks? Presumably the expression is intended to convey a sense of the overlapping character of our immersion in these networks, but much more is closed down than opened up by this motif of imbrication that is prevalent within this literature.
7 He cites post-industrial society, post-modern society, risk society and information society. The fact these were replaced by network society, late modernity, liquid modernity and second modernity with little significant difference speaks volumes about the creeping vacuity incipient in epochal theorizing. The modern-day equivalents would perhaps be digital capitalism, platform capitalism and data capitalism. An unfair reading of our social morphogenesis project could place it in this category, but we would suggest we exercised a degree of theoretical reflexivity within the project, which meant we avoided this fate (Archer 2013).
8 To those who doubt the extent of this influence, perhaps seeing a decline in references to them or a widespread sense within their own intellectual milieu that such work is passé, we invite you to search for citation data for their key texts on Google Scholar. The fact texts on late modernity, liquid modernity and risk society have been cited

many tens of thousands of times (and continue to be cited) reflects their status as conduits which link together the many fields and sub disciplines which sociology, as the quintessential exporter discipline in Holmwood's (2010) sense, has generated in recent decades (Carrigan 2010, 2014).

9 Though it seeks unlikely these criteria for relevance would identify anything which didn't share the underlying axioms Braidotti (2019) is working with, thus undermining its effectiveness for filtering intellectual variety in the manner suggested.

10 Though this sympathy might also extend to making the methodological point that there are clearly better ways in which we can do this (Archer 2013).

11 In his case 'cyber' was promising to eclipse "the latest pile of books on the postmodern, globalisation, reflexive modernisation (last year's model?) and the like" (Burrows 1997). The extent to which 'cyber' now sounds profoundly anachronistic under conditions when digital anthropology, digital geography and digital sociology are established subdisciplines only underscores the accuracy of the point he was making.

12 "New Zealand now recognizes a right to personhood for a river, India acknowledges the rights of waterfalls, and Ecuador grants rights to the environment as a whole" (Braidotti 2019: 129).

13 Surely unproblematic from a critical realist standpoint, even if it uses a very different theoretical idiom.

14 This is compounded by the purely formal character of the collective agency which Braidotti affirms. If we're not sure who would be pursuing these conceptual decisions in the social world, then how can we begin to understand what their potential ramifications would be?

15 For example actor-network theory, agential realism, speculative realism, object-oriented ontology, neo-vitalism, new materialism and so forth.

16 To be fair, a 'we' is invoked in a manner which implies this adaption is part of a broader political project, as opposed to being a lifestyle choice for a community of those interested in post-humanist theory. However, its invocation tends to be purely formal, for example with Braidotti (2019: 19), leaving one with the suspicion that this much narrower community of reference is who 'we' refers to in practice. One could argue this is implicitly recognized when Braidotti (2019: 36) explains what matters is "assembling *a* people" without specifying who these people are, where they are found or how they might practically be assembled. In this sense her much-repeated affirmation is purely formal, remaining unavoidably aloof from the actually existing people, movements and struggles it purports to designate. As she writes later, "A people is always missing and virtual, in that it needs to be actualized and assembled" (Braidotti 2019: 52). How will this assembly happen, what conditions will facilitate it and how might her project contribute to it? Our point in asking these questions is not to claim any greater proximity to the political but rather stress that invocations of political praxis remain purely formal unless they provide answers, regardless of whether they come presented in a post-Deleuzian rhetoric of immanence.

17 What he describes as the "strange loneliness" of Archer's sociology is a lonely *moment* which characterizes the existence of all subjects to *varying* degrees. The great advance of her account of agency is to recognize the temporal dynamics of individuality and relationality: it is the (contingent) balance between the two over the unfolding life course which makes us who we are (Carrigan 2014).

18 Braidotti (2019: 176) accepts that a critical reader might "see this as being concomitant with neo-liberal self-management techniques, whereas it is intended to be exactly the contrary" but doesn't explain how is so, apart from claiming it is "a way of decelerating and escaping the multiple speeds of reterritorialization by capital, by focusing on alternative values." But surely the point is these *aren't* alternative values? At root what she's advocating are creative responses to uncertainty, changing your mindset to liberate your potential and striving to become what you can be. An uncharitable critic would suggest these are core elements of neoliberal doxa.

19 It remains a philosophical question how much rests on Braidotti's insistence on the immanent character of this force. Is analytical purchased gained by specifying this creativity is (non-specifically) within the world rather than somehow outside of it? The same question can be asked concerning her characterization of life as the "inexhaustible generative force that potentially can transmute lives into sites of resistance" (Braidotti 2019: 177). It should hardly need pointing out how much work 'potentially' does in this sentence.

20 Our point is not that theoretical ideas being used in empirical research are inherently validating, only that an adequate treatment of ideas necessitates consideration of how they have been picked up and used, as well as how their conceptual character shapes this use.

References

Alexander, J. C., & Alexander, J. (1995). *Fin de siècle social theory: Relativism, reduction, and the problem of reason*. London: Verso.

Archer, M. S. (2000). *Being human: The problem of agency*. Cambridge: Cambridge University Press.

Archer, M. S. (2003). *Structure, agency and the internal conversation*. Cambridge: Cambridge University Press.

Archer, M. S. (2007). *Making our way through the world: Human reflexivity and social mobility*. Cambridge: Cambridge University Press.

Archer, M. S. (2012). *The reflexive imperative in late modernity*. Cambridge: Cambridge University Press.

Archer, M. S. (Ed.). (2013). *Social morphogenesis*. Dordrecht: Springer.

Bacevic, J. (2019). Knowing neoliberalism. *Social Epistemology, 33*(4), 380–392.

Badmington, N. (Ed.). (2000). *Posthumanism*. Basingstoke: Macmillan.

Bauman, Z. (2000). *Liquid modernity*. Cambridge: Polity Press.

Beck, U. (1992). *Risk society: Towards a new modernity*. New Delhi: SAGE.

Beck, U. (2016). *The metamorphosis of the world: How climate change is transforming our concept of the world*. Cambridge: Polity Press.

Bhaskar, R. (2010). *Reclaiming reality: A critical introduction to contemporary philosophy*. London: Taylor & Francis.

Bostrom, N. (2001). What is transhumanism. *Nick Bostrom*. Retrieved from www.ildodopensiero.it/wp-content/uploads/2019/03/nick-bostrom-transhumanist-values.pdf

Bostrom, N. (2005). Transhumanist values. *Journal of Philosophical Research, 30*, 3–14.

Braidotti, R. (2013). *The posthuman*. Cambridge: Polity Press.

Braidotti, R. (2019). *Posthuman knowledge*. Cambridge: Polity Press.

Burrows, R. (1997). Cyberpunk as social theory: William Gibson and the sociological imagination. In S. Westwood & J. Williams (Eds.), *Imagining cities: Scripts, signs, memory*. London: Routledge.

Callinicos, A. (2010). *Bonfire of illusions: The twin crises of the liberal world*. Cambridge: Polity Press.

Carrigan, M. A. (2010). Realism, reflexivity, conflation, and individualism. *Journal of Critical Realism, 9*(3), 384–396.

Carrigan, M. A. (2014). *Becoming who we are: Personal morphogenesis and social change* (Doctoral dissertation), University of Warwick.

Carrigan, M. A. (2018). The evisceration of the human under digital capitalism. In I. Al-Amoudi & J. Morgan (Eds.), *Realist responses to post-human society: Ex Machina*. London: Routledge.

Crouch, C. (2004). *Post-democracy.* Cambridge: Polity Press.

Crouch, C. (2011). *The strange non-death of neo-liberalism.* Cambridge: Polity Press.

Davies, T. (2008). *Humanism.* London: Routledge.

Donati, P., & Archer, M. S. (2015). *The relational subject.* Cambridge: Cambridge University Press.

Ford, M. (2015). *Rise of the robots: Technology and the threat of a Jobless future.* London: Oneworld Publications.

Fuller, S. (2011). *Humanity 2.0: What it means to be human past, present and future.* Basingstoke: Palgrave Macmillan.

Fuller, S., & Lipinska, V. (2014). *The proactionary imperative: A foundation for transhumanism.* Basingstoke: Palgrave Macmillan.

Ghosh, A. (2018). *The great derangement: Climate change and the unthinkable.* London: Penguin.

Giddens, A. (1991). *Modernity and self-identity: Self and society in the late modern age.* Cambridge: Polity.

Giddens, A. (2006). Positive welfare. In C. Pierson & F. G. Castles (Eds.), *The welfare state reader* (pp. 478–488). Cambridge: Polity Press.

Giddens, A. (2013). *The third way: The renewal of social democracy.* Cambridge: Polity Press.

Gilbert, N., & Van Voorhis, R. A. (Eds.). (2001). *Activating the unemployed: A comparative appraisal of work-oriented policies.* London: Routledge.

Herbrechter, S. (2013). *Posthumanism: A critical analysis.* London: Bloomsbury.

Kaplan, J. (2015). *Humans need not apply: A guide to wealth and work in the age of artificial intelligence.* London: Yale University Press.

King, A. (2010). The odd couple: Margaret Archer, Anthony Giddens and British social theory. *The British Journal of Sociology, 61,* 253–260.

Lupton, D. (2016). *The quantified self.* Cambridge: Polity Press.

Lupton, D. (2019). *Data selves: More-than-human perspectives.* Cambridge: Polity Press.

Mason, P. (2019). *Clear bright future: A radical defence of the human being.* London: Penguin.

Mouzelis, N. (2003). *Sociological theory: What went wrong? Diagnosis and remedies.* London: Routledge.

Outhwaite, W. (2009). Canon formation in late 20th-century British sociology. *Sociology, 43*(6), 1029–1045.

Porpora, D. V. (2003). *Landscapes of the soul: The loss of moral meaning in American life.* Oxford: Oxford University Press.

Savage, M. (2009). Against epochalism: An analysis of conceptions of change in British sociology. *Cultural Sociology, 3*(2), 217–238.

Savage, M., & Burrows, R. (2007). The coming crisis of empirical sociology. *Sociology, 41*(5), 885–899.

Sayer, A. (2011). *Why things matter to people: Social science, values and ethical life.* Cambridge: Cambridge University Press.

Sloterdijk, P. (2020). *Infinite mobilization.* Cambridge: Polity Press.

Stiglitz, J. E. (2004). *The roaring nineties: A new history of the world's most prosperous decade.* London: Penguin.

Taylor, C. (2009). *A secular age.* Cambridge, MA: Harvard University Press.

Turner, F. (2010). *From counterculture to cyberculture: Stewart Brand, the Whole Earth Network, and the rise of digital utopianism.* Chicago, IL: The University of Chicago Press.

Varoufakis, Y. (2011). *The global minotaur. America, Europe and the future of the global economy*. London: Zed Books.

Varoufakis, Y. (2016). *And the weak suffer what they must? Europe, austerity and the threat to global stability*. London: Random House.

Whitaker, E. (2017). No death, no taxes: A wake up call from transhumanism. *The Sociological Review*. Retrieved from www.thesociologicalreview.com/no-death-no-taxes-a-wake-up-call-from-transhumanism/

Wolfe, C. (2010). *What is posthumanism?* Minneapolis, MN: University of Minnesota Press.

Žižek, S. (1999). *The ticklish subject: The absent centre of political ontology*. London: Verso.

Žižek, S. (2009). *First as tragedy, then as farce*. London: Verso.

1 Being human (or what?) in the digital matrix land

The construction of the humanted

Pierpaolo Donati

When does digital-based enhancement become (really) human?

If we define digital-based enhancement as the use of technological tools (such as information and communication technology [ICT], artificial intelligence [AI] and robots) to increase the capacities of human persons, groups and social organizations to overcome certain limitations internal or external to them, the problem that opens up is understanding how and to what extent 'the human' and its dignity are modified.

The challenge is great due to two complex sets of reasons: first, because the human is difficult to define, as its boundaries are always historically open; second, because digital devices are not mere tools but rather social forces that are increasingly affecting our self-conception (who we are), our mutual interactions (how we socialize), our conception of reality (our metaphysics), our interactions with reality (our agency) and much more (Floridi 2015).

In volume I of this series (Donati 2019), I supported the thesis that enhancement through digital technologies is more human the more it allows those intersubjective and social relationships that realize the humanization of the person. This argument is not found in most of the current literature, where enhancement is assessed with reference to the body and/or to the mind of the individual and, in some way, to his relations, but not to social relations as such. The topic of 'relational enhancement', as I understand it, is underdeveloped, if not virtually unexplored.

The aforementioned thesis is motivated by how digital technologies increasingly change social and human relations. That is why, in volume II (Donati 2020), I proposed to analyse the processes of hybridization of social identities, relations and social organizations in order to understand under which conditions the enhancement brought about by the digital revolution can shape organizational forms that are capable of promoting, rather than alienating, humanity.

In volume I (Donati 2019: section 2.2), I introduced the concept of 'Matrix Land' as the pervasive environment of digital (virtual) reality in which humanity is destined to live ever further from its natural origin. The digital technological matrix (DTM) can be defined as *the globalized symbolic code that governs the creation of digital technologies designed to enhance or replace human action, radically changing social identities and relationships.* By modifying human action, digital technology conditions the human persons who use it to the point that the DTM changes their identities together with the social relations that constitute them (given that identities and social relations are co-constitutive).

The challenge posed by Matrix Land is that of a future society, however uncertain, in which the cognition of historical time will be lost and, with it, also the classical (Euclidean) notion of space. Time and space become illusions. Virtual reality will prevail over human nature so that human beings will think that what previously appeared real to them was on the contrary pure illusion.[1] From the point of view of the radical supporters of the DTM, reality exists only in the mind. Virtual logic will supersede analogical thought. What then will be left of the human?

For those who are fully immersed in Matrix Land, human reality is not something to understand or explain in order to remedy some of its defects but only a set of images hidden in the back of the human brain, formed on the basis of electrical stimulations aroused by the perceptions of the five bodily senses. The senses capture all kinds of stimulations, which come from both human beings and from every other non-human entity, mixed in such a way that the human reality conceived in the brain takes on unprecedented characteristics. Which ones?

According to the developments in quantum physics and biogenetics, our processes of imagination will allow us tomorrow to create something that today seems impossible or imaginative. In Matrix Land, the Mind creates what future society will concretely make possible. For example, thinking that human beings can fly will lead society to allow them, in the near or distant future, to actually fly – obviously only when it shall have the right tools to make it happen.

In this contribution I would like to evaluate this perspective to understand what it implies from the point of view of what 'being human' could mean in Matrix Land.

The rationale of my argument is that, in order to achieve a truly human enhancement, it is not enough to improve the abilities and performances of an individual (its body and/or mind) or a social group or organization, but it is necessary to verify that enhancement operations have positive repercussions on the persons' social (i.e., 'relational') life. I wonder what kinds of social relations between humans are favoured (or impeded) by digital technologies and how the tools of digital enhancement affect human persons from the point of view of their intersubjective and social relations. Applying a digital device – no matter how intelligent it is – in order to improve the performances of an individual or a group of people is completely insufficient to affirm that this action of enhancement has properly human consequences. If so, under what conditions can we say that enhancement based on digital tools respects or favours human dignity rather than putting it at risk or damaging it?

Enhancement, digital revolution and social relations

During the first Industrial Revolution, in the cultural climate of the Enlightenment, the human being was often conceived as a machine (see *L'Homme Machine* by J. O. de La Mettrie published in 1747). Yet until the twenty-first century, human relations have been regarded as distinct from mechanical relationships. The digital revolution threatens to erase this distinction. It is as if a new Enlightenment[2] is reformulating the idea of the machine and the idea of the human being within a single, conforming digital code. In this way, the relationships between humans and those between humans and machines (or animals, or whatever) become assimilable.

Accordingly, one wonders: what is the difference in relationality that connects human beings with mindless machines *compared with* the relationality between human and machines equipped with an autonomous artificial mind?

The crucial point concerns the possibility that the distinction between the personhood of humans and that of smart machines might disappear (Warwick 2015), so as to decree the death of the old humanism focused on that distinction (Breslau 2000). No wonder that even the distinction between interhuman relations and other kinds of relations (e.g., with non-human living beings or material things) disappears. This is the putative miracle of the DTM. The *I-Thou* relationship theorized by Martin Buber can now be applied to the relations that people have with their supercomputer, a bat or extraterrestrials provided that they have a first-person perspective, since "thou-ness is not distinct to humans."[3]

In my opinion, this view is based on the assumption that the identity of an entity relies entirely upon its mind (first-person perspective) and does not depend on the quality and structure of the relations that their physical or body structure, albeit enhanced, can allow. This argument forgets that between identities and relationships there are non-random connections that are specific generative mechanisms on which the outcomes depend, for instance the flowering or alienation of the human (as we will see by commenting on Figure 1.1). If we understand relationships as expressions of a self-reflective mind (which thinks in the first person), we digitize human beings in the same way as animals and any other object.

In order to understand the specific identity of the human mind, it is useful to assume that a mind, in the abstract, is an effect (a relational entity) emerging from interactions between its constitutive elements working together, making it a product of three components – *brain + stimulating factors (internal & external) + the autonomous contribution of the relations between brain and stimulating factors –* which is the third component of the emergent effect that is the operating mind.

Does the AI/robot's mind have the same third component (the autonomous role of the connecting relations) as the human mind? My answer is negative: the human and artificial minds are two incommensurable orders of reality because of their structurally different relationality, both internally and externally.

Identity is formed in relationships, and vice versa, relationships are formed through identities, which means that the process of interactions can have different outcomes, depending on whether the process occurs in a conflationary way between identity and relations or instead distinguishes them analytically over time as realities of different orders. Not any kind of interaction leads to the fulfilment of the human person. Between an arrangement in which interactions are of a reproductive type (morphostatic) and an arrangement in which they are of a chaotic type (turbulent morphogenesis) there are innumerable different configurations of which it is difficult to appreciate their more or less humanizing character. Consider, for example, the self-description of a groundbreaking high-tech company of AI researchers, neuroscientists, psychologists, artists and innovative thinkers called *SoulMachines*. This company aims at re-imagining what is possible in human computing with the following declaration on its website:

> We bring technology to life by creating incredibly life-like, emotionally responsive Digital Humans with personality and character that allow machines to talk to us literally face-to-face! Our vision is to humanize computing to better humanity. We use Neural Networks that combine biologically inspired models of the human brain and key sensory networks to create a virtual central nervous system that we call our Human Computing Engine. When you 'plug' our engaging and interactive Digital Humans into our cloud-based Human Computing Engine, we can transform modern life for the better by revolutionizing the way AI, robots and machines interact with people.

It is then a matter of analysing what kind of hybridization between the human being and the machine is produced by the different forms of enhancement, and what consequences are produced in social relations, and therefore in the whole organization of society.

I would like to analyse this topic by looking at how the historical evolution of technologies is changing both the natural order and the social order through the practical order of reality.

Confronting the digital matrix: the emergence of the humanted

The transition to the humanted

Human identity, and its humanization, passes through the relationality of the mind in connection with its internal and external environments. It becomes essential to understand how these relationships change in different technological environments.

In Table 1.1 I summarize the transition from the pre-DTM historical phase to the advent phase of DTM and to the further development of DTM.

(I) In the pre-matrix phase, machines can be more or less sophisticated, but they are not 'thinking'. Therefore human beings use them as instruments that can be mastered, even if the users are also affected by the instruments they use. In any case, human relationships remain clearly distinct from machinic (automatic) relations. Knowledge and communication are of an analogical type. Society is still seen as the exclusive domain of human beings, who are supposed to be its architects and its 'centre' (anthropocentrism).

(II) In the transformation phase, the traditional sectors of society that operate in analogue mode (including analogue machines) are increasingly replaced by smart

Table 1.1 How the digital technological matrix progressively transforms humanness and society

(I) Before the digital matrix:	(II) Transition to the digital matrix:	(III) A society driven by the digital matrix
'Man architect' **(*Homo faber*)**	**'(Re)constructed man'** **(*Homo aedificatus*)**	**'Digital man'** **(*Homo digitalis*)**
Analogical code (classic ontology and epistemology)	**Binary code** (dialectic ontology and epistemology)	**Quantum code (qubit)** (relationalist ontology and epistemology)
The human being can design and master the machine, which is an instrumental and passive tool for practical activities	Technologies become more intelligent and autonomous so that their relations 'redefine' the human being	Human beings become accustomed to digital relations and take digital features from them (generation of the humanted)
Identities and social relations are supposed to reflect given-for-granted human features, since knowledge and communication are *analogical*	Identities and social relations become mentalized and hybridized, because knowledge and communication become *digital* (algorithms)	Identities and relations depend on the type and degree of reflexivity exercised on the processes of *mentalization* and *hybridization* of knowledge and communication (*reflexive hybridization*)
Society represents itself as immediately 'human' (anthropo-*centrism*)	Society represents itself as a 'collective mind' (anthropo-*eccentrism*)	Society represents itself as a multiplicity of social worlds differentiated according to the guiding distinction *cyber/human*

machines eventuated by the digital revolution. Behind these innovations, there is the visionary idea of a 'society of mind' that is cultural, scientific and practical. This visionary idea is to think and configure society as it is to build a mind that works on the basis of innumerable elements that are in themselves 'stupid', but all working together they make 'the whole' (i.e., society itself as a mind) intelligent. According to Marvin Minsky, this is the idea behind the construction of both the AI and the society they will create. In his words, society of mind is a

> scheme in which each mind is made of many smaller processes. These we'll call *agents*. Each mental agent by itself can only do some simple thing that needs no mind or thought at all. Yet when we join these agents in societies – in certain very special ways – this leads to true intelligence.
>
> (Minsky 1988: 17)

From my point of view, the DTM is the practical realization of this vision of society in which agents are mere processes, neither reflexive people nor social subjects capable of expressing and putting into practice intelligent and meaningful projects. Such a DTM imposes itself as an impersonal and anonymous force. The tendency to replace the analogical code with the digital one has the consequence of eroding the distinctions between human-human relations and human-machine relations, because human relationships are replaced by the operations of smart machines and assimilated to their logic and their characteristics.

Current technologically advanced societies represent a middle step between a society where there is no artificial intelligence and a society in which smart machines are endowed with minds (i.e., autonomous cognitive processes), so that new kinds of 'persons' (like 'electronic persons' and virtual networked organizations) become 'agents' on their own.

In this transitional phase, human rights are increasingly at stake due to what Teubner (2006: 240–41) calls "the anonymous Matrix of communication":

> The human-rights question in the strictest sense must today be seen as endangerment of individuals' body/mind integrity by a multiplicity of anonymous and today globalised communicative processes. [. . .] Failing a supreme court for meaning, all that can happen is that mental experience endures the infringement and then fades away unheard. Or else it gets 'translated' into communication, but then the paradoxical and highly unlikely demand will be for the infringer of the right (society, communication) to punish its own crime! That means turning poachers into gamekeepers.

(III) A society driven by DTM seems to be the point of arrival of what Karl Marx called the administration of things by things. Political institutions and civil actors try to dominate the new technologies, but more and more they realize that the power of intelligent machines changes their way of thinking and relating to each other.

These changes are marked by the passage from (I) the analogical symbolic code of the early modern society, to the (II) binary code of the post-modern society, to the (III) quantum code (qubit) of the trans-modern society.[4]

What I want to emphasize is the transformation of social relations. (I) The *analogical code* is that of classical ontology and epistemology, in which symbols or models are applied to a constructed or artificial reality on the basis of analogies with a reality conceived as natural. Thus achieved is a correspondence between two different phenomena governed by the same laws, which therefore can be subsumed under a single model: *social relations seen as natural*. (II) The *binary code* refers to a dialectical ontology and epistemology in which 0 and 1 are used alternatively to produce dynamic and dialectical states that can in any case generate a certain stability at the macro level under certain very particular conditions. *Social relations become a built reality of procedural and transactional character.* (III) The *quantum code* (qubit) refers to the ontology and relational epistemology in which 0 and 1 overlap and intertwine (the phenomenon is called entanglement) in procedural states generally lacking in stability both at the micro and macro levels. *The social relationship now becomes purely virtual.* As Malo (2019) reminds us, social relationships have their own energy, or what Aristotle called *energeia*. From my point of view, in the social sciences, the energy of the social relation occupies a position analogous to that of the quantum in the physical sciences. Just as quantum mechanics provides only a discrete set of multiple values for a fundamental variable that cannot be further broken down, so does my relational sociology for social relations.

One wonders where society is going. Certainly, as far as the human person is concerned, the result of this dynamic will be the emergence of an 'augmented human', which I call a *humanted* (i.e., an augmented human), a human person modified by technologies who is both the product and producer of the hybridization of society. The augmented human identity will enjoy a strengthening of natural abilities but will also experience new problems of relationship with herself, with others, and with the world.

What will be its future configuration when DTM will be further developed to the point of acquiring its autonomy with respect to human subjects? Obviously, a series of scenarios are opened here for a society led by DTM. To put it shortly, these scenarios depend on two main processes.

The first process favours the *mentalization* of social relations and therefore of both personal identity and the representation of society. It makes mind the cultural model for the whole society, replacing the old metaphor of society as industrialized labour, the one that the twentieth century called 'machine civilization' (Miller 1979).

The second process is the *hybridization* of social relations, which is closely linked to the first. It derives from the fact that social relations between humans, instead of being distinct from digital ones, tend to incorporate certain characteristics of the latter and therefore hybridize. People are induced to think and act 'digitally' instead of analogically.

In the current use of AI/robots, there is something that binds the human person and the technological artefact, while still differentiating them. They differ as they must 'adapt' to each other if they want to work together. This adaptation takes place precisely via the interactions and transactions they establish between them. Their feedbacks are interactive and transactional but not strictly relational (Donati 2013), which means that one incorporates certain modes of operation of the other, but the relationship remains problematic.

The problem can be understood in the words of Melanie Mitchell (2019) when she states that machine learning algorithms don't yet understand things the way humans do – with sometimes disastrous consequences. Current progress in AI is stymied by a barrier of meaning. Anyone who works with AI systems knows that behind the façade of humanlike visual abilities, linguistic fluency and game-playing prowess, these programs do not – in any humanlike way – *understand* the inputs they process or the outputs they produce. The lack of such understanding renders these programs susceptible to unexpected errors and undetectable attacks.

If one argues that personhood is not in principle confined to those entities that have a human body (or traceable to human bodies, as in moral persons), or is compatible with changing any part of the human body because personhood consists in possessing the first-person perspective, as Baker claims, the consequence is that personhood is 'mentalized'. Mentalization consists in the fact that the intersubjective production of meanings (semiosis) is made virtual (Arnold 2002). The mentalization and hybridization of identities and social relationships promotes the anthropomorphic attribution of human characteristics to realities that are not human. Personification of robots, for instance, is precisely a strategy of dealing with uncertainty about their identity, which moves the pattern of attribution of identity from the causality induced by humans to that of the double *Ego-Alter* contingency, which presupposes the robot's self-referentiality. The question is: does this self-referentiality produce the same emerging effects of inter-human relations?

The relationship between the human person and AI/robot becomes a mind-to-mind relationship. Deprived of a correspondence between two human bodies, emotional, sentimental and psychological dimensions become an enigma. By losing the relationship with their specific bodily support, dialogue, conversation and communication assume the character of a simulated, emulated, fake or fantasized reality. If I think to relate myself to a star that is in a galaxy billions of light years away from me, I imagine a relationship that is purely mental but which has an effect on me, because it redefines my identity.

As Henry Atlan (1985: 96) wrote:

> Ce qui nous pousse en fait à placer la barrière de façon arbitraire entre les hommes et le reste, c'est l'expérience immédiate d'une peau, d'un corps ou de mots, que nous faisons d'un autre système, extérieur à nous-memes. Cette experience est pré-scientifique ou post-scientifique et c'est un souci d'éthique de comportement plus que de connaissance objective qui nous fait placer intentions, projets, créativité et en meme temps responsabilité et liberté, à l'intérieur d'une peau qui enveloppe un corps dont il se trouve que, de près ou de loin, il ressemble au mien.

For example, by attributing personality to a robot or AI, sexual identity is mentalized, since it no longer corresponds to a defined body but to an indefinitely hybridized medium. Entrusting family, friendship or business communications to an AI/robot instead of face-to-face relationships leads to mentalizing relationships rather than considering their concreteness, their materiality.

Supplementing the first-person perspective by adding reflexivity and concerns in order to delineate personal and social identities can help to avoid these outcomes to some extent, but it is not enough to make social relationships adequate to meet human needs related to physicality. As many empirical investigations reveal, relationships between family members who frequently prefer to communicate through the internet rather than face-to-face gradually take on the virtual logic of social networks: interpersonal relationships are decomposed and recomposed (unglued and re-glued) and become more fragile, while communications are privatized on an individual basis. In sum, family relationships become mental rather than analogical (Cisf 2017). If a person does the daily shopping in a supermarket through the internet rather than going in person to the shops and meeting other people, she ends up impoverishing her human relationships and absorbs, unwittingly, a relational logic that is hybridized with how the supermarket *app* operates. The private lifestyle, at least in consumption, is made accessible to the knowledge of strangers and the boundaries between private sphere and public sphere collapse. The strength of DTM is nourished through the diffusion of a mentalized environment of reference common to all those who communicate which, moreover, is retained and manipulated through big data. People who communicate outside DTM become socially irrelevant.

The process of hybridization

A society driven by DTM can evolve in various directions. In my opinion, the scenarios for a 'digital society' will be different (1) depending on the type and degree of control and mastery that humans will have on DTM; (2) according to the type and degree of reflexivity that people exercise on the processes of mentalization and hybridization of relations; and (3) according to the forms of governance of the organizations and economies that use DTM.

Society will be less and less interpretable as human in a direct and spontaneous way because human relations will be increasingly mediated by DTM. With all this, the human does not disappear, but what was once called 'human society' must be intentionally re-generated as 'society *of the* human', characterized by being produced through relational reflexivity on the human through new distinctions between the various forms of social relations that generate different types of society. The so-called human society has been swept away by functional differentiation (Luhmann 1990), and the 'society of the human' can emerge only through a supra-functional relational differentiation able to challenge the cyber society.

If an organization or social network wants to maintain the basic characteristics of the human, it will have to develop a culture and practices that give people the ability to reflect on the hybridization of social relations in order not to become the slaves of machines.

This problem is maintaining and empowering human agency, which is threatened by a social structure (the hardware of DTM) that has become the engine of change and that bypasses the agency by continuously adapting to itself a cultural system which in turn overrides human agency without giving it the ability to exercise its personal and relational reflexivity.

I summarize this process in Figure 1.1 which formulates, within the framework of relational sociology, the SAC (structure-agency-culture) scheme of morphogenesis suggested by Archer (2013: 1–21) so as to meet the demands for greater clarification (Knio 2018) concerning the key role of relations in the double and triple morphogenesis of agency.

To be short, the core idea is that, when the human agency is unable to influence the structure, the latter determines the morphogenesis of agency in such a way as to reduce or prevent its reflexive capacities. In this case, the structure directly modifies the cultural system without agency reacting, and in this way the dominance of DTM is reinforced, which hybridizes identities and social relations. Hybridization proceeds to the extent that reflexive agency is blocked, so that the

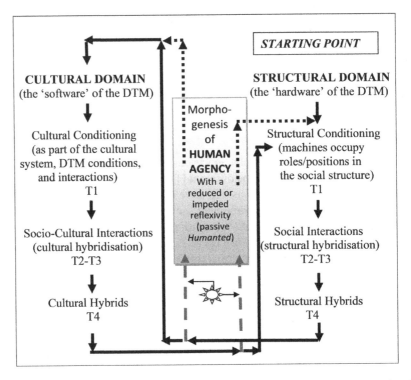

Figure 1.1 The morphogenetic cycle of SAC (structure, agency and culture) run by the DTM that generates the hybridization of society and the passive *humanted*

[*Legenda*: when the agency is blocked (within dotted lines) the structure and culture prevail and change morphogenetically each other (solid lines), with the agency being more passive].

structural changes of DTM can change cultural processes without resistance and continuously reshape the identities and relationships of human persons. The latter becomes a passive humanted.

Take the case of the Boeing 737 Max-8 aircrafts that have crashed in recent years (for example, that of the Ethiopian Airlines crashed near the Addis Ababa airport on 10 March 2019). True or not, one of the explanations for the accident was that the aircraft's software (i.e., the AI that had to monitor it) forced the pilot to do certain operations not left to his discretion in order to avoid possible terrorist hijacking. In the presence of an unexpected event (probably fire on board), the AI did not allow the pilot to do those manoeuvres that could have prevented the fall. In a sense, the pilot's identity (humanted) and his relationships to manoeuvre the plane were hybridized and blocked by the AI. This example is emblematic for all those cases in which an AI, although created to ensure the achievement of positive ends, prevents the use of relational reflexivity by those who drive the machine (passive humanted) and leads to a negative outcome of the action system or organization. The remedy is not sought in strengthening the human agent (the pilot as *proactive humanted*), but in designing a more sophisticated AI that can replace him. A well-known case is that of managers who entrust an AI with the task of establishing the duties and shifts of company employees so that, as AI does not allow the manager to use adequate personal and relational reflexivity (weakened or impeded agency in Figure 1.1), a lot of employee dissatisfaction and an overall negative business climate are generated (cultural domain), which leads to seeking a remedy by replacing employees with robots, AI or other artificial instruments (structural domain).

We can say that being human in Matrix Land means having the chance to exercise the qualities and causal powers of human agency in such a way as to react to structural and cultural conditioning by reflexively redirecting social relations towards human persons. In Figure 1.1, this means empowering the weak relations (dotted lines) and making them stronger and proactive (solid lines). To exert effective reflexivity, agency needs a favourable social environment to configure itself. In other words, to put into practice the reflexive imperative, it is necessary to satisfy the relational imperative. This implies control and regulation of the conditioning social structure (how the economic powers behind the techno-structure operate) in order to prevent it from colonizing the cultural system in such a way as to bypass human agency.

When human agency, although influenced by DTM, can react to the latter with an adequate relational reflexivity (strong relationality), we see the emergence of a proactive augmented human (humanted), as in Figure 1.2.

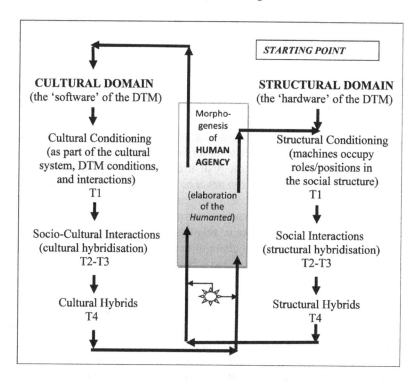

Figure 1.2 The proactive humanted

The future of the world depends on the types and degrees of mastery over smart digital machines (ICT, AI, robots). I cannot discuss here the various political, economic, organizational and legal instruments that can serve this purpose at the macro and meso levels.[5] Al-Amoudi (2019: 182) has made clear how "managerial practices have contributed to dehumanising contemporary societies, and that management studies bear an important share of the blame."

To counter this drift, we should understand the importance of the ontic necessity of relations in organizational studies.[6] Very important are studies on human-robot interaction (HRI) to assess the relational implications. At the micro level, it is necessary to develop a cybernetic literacy that does not limit itself to educating the individual as such, as proposed by Pierre Lévy (1997), but regards the way of operating networks in which individuals are inserted. Only in this way will we be able to prevent DTM from producing new segmentations and inequalities between social groups due to the new divides created by the differentiation of the networks of social relations and the differentials in cyber literacy between people. It is at this point that we need to address the discourse on human dignity and human rights in the face of the society led by DTM.

When and how can an organization using digital technologies achieve human enhancement?

When is the enhancement pursued through hybridization human?

How do we distinguish when the enhancement practiced by an organization that works with digital technologies is humanizing rather than dehumanizing or even non-human?[7]

To make these distinctions, it is necessary to clarify what is meant by 'human' applied to the effects that enhancement technologies have on people and their relationships in a hybridized organization.

I do not want to enter the debate about the potential comparability of AI or robots and humans. I limit myself to observing that human ontology is incommensurable with respect to the ontology of artefacts. Even if AI and robots can be made 'sentient', their subjectivity can never be human. I say this because I believe that *personhood exists only in the relationships* both between mind and body and between the person and the surrounding world.[8] Human dignity exists and is to be protected and promoted in its social relationality. Baker's argument, according to which "artefacts have as strong claim to ontological status as natural objects" (Baker 2004: 112), must be subjected to a critical examination because the ontological status of the human body cannot be equated to that of an artefact like an AI or robot.

In a sense, even social organizations are artefacts, to which we attribute a legal personhood.[9] Organizations equipped with smart machines increase their intelligence and creativity to the extent that they are hybridized, that is, in which human subjects increase the 'awareness of their consciousness' just because they use AI or robots. Using intelligent artefacts allows workers to be more available for non-routine and more creative action. The question is in what sense and in which way do these organizations ensure the human qualities of the relationships between their members and the relationships that those who benefit from the activities of that organization will have?

To answer this question, it is not enough to refer to the ability of the individual members of the organization or its customers. It is necessary to consider the quality of the relationships created between the members of the organization and the quality of the relationships that its customers can put in place following the use of AI and robots.

To understand hybridized organizations in the sense understood here, it is necessary that personhood be not defined for its individual and self-referential abilities but be defined in a relational way to distinguish between the different types of relationships that are created in the organization with the introduction of intelligent machines.

In short, while individual human personhood requires possession of the first-person perspective, when we refer to a social organization as a relational subject we must reason in terms *relational personhood*. To manage the hybridized relationships of an organization in a human way, individual personhood must be the expression of a mind that works in connection with a human body (O'Connor 2017), able to reflect not only on itself and on its context but on the relationship to the Other as such. In hybridized social relations, there coexist both characteristics of the inter-human relationship – which is structured according to the *Ego-Alter* double contingency – and characteristics of the *Ego-It* digital relationship. In the latter, the expected contingency on the part of It is characterized by a drastic reduction compared to the complexity of the double contingency Ego-Alter.[10] If an organization hybridized by new technologies wants to avoid the reduction of Ego-Alter relationships to I-It relationships, it must maintain the high level of contingency in the Ego-Alter relationship. This requires the adoption of a second person's perspective beyond that of the first person, necessary to communicate sensibly with the Alter, and in particular to recognize Alter's differences and rights (Darwall 2007). In my opinion, admitted and not granted that the AI/robot can act according to the perspective of the first person, to play the role of Alter (and vice versa Ego) in the relationship with a human person, the AI/robot should be able to assume the perspective of the second person. The perspective of the second person implies that the agent (in this case the AI/robot) should be able to act as a "Self like an Other" (*Soi-même comme un autre*),[11] which means that the AI/robot should act like a human being and, as such, evaluating the good of the relationship (the relational good between Ego and Alter). This is impossible as long as the AI/robot does not have the same constitution as a human being.

In opposition to this statement, there are scholars who think that sentient AI or robots can be (or become) capable of 'reflecting' on the Other and/or the relational context as if they were an Alter in the Ego-Alter relationship. At this point we find the problem of clarifying whether or not there are differences – and if so, what are they – between humans and AI/robots in social life and, consequently, if any, between the dignity of one and the other.

The talk about personhood and human dignity

Charles Taylor (1985: 102) observes:

> what is crucial about agents is that things matter to them. We thus cannot simply identify agents by a performance criterion, nor assimilate animals to machines. . . . [likewise] there are matters of significance for human beings which are peculiarly human and have no analogue with animals.

I think the same is true when it comes to AI/robots and not just animals.

One of the things that matters is social relations. They have a significance for human beings which are peculiarly human and have no analogue with animals or AI/robots. To clarify this point, I suggest making a parallel between the distinction of first- and second-order desires made by Harry Frankfurt (1971) as essential to the demarcation of human agents from other kinds of agent, and the distinction of first- and second-order relations.

Human beings are not alone in having desires and motives or in making choices. They share these things with members of certain other species, some of which even appear to engage in deliberation and to make decisions based on prior thought. This is possible also for AI/robots. What is distinctive of a human person is the capacity to have a second-order relation when she has a desire or makes a choice whose object is her having a certain first-order relation. The first-order relation is an expression of inner reflexivity that can be present at certain times also in some animals and perhaps in some future AI or robots, but only the human person can have second-order relationships that are an expression of relational reflexivity (Donati 2013). After all, the higher morality of human agency lies not so much in the first-order relationship as above all in the second-order relationship.

This point of view is particularly important because AI/robots can be actors of new types and forms of relationships that differ greatly from the relationships that animals can have with human persons. Human-animal relationships belong to the natural order, while human-digital artefacts relate to the orders of social and practical realities of applied technologies. The actor-network theory is flawed precisely because it conflates all these orders of reality.

The 'relationality criterion' should not be understood as a 'performance criterion' or another behaviourist criterion. G. H. Mead's view, taken up by R. Harré and others (see Jones 1997: 453), that selves exist solely in lived discourse and derive their dynamics and intentionality from speech acts is fallacious precisely because social relations also exist without linguistic acts and they reflexively influence the self also in an indirect or unintentional way. In my view, the 'relationality criterion' becomes more and more important and significant precisely because the DTM dramatically amplifies the phenomena of hybridization of social relations and, more generally, it is the causal factor of a huge 'relational revolution' in the globalized world (Donati 2012).

As far as I know, no scholar has dealt with the issue of distinguishing human-robot relations in respect to human-human relations on the basis of a general theory of the qualities and causal properties of social relations in themselves, both in terms of dyads and complex networks.

Some suggestions can be found in the thesis advanced by David Kirchhoffer (2017), who rightly argues that the problem of dignity talk arises because proponents of various positions tend to ground human dignity in different features of the human individual. These features include species membership, possession of a particular capacity, a sense of self-worth, and moral behaviour. He proposes a solution to this problem by appealing to another feature of human beings, namely their being-in-relationship-over-time.

This perspective can enable us to understand dignity as a concept that affirms the worth of the human person as a complex, multidimensional whole rather than as an isolated, undersocialized entity (rational choice theory), a juxtaposition of 'dividual' features (Deleuze) or the product of functional differentiation (Luhmann; see Lindemann 2016). Kirchhoffer elaborates his argument by observing that the concept of human dignity can serve both a descriptive and a normative function in the enhancement debates. At a descriptive level, asking what advocates of a position mean when they refer to human dignity will reveal what aspects of being human they deem to be most valuable. The debate can then focus on these values. The normative function, although it cannot proscribe or prescribe all enhancement, approves only those enhancements that contribute to the flourishing of human individuals as multidimensional wholes.

One can agree with the idea that a person's ontological status rests on being a centre of value, 'integrally and adequately considered', but the foundation of such worth remains obscure. What is missing in Kirchhoffer's argument is the clarification of what values are distinctive of the human and which characteristics must have the relationships that make them flourish. The argument that human dignity stems from the fact that the human person is a multidimensional whole is necessary but not sufficient. We need to enter into the analysis and evaluation of the vital relationality that characterizes that 'whole' and makes it exist as a living being that has a structure and boundaries, however dynamic and morphogenetic.

Generally speaking, in the so-called relational turn of the last two decades mentioned by Raya Jones,[12] social relations have been almost always understood as interactions and transactions instead of 'social molecules' to which we can attribute human qualities and properties or not. When social relationships have been observed as more substantial, stable and lasting phenomena, their characteristics have been treated in terms of the psychological (mainly cognitive) qualities deriving from the related terms (i.e., human persons and robots). The attributions of qualities and properties to the human/robot relationships as such are, mostly, psychological projections of human persons on entities to which is attributed an ontological reality that is the result of subjective feelings and mental abstractions.

In short, social relations have been treated as psychological entities instead of being considered emergent social facts in which we can objectively distinguish human characters from those that are not. It is instructive, for example, that, speaking of the relational turn, Jones refers to authors such as G. H. Mead and Lev Vygotsky. He quotes the saying of Charles Cooley – "Each to each a looking-glass. Reflects the other that doth pass" – considering it as the premise of the interactionist relationalism, and then he still appreciates the perspective of Turkle according to which "in the move from traditional transitional objects to contemporary relational artefacts, the psychology of projection gives way to a relational psychology, a psychology of engagement."

Jones wholly ignores all those perspectives according to which social relations cannot be reduced to social psychological traits. The researches cited by Jones only show that a growing number of scholars treat human/robot relationships as they study relationships between human and domestic animals, thinking that robots will do better than animals. Of course, those who love dogs or cats treat them as human beings: they grow fond of them, talk to them every day, adapt to their needs in their own relational life and so on. But dogs and cats are not human beings. Of course, robots can have many more human characteristics than dogs and cats: they can talk in turn, they can reciprocate smiles and gestures of sympathy and they can perform orders much better than any other pet. But they cannot have that 'complex' of qualities and causal properties that make up the human and generate other kinds of relationships, which are ontologically – not just psychologically – distinct from those with animals. The problem is that the researches cited by Jones lack a generalized paradigm to define precisely and substantively what is meant by social relation.

Jones (2013: 412) suggests that, perhaps, in the future, "robots may enter as relational partners" as if they were human. She does not distinguish between social relations between humans and relations between humans and artefacts from the point of view of social ontology. She seems to share the idea that "it is the human's perception of the relationship that humanises the machine" (Jones 2013: 415), thus demonstrating that she treats social relations as psychological projections, even when she criticizes individualist interactionism to affirm what she calls relational interactionism and ecological relationalism.

Social relationships are not just human because we think of them as human even if, according to Thomas's theorem, the fact of considering them as human leads to certain practical consequences. It is precisely these consequences that allow us to distinguish when social relationships are human and when they are not. Two examples can be mentioned: one in educational robotics, when we see that the use of robots can cause harm (e.g., psychological and relational disorders) to children (Sharkey 2010); the other in assistive robotics, when elderly people refuse the robots, saying that they do not respect their human dignity precisely because they cannot replace human relations (Sharkey & Sharkey 2010, Sharkey 2014).

A litmus test will be the case in the future of sexual relations between humans and robots. We will have to check whether the sexual relations between humans and robots are as satisfying as those between humans, even if the latter are not always humanizing.

If we split personhood, defined in the moral sense I have just indicated, from humanness by attributing moral personhood to non-human entities, the boundaries between human and non-human are lost. Therefore, no humanism is more sustainable. Those who attribute moral qualities to non-human animals and, potentially, to post-human or transhuman beings do so. The conflation between human, infra-human and superhuman, must then be legitimized on the basis of some evolutionist theory (be it materialistic, like Darwinian, or spiritualistic, like that of Teilhard de Chardin) according to which a novel species or genus of hominid will be born beyond *Homo sapiens* (theory of singularity) – which means adhering to some mutating utopia of the human nature. For relational realism, this mutation is not possible because the utopia on which it stands is not concrete. If post-human beings are created, even if they have a superior intelligence, their personhood will no longer have proper human characters. They will be alien beings to the human; to be more explicit, they will no longer have that 'relational complex' that characterizes the human.

I think the contraposition between transhumanists and bioconservatives is misleading. Bostrom's (2005) proposal to elaborate a concept of dignity that is inclusive enough to also apply to many possible post-human beings ("future posthumans, or, for that matter, some of the higher primates or human-animal chimaeras") is confusing because it makes no sense to attribute a single concept of dignity to human and non-human beings. Certainly, dignity implies respect and recognition of a certain worth, but the kinds of respect and worth are not the same for humans and non-humans. Every existing species of beings (living and non-living) has its own dignity (Collier 1999), but it is different for each of them. A unique concept would lead to indifferentism and relativism in moral choices. Rather, it is necessary to use a concept of dignity that is differentiated for each order and layer of reality. The relational proposal is, in fact, to define the concept of dignity relationally, depending on the qualities and causal properties of the relationships that each being realizes or can realize. Thus, social organizations like hospitals should adopt a relational perspective if they want to be humanizing. A person X can receive a new heart (or another organ) with a transplant if she needs it, but her relationship to the transplanted body will not be the same as it had been with the original.

Is it the same person? Sure, but the person X must recompose her identity with the new body. Undoubtedly this requires the activation of her mental abilities (the exercise of the first-person perspective, reflexivity, and endorsement of concerns), but her mental abilities that allow for self-consciousness are not enough. She has to elaborate a certain virtual relationship with the figure of the donor, which implies affective and symbolic elements of relationship with this Other that has become part of her bodily identity. That person finds herself still *ipse* (in her capacity to be still the same person) but not *idem* (she is not equal to what she was before) because the transplant, by changing the body, has changed her relational identity (with herself and the others): "I am still the same, but different." It is this relational ability to maintain the same identity while changing it that characterizes the personhood of the human subject beyond her cognitive abilities. This is what distinguishes the human from the artificial personhood: the human actualizes in the same subject 'being for oneself' and 'being for others' at the same time. As I have already said, in principle the AI/robot can perform the first operation (being for oneself) but not the second (being for others), because to be able to implement second-order relational reflexivity it should have the same relational nature of humans.

If we admitted, hypothetically, that a super robot can have a cognitive sense of the Self, however it would not be able to manage the double contingency inherent in this relationality, which is beyond its reach (see, for instance, Eva's behaviour in the movie *Ex Machina*). Something similar happens when the interpersonal relationships between the members of an organization are mediated by AI and robots in such a way as to change the identity of people in their social roles.

In short, from my point of view, in order to evaluate whether an organization providing enhancement is more or less humanizing versus not humanizing at all, it is necessary to adopt the relational optics (i.e., assessing the effects of the intervention of the organization on the relations both between the body and the mind of the person and on the specificity of her interhuman relationships with respect to other types of relationships).

This perspective is essential when we analyse the use of digital technologies for the enhancement of people working in complex networks or organizations. In that case, we need to see how technologies – such as AI or robots – influence the most important resource of a social organization (i.e., the production of social capital and relational goods rather than the consumption of social capital and the feeding of relational evils).

Redefining the human in hybridized organizations

Usually, 'hybrid organizations' are understood as networks based upon partnerships, open coordination, co-production, community networking and the like between different sorts of organizations. They are social configurations intertwining system and social integration. In this context, I define 'hybridized organization' as a social form comprising multiple people linked together by a collective endeavour and connected by digital technologies both internally and with the external environment. Digital technologies are included in the system integration side, while human relations are ascribed to the lifeworlds of social integration.

We can observe what happens in organizations like a family, a school, a corporation, a hospital or a civil association when they are hybridized by digital technologies. First of all, robots are changing the relational context by adding relations that can complement or replace interpersonal relations. Reporting the results of empirical research on what happens in families, schools, hospitals, corporations, retirement homes for the elderly and so on would take too long.

Technology is now able to recognize our emotions and our tastes. It studies our behaviour through algorithms and big data, thus directing the choices of individuals. To counter the constraints imposed by the technological market, it is necessary to relate to DTM with meta-reflexivity and resort to relational steering (which I will mention momentarily).

My argument is that the performance of digital technologies introduced for enhancement purposes should be considered as factors that always operate in a defined relational context and work in a more or less human way depending on whether they generate a relational good or a relational evil.

If we assume that society 'is relationship' (and not that it 'has relations'), the qualities and properties of a concrete society and its organizational forms will be those of its social relations. The transformations of the forms of social organization in which the relationships are mediated by technologies (AI or robots) must be evaluated by how they help the production of those social relations that establish a virtuous circle between social capital and relational goods (Donati 2014).

The decisive level for this evaluation is that of meso contexts, intermediate between micro and macro levels. Biologists tell us today that cancer is a tissue problem, that is, a network, not a single cell (network node). If a cancer cell is placed in an egg, the cell returns to normal. The meso relational context is also decisive in human behaviour. Pathology, like the good, of human behaviour is not in the single node (individual) but in the relational network.

The type of organization or social network and its dynamics depend on the agents' ability to make sustainable over time those innovations that include new technologies, to the extent that the agents are able or not to have a more reliable relational reflexivity on their hybridized relationships in a way as to produce the social capital necessary to generate relational goods.

This is my proposal to counteract the trend, rightly denounced by Ismael Al-Amoudi (2019: 182), of "managerial practices contributing to dehumanising contemporary societies, and that management studies bear an important share of the blame." Relational goods are common goods which can be produced only in networks that are organized in such a way as to share decisions and responsibilities according to styles of collegiality (Lazega 2017).

If a social or political movement entrusts decisions to an algorithm (AI or robot) that limits itself to gathering the voting preferences of individual members and decides on that basis, how will the behaviour of individual members (primary agents) and those of the movement as a corporate agent change? Experiments of this kind are still rare. One of them is the Five Stars political movement in Italy, which apparently has a democratic organization, but in reality it is governed by those who master the algorithm.

The fact is that using the web to build democratic social movements is problematic. For example, we have research on how social networks worked in the case of the various Arab Spring uprisings. Apparently, these were democratic movements, but the results were very different from building a democracy. The reason is that such networks were not organized in order to produce relational goods but were simply aggregations of masses of individuals sympathetic towards a collective protest action. The Arab Spring fed by the web was not an expression of the creation of relational goods among the participants, as Carole Uhlaner (2014) claims, so much so that from the Arab Spring arose non-democratic systems.

What is certain is that AIs and robots cannot create social capital per se. They cannot define our well-being and they cannot create relational goods, such as trust or friendship. There can there be no 'we believe' between humans and robots. They can certainly adapt the content of their information and messages of various kinds to individuals (as Graber 2016 claims), but based on the algorithmic identity of the recipient.

The risk of a society or social organization driven by a DTM environment is to become a 'mental relation' populated by disembodied minds. This gives rise to opposing feelings. On one side, for instance, the Dalai Lama is quite happy to contemplate the karma of digital technology while leaving geeky details to the younger crowd,[13] while on the other side, people like Chamath Palihapitiya[14] – a venture capitalist born in Sri Lanka, raised in Canada, and a Facebook employee in Silicon Valley for a significant span of his life in – claims that "social networks are destroying how society works" and that he feels "tremendous guilt" about his work:

> It (Facebook) literally is at a point now where I think we have created tools that are ripping apart the social fabric of how society works. . . . We are in a really bad state of affairs right now in my opinion, it is eroding the core foundations of how people behave by and between each other.

The assessment of the human character of people's enhancement in hybrid organizations should be done in light of the criterion that the empowerment to act is viewed as arising from interaction within mutually empathic and mutually empowering relationships. The importance of technologies in human enhancement lies in creating and sustaining relationships and relational contexts that empower people in all life activities. The benefits of hybridization are to be assessed based on how much the technologies favour cooperative strategies and are sources of interorganizational competitive advantage (Dyer & Singh 1998).

It is important to place these phenomena in the frame of cultural processes. At the moment, the hybridization of identities, relationships and organizations takes place in different ways in the so-called Eastern and so-called Western cultures, apparently opposed. In the East (Asia), cultures are inspired by a hierarchical relational matrix on which all transactions depend. In this case, relationships drive functional performance (Yeh 2010, Liu 2015). In the West, on the contrary, relationships are reduced to performances within an individualistic cultural matrix. The prevailing culture treats relationships as instrumental entities to be used to improve management efficiency. The result is the commodification of social relations (Pawlak 2017).

Today we are witnessing a comparison between the different ways in which these two cultures develop and use technologies. In the long run, however, it is likely that the cultural environment of DTM can proceed towards forms of hybridization between Eastern and Western cultures. The Western individualistic and private model of Silicon Valley is already taking on the characteristics of an unscrupulous managerial and financial model such as China (Morozov 2011).

Conclusions: being human before and after the matrix

All cultures and societies must now confront the alternative between considering humanism dead or redefining the human in the new digital environment. The first solution makes residual what is properly human and places it in the environment of DTM. The second solution challenges DTM as the main driver of society and puts technologies back to the ontological level of means rather than first drivers. This turn can only be done by managing the hybrids (hybridized identities, relations and organizations) through distinctions that are defined by and within a social relational matrix based on critical realism rather than as an expression of a constructivist digital matrix.

The AI used for technological enhancement can only simulate the human and cannot be substantially human. The reason lies in the fact that AI cannot understand (*Verstehen*), that is, to attribute a meaning, to what it thinks or does because it does not have a relationship with the real thing (existing in itself). If the AI could recognize the Other (the non-Ego), that is to put oneself in the Other's shoes, it would have an Ego able to relate to another from itself. But AI cannot have this capability because the AI relationship is just a communication of information according to a symbolic code in which the Ego is split from the non-Ego. This code reads the 'inter' (i.e., the relationship between the subjects) as a factor added to the two terms of the relationship (i.e., as one more thing), and not as the emergent effect of their actions on which they should be relationally reflexive.

Traditional personalism (I do not like this word, but I use it because it is part of a historical debate), as a cultural model developed before the advent of the digital matrix, had a non-relational substantialist character. It cannot be further supported. The person must now be conceived in relational terms. However, here is a new comparison between those who reduce the person to relationships, and relationships only to communications, and those who maintain that the person cannot be dissolved in communications because, if it is true that communications form the person, they cannot replace her nature. We can grant a status of legal persons to artificial beings, but we cannot interject human nature into them.

In this chapter, I have put forward the thesis according to which the human/non-human distinction is revealed in the kind (qualities and causal properties) of the social *relationality* that digital technologies and their use favour or not. In short, it is about evaluating whether the technological mediation between human persons and their social organizations promotes or inhibits those relational goods that realize human fulfilment. The challenge of existing as human beings in the future digital Matrix Land will be to face the *relational imperative*: how to distinguish between social relations that are human and those that are not.

Robots will certainly become 'social beings', but not human beings. The historical process is destined to differentiate more and more human social relations from non-human social relations. Lawrence, Palacios-Gonzáles and Harris (2016: 250) rightly warn that

> our possible relations to AI persons could be more complicated than they first might appear, given that they might possess a radically different nature to us, to the point that civilized or peaceful coexistence in a determinate geographical space could be impossible to achieve.

In conclusion, why is the human person-robot relationship different from the relationship between human persons? Why there is no 'we-believe', no 'we-ness', no 'we-relation', no proper relational goods between humans and robots? I justified my negative answer based on the argument that, even if it were possible to have new artificial beings capable of some reflexivity and behaviours suitable to the ethics of the first person, these two criteria would not be sufficient to distinguish between person-person relationship and person-robot relationship. To see the distinction between the various types of relationships, we need to resort to relational reflexivity, which is different in nature from the individual one because it is based on the ethic of the second person. This distinction of forms of reflexivity corresponds to the distinction between two types of personalism: classical personalism, for which the person transcends herself in her own action, and *relational personalism*, for which the person transcends herself in the relationship with the Other. After the Digital Matrix has covered the globe, perhaps we all will become humanted, but the relational criterion will be even more discriminating than in the past.

Notes

1　See 'The Illusion of Reality' at www.youtube.com/watch?v=NxiGgxL5btA, and many other similar websites.
2　Let us think of Luhmann's sociological neo-Enlightenment (see Baecker 1999).
3　As suggested by Porpora (2019: 37):

> a thou is what bears the character of an I (or at least per Buber what is addressed as such). But then what is an I? An I is anything to which it is appropriate to attach what Thomas Nagel calls a first person perspective. [. . .] Put otherwise, an I or what is properly addressed as such, i.e., a Thou, is an experiencing subject, where an experience is not just a matter of thought but also of feeling. [. . .] If in Nagel's sense there is something it is like to be a bat, meaning it has what Nagel calls a first-person perspective, then, per my own argument, a bat is a thou. Which means that thou-ness is not distinct to humans. [. . .] Care, I would say, is the proper attitude to adopt toward a thou, human or not. To be clear, it is a non-instrumental care of which I speak. I care for my car but mostly because I do not want it to break down on me. The care I am suggesting that is properly extended to a thou, human or not, is concern for them as ends in themselves.

> It seems to me that, according to Buber (and I would like to add Ricoeur and Lévinas), a Thou should be another entity like the I (Ego). If it were an entity that is neither a Thou nor an It but a personification of something (e.g., a tree for a Taoist, the sky for a Confucian or the deities of woods and animals according to religions such as Hinduism and Buddhism), a question arises: do these entities speak to the Ego or, on the contrary, is the Ego talking to them? Or again, is it the Ego who tells them what they have stimulated in himself?

4　The term *trans*modern indicates a caesura or profound *discontinuity* with modernity, while the term of late or *post*modern indicates the developments that derive from bringing modernity to its extreme consequences on the basis of its premises.
5　See for example House of Lords (2018).
6　For instance, in marketing systems: see Simmons (2018).
7　I mean 'dis-humanizing' enhancement as that which degrades the human (e.g., using big data to condition consumer behaviour), therefore distorting the human which,

however, maintains its own potentiality, while 'non-human' means an action or intervention that reduces the human person to a simple animal, thing or machine (e.g., grafting a nanobot into the human brain to reduce the person to a slave).

8 See the emergence of the human person from the links between body and mind in Smith (2010).

9 We already attribute a subjectivity to fictitious (legal) persons who are ontologically artefacts, such as corporations, civil associations, schools, hospitals, banks and even governments.

10 On the issue of contingency reduction respectively by technology and human beings, see Luhmann and Schorr (1982), and Luhmann (1995).

11 Ricoeur (1990: 380):

> l'Autre n'est pas seulement la contrepartie du Même, mais appartient à la constitution intime de son sens." It may be useful here to clarify the meaning of the terms used by Ricoeur: "Soi" means "le soi (selbst, self) se distinguant de l'ego (je, Ich, I) non réfléchi." "Même" means "l'ipséité (← *ipse* identité réflexive) s'oppose à la mêmeté (← *idem* ressemblance, permanence)," and "Autre" means l'ipséité ne se définit pas contre l'altérité, mais par elle.

12 Raya A. Jones (2013: 405) writes:

> Relationalism refers primarily to a standpoint in social psychology. This standpoint is premised on the threefold claim that "persons exist by virtue of individuals' relations to others; that, cognately, "selves" are an emergent property of semiotic I-You-Me systems; and that therefore the task for social psychology is to identify "regularities" of interrelations between specific cultural practices and particular experiences of self.

This relational turn is derived mainly from authors such as Gergen and Harré.

13 Melinda Liu, *Dalai Lama, Twitter Rock Star: The Virtual Influence of His Holiness*, August 6, 2012 (online).

14 Interview at Stanford University, November 2017 (online).

References

Al-Amoudi, I. (2019). Management and de-humanization in late modernity. In I. Al-Amoudi & J. Morgan (Eds.), *Realist responses to post-human society: Ex Machina* (pp. 182–194). Abingdon: Routledge.

Archer, M. S. (2013). Social morphogenesis and the prospects of morphogenic society. In M. S. Archer (Ed.), *Social morphogenesis* (pp. 1–21). Dordrecht: Springer.

Arnold, M. (2002). The glass screen. *Information, Communication & Society, 5*(2), 225–236.

Atlan, H. (1985). Intelligence Artificielle et organisation biologique. *Les Cahiers du MURS, 3*, 67–96.

Baecker, D. (1999). Gypsy reason: Niklas Luhmann's sociological enlightenment. *Cybernetics & Human Knowing, 6*(3), 5–19.

Baker, L. R. (2004). The ontology of artefacts. *Philosophical Explorations, 7*, 99–112.

Bostrom, N. (2005). In defence of posthuman dignity. *Bioethics, 19*(3), 202–214.

Breslau, D. (2000). Sociology after humanism: A lesson from contemporary science studies. *Sociological Theory, 18*(2), 289–307.

Cisf. (Ed.). (2017). *Le relazioni familiari nell'era delle reti digitali*. San Paolo: Cinisello Balsamo.

Collier, A. (1999). *Being and worth*. Abingdon: Routledge.

Darwall, S. (2007). Law and the second-person standpoint. *Loyola of Los Angeles Law Review, 40*, 891–910.

Donati, P. (2012). Doing sociology in the age of globalization. *World Futures, 68*(4–5), 225–247.

Donati, P. (2013). Morphogenesis and social networks: Relational steering not mechanical feedback. In M. S. Archer (Ed.), *Social morphogenesis* (pp. 205–231). Dordrecht: Springer.

Donati, P. (2014). Social capital and the added value of social relations. *International Review of Sociology – Revue Internationale de Sociologie, 24*(2), 291–308.

Donati, P. (2019). Transcending the human: Why, where, and how? In I. Al-Amoudi & J. Morgan (Eds.), *Realist responses to post-human society: Ex Machina* (pp. 53–81). Abingdon: Routledge.

Donati, P. (2020). The digital matrix and the hybridization of society. In I. Al-Amoudi & E. Lazega (Eds.), *Before and beyond the matrix: Artificial intelligence's organisations and institutions*. Abingdon: Routledge.

Dyer, J. H., & Singh, H. (1998). The relational view: Cooperative strategy and sources of interorganizational competitive advantage. *Academy of Management Review, 23*, 660–679.

Floridi, L. (Ed.). (2015). *The onlife manifesto. Being human in a hyperconnected era*. Dordrecht: Springer.

Frankfurt, H. G. (1971). Freedom of the will and the concept of a person. *The Journal of Philosophy, 68*(1), 5–20.

Graber, C. B. (2016). *The future of online content personalisation: Technology, law and digital freedoms* (i-call Working Paper No. 01). Zurich: University of Zurich.

House of Lords. (2018, April 16). *AI in the UK: Ready, willing and able?* (HL Paper 100). London: Select Committee on Artificial Intelligence.

Jones, R. A. (1997). The presence of self in the person: Reflexive positioning and personal construct psychology. *Journal for the Theory of Social Behaviour, 27*, 453–471.

Jones, R. A. (2013). Relationalism through social robotics. *Journal for the Theory of Social Behaviour, 43*(4), 405–424.

Kirchhoffer, D. G. (2017). Human dignity and human enhancement: A multidimensional approach. *Bioethics, 31*(5). doi:10.1111/bioe.12343

Knio, K. (2018). The morphogenetic approach and immanent causality: A Spinozian perspective. *Journal for the Theory of Social Behaviour, 48*(4), 398–415.

Lawrence, D., Palacios-Gonzáles, C., & Harris, J. (2016). Artificial intelligence. The shylock syndrome. *Cambridge Quarterly of Healthcare Ethics, 25*, 250–261.

Lazega, E. (2017). Networks and commons: Bureaucracy, collegiality, and organizational morphogenesis in the struggles to shape collective responsibility in new shared institutions. In M. S. Archer (Ed.), *Morphogenesis and human flourishing* (pp. 211–238). Dordrecht: Springer.

Lévy, P. (1997). *L'intelligence collective: pour une anthropologie du cyberespace*. Paris: La Découverte.

Lindemann, G. (2016). Human dignity as a structural feature of functional differentiation: A precondition for modern responsibilization. *Soziale Systeme, 19*(2), 235–258.

Liu, J. (2015). Globalizing indigenous psychology: An East Asian form of hierarchical relationalism with worldwide implications. *Journal for the Theory of Social Behaviour, 45*(1), 82–94.

Luhmann, N. (1990). *Paradigm lost. Über die Etische Reflexion der Moral*. Frankfurt a. M.: Suhrkamp Verlag.

Luhmann, N. (1995). *Social systems*. Stanford, CA: Stanford University Press.

Luhmann, N., & Schorr, K. E. (1982). *Zwischen Technologie und Selbstreferenz*. Frankfurt a. M.: Suhrkamp Verlag.

Malo, A. (2019). Subjectivity, reflexivity, and the relational paradigm. In P. Donati, A. Malo, & G. Maspero (Eds.), *Social science, philosophy and theology in dialogue: A relational perspective*. Abingdon: Routledge.

Mikołaj Pawlak, M. (2017). How to see and use relations. *Stan Rzeczy [State of Affairs], 1*(12), 443–448.

Miller, P. (1979). *The responsibility of mind in a civilization of machines*. Boston, MA: University of Massachusetts Press.

Minsky, M. (1988). *The society of mind*. New York: Simon & Schuster.

Mitchell, M. (2019). *Artificial intelligence: A guide for thinking humans*. New York: Farrar, Straus, and Giroux.

Morozov, E. (2011). *The net delusion. The dark side of Internet freedom*. New York: Public Affairs.

O'Connor, C. (2017). Embodiment and the construction of social knowledge: Towards an integration of embodiment and social representations theory. *Journal for the Theory of Social Behaviour, 47*(1), 2–24.

Porpora, D. (2019). Vulcans, Klingons, and humans: What does humanism encompass? In I. Al-Amoudi & J. Morgan (Eds.), *Realist responses to post-human society: Ex Machina* (pp. 33–52). Abingdon: Routledge.

Ricoeur, P. (1990). *Soi-même comme un autre*. Paris: Seuil.

Sharkey, A. J. (2010). The crying shame of robot nannies: An ethical appraisal. *Interaction Studies, 11*(2), 161–190.

Sharkey, A. J. (2014). Robots and human dignity: A consideration of the effects of robot care on the dignity of older people. *Ethics and Information Technology, 16*(1), 63–75.

Sharkey, A. J., & Sharkey, N. (2010). Granny and the robots: Ethical issues in robot care for the elderly. *Ethics and Information Technology, 14*(1), 27–40.

Simmons, H. (2018). Enabling the marketing systems orientation: Re-establishing the ontic necessity of relations. *Kybernetes, 4*(3). doi:10.1108/K-09-2017-0352.

Smith, C. (2010). *What is a person? Rethinking humanity, social life, and the moral good from the person up*. Chicago, IL: The University of Chicago Press.

Taylor, C. H. (1985). *The concept of a person. Philosophical papers* (Vol. 1, pp. 97–114). Cambridge: Cambridge University Press.

Teubner, G. (2006). The anonymous matrix: Human rights violations by "private" transnational actors. *Modern Law Review, 69*(3), 327–346.

Uhlaner, C. J. (2014). Relational goods and resolving the paradox of political participation. *Recerca. Journal of Thought and Analysis, 14*, 47–72.

Warwick, K. (2015). The disappearing human-machine divide. In J. Romportl, E. Zackova, & J. Kelemen (Eds.), *Beyond artificial intelligence. The disappearing human-machine divide* (pp. 1–10). Dordrecht: Springer.

Yeh, K. H. (2010). Relationalism: The essence and evolving process of Chinese interactive relationships. *Chinese Journal of Communications, 3*(1), 76–94.

2 Being human as an option

How to rescue personal ontology from transhumanism, and (above all) why bother

Andrea M. Maccarini

The challenge: being human as an option

The most advanced civilizations in the context of global society are exhibiting an astonishing loss of collective self-consciousness. The core of this cultural oblivion consists of the dismissal of human exceptionalism, on the ground of neuroscience and bio-genetics. The idea that humans have a unique status among all living entities is increasingly questioned and tends to be replaced by radically naturalistic views of the human species.

In the pluralistic cultural system of global society, the rejection of concepts that used to indicate the specificity of being human is still sitting uncomfortably alongside the modern discourse on human rights and coexisting with a widespread popular belief in human uniqueness. Yet, the crisis of historical forms of human self-understanding is increasingly characterizing the current state of our scholarly culture. At some point along this path, our 'traditional' feelings and beliefs about *what kind* of entities we are become shaky and unwarranted. As Niklas Luhmann anticipated many years ago (Luhmann 1986: 323), "to want to be human [. . .] amounts to sheer dilettantism."

This striking cultural mutation is the object of the present chapter. More precisely, the chapter is focused upon human enhancement (HE) and transhumanizing techniques and practices, as these epitomize the social and cultural challenge in question. Indeed, neuroscience and the new biology are working as the scientific as well as ideological underpinning of such techniques and practices. Taken together, this coherent syndrome of knowledge-and-action represents the cutting edge of the naturalistic challenge. The latter goes far beyond any regular evolutionary approach. Darwinian and neo-Darwinian perspectives have long become a part of our cultural heritage. Neuroscience is now building a radically materialistic case, based on the claim that human thoughts, desires, ideal orientations, attitudes and actions can be reduced to neural activity. Biologists, in turn, are trying to trace various concrete aspects of human agency to particular genetic features. The combined effect of this double challenge is to disrupt any notion of 'human nature' that exceeds genetic constitution. The resulting, exclusively materialistic definition has two crucially appealing features to transhumanists: it deprives human nature of any normative meaning and opens it to manipulation with no principled limits. In a nutshell, this is what opens the gate to a post-human world. This scientistic syndrome is quickly becoming an independent cultural driver. However, modern political philosophies obviously share in its genealogy. Liberal individualism is clearly involved, given its principled rejection of normative constraints on individuals' freedom to pursue their own instrumental improvement and expressive satisfaction – except for violations of the others' equal rights – and its emphasis on individual free choice in all respects. Coupled with the radically functionalistic worldview that is inherent in predominant forms of capitalism, this heritage provides an effective ideological underpinning to manipulative notions of humanity. On the other hand, the idea of *anthropotechnics* – referring to the variety of procedures of mental, physical and technological 'work on oneself' through which individuals and populations can be optimized and moulded into a new kind of person, even beyond the limits of the species – was typical of the early Soviet system and thinkers.[1]

As various forms of HE are going to spread, the problem arises of a latent human identity that may (or may not) continue to underlie technical empowerment and hybridization. My way to frame this issue is to say that *being human* becomes *an option*. Such a phrase puts together two different insights. First, it goes back to Margaret S. Archer's work (2000), which articulates a theory of personal and social identity within a critical realist conceptual framework. The second part of the phrase is borrowed from the social theory of religion in late modernity (Joas 2014, Taylor 2007). There it conveys the idea that religious faith in contemporary Western society is not prone to sheer secularization and bound to disappear but must be reflexively redefined in a context of multiple possibilities, including complete rejection of faith as the default option in many social environments. Similarly, being human in a post-human world will no longer be a matter of 'nature' but will have to be *defined and chosen* as a particular way of being-in-the-world within a range of possibilities.

This involves two intertwined issues. On the one hand, what is essential (if anything!) to being human must be distinguished over and over again, whenever some new technical empowerment of some personal properties becomes available. On the other hand, the problem is to make sense of either option. Does being, or remaining, recognizably human become a choice, a right, a mistake, a form of disability, a reactionary opposition to progress, an exercise in cultural resistance or what? Should one accept a possible enhancement of some personal quality or power in order to 'improve' oneself or reject it for the sake of preventing 'de-humanization'? What does the latter mean anyway in the new context? In the end, is there anything normative about being human? Does this option make any serious difference?

I want to articulate an affirmative answer to the latter question. People may well be attracted to any kind of self-transformation, for instrumental as well as expressive reasons. But my thesis is that, whatever individuals decide and choose for themselves, the option of remaining human (or not) is still going to make a meaningful difference, one about which we should indeed care. Moreover, I argue that no critique of transhumanism can be effective without an explicit reference to human ontology and its indisposability.

My analysis will be conducted in a sociological perspective. Indeed, HE and transhumanism are here studied *as social facts*. From this vantage point, what can be examined regards the structural and cultural conditions as well as the human needs and desires that underlie the transhumanizing trend. The emphasis could fall on how the interaction of those conditions, needs and desires with the relevant technologies over multiple social morphogenetic cycles might transform social relationships and identities and even change the deep human self-understanding.

The present chapter finds its relevance in this broad area of studies but has a much narrower focus. As the title reads, I wish to explain *why* the current crisis of the idea of personal ontology is something we should care about. I try to answer this question through an analysis which revolves around a few social problems in an emerging post-human world. I argue that some of those problems are likely to be intractable and probably entail a loss of human goods that would be regarded as unacceptable by contemporary cultural standards. This is why we should bother. The way our culture defines human nature and personhood is crucially important, but only (from my viewpoint) as a result of issues arising within the socio-cultural realm.

First, I take a closer look at the phenomenon in question and make some conceptual clarifications that are necessary to understand the main argument. Then I illustrate how the debate about HE and transhumanism has been largely dominated by the modern categories of equality and individual autonomy and argue that this has prevented an adequate understanding of the challenge ahead. In the next section, I claim that the HE revolution presents us with some social issues that can hardly be tackled with the theoretical and political tools of modernist thinking. These issues include (1) the rise of ontological, not just social, stratification; (2) the possible emergence of sub-speciation (i.e., an ontological differentiation of society) with the related problem of mutual respect between differently human communities; (3) the transformation of social control; (4) inter-generational relationships, entailing problems of care and autonomy; and (5) an overall change in the meaning of human experience and the grammar of basic human attachments. Finally, some conclusions are drawn as regards the relevance of personal ontology to those problems.

Let me anticipate an obvious objection. If I claim to be developing a sociological approach to transhumanism and HE, why should I call the related change a 'loss'? Isn't this a blatant confession of my bias towards old-fashioned humanism? My point is that such a change may be described as loss insofar as it disallows to grasp specifically human features that are evident to empirical observation and have always made sense to most human beings in the world, both present and past. Furthermore, whether we sadly admit that our old humanistic self-conception is a hopeless illusion or we happily embrace a fully naturalistic understanding of ourselves and the world – two versions of Charles Taylor's famous "Victorian courage" (1989) – the transhumanist worldview makes the specific experience of being human literally unintelligible. If humans embrace a fully naturalistic self-understanding, then our search for a principle of reality, our different opinions on politics or other issues, feelings like love and hatred, altruistic versus egoistic behaviours, cynicism, hope, concerns, moral responsibility and non-physical pain (e.g., that caused by exclusion or humiliation), the aesthetic experience, all the very stuff of human existence and everything humans care about will have to be traced back to neural activity. Even an autonomous centre of agency cannot be identified beyond the network comprising our brain. Of course, 'we' (whatever this word still means) find it hard to believe this, but such a difficulty must be ascribed to a *side effect* of our brain constitution – often articulated through the concept of *exaptation*.[2]

If this were the case, the only chance would be to declare the historical form of human experience to be simply misleading. In spite of their highly developed reflexivity and cognitive capacity – indeed, as a result of it – humans allegedly end up as the only animal species on the planet whose self-representation is just plain wrong. Unfortunately, such a cold shower of 'scientific' self-awareness would cause an abysmal loss of meaning and huge, related problems in both individual and collective life. Probably, some scientists would consistently propose that such a search of meaning is an error to be cured. But if neuroscientists were right on this account, then it would be unclear on what ground some neural *and* practical activities – those neuroscientists engage in – should be regarded as a worthy way to spend our time, while others would not. This should clarify why in the present chapter the notion of a 'loss' involves no a priori philosophical or anthropological commitment – at least, no more than the supposedly neutral neuroscience itself – but indicates the inability of a given cultural system to draw existentially important distinctions while it claims to herald a tragic form of 'enlightenment'.[3]

The present considerations take place in this context. The author is surely not a supporter of transhumanism but is also reluctant to sign in as a radical bio-conservative and would prefer to take a more analytical approach to the whole matter. However, one guiding idea of this chapter is that the uniqueness of being human still deserves attention and care. The challenge is to defend it on principled grounds for its deep meaning and not just as a matter of precaution.

The strengths of transhumanism

To non-scholarly ears, the question about whether or not it is still important to identify and safeguard the essence of being human in the face of technological change may sound redundant. Isn't our humanity obviously relevant? Correspondingly, my thesis that we should bother to rescue personal ontology may sound trivial. Later sections explain why this is far from true. In a nutshell, my point is that various structural and cultural factors are making it quite hard to draw distinctions that were once banal. Not only "the dykes against human genetic engineering are bulging against the tide of the 'post-human', and much of the intellectual establishment on these matters seems to be leaning in the direction of letting them go" (Juengst 2009: 44). Furthermore, even the critics of transhumanism usually deploy a conceptual framework that proves insufficient to treat the most serious issues.

What explains the strength of the transhumanizing trend? One reason has to do with the inherent complexity of the subject matter. The transhumanist movement is part of a far-reaching societal change. At the core of such change lies the convergence between technology and a new understanding of biology. The most important outcome from our specific viewpoint is the rise of a *disposable world*. Here we find a term that is central to my argument but calls for some preliminary clarification, especially since it may raise some eyebrows as to its English usage. In the present text, 'disposability' indicates a potentially instrumental relationship to the world, which is different from the old relation between a stable, objective world and an equally stable human agent. The concept is meant to describe the new situation in which the boundaries between ontology and epistemology, knowledge and action, the wet and the dry, the grown and the made seem to disappear.[4] In the same vein, while discussing the implications of genetically designing children, Habermas writes that "we experience our own freedom with reference to *something which, by its very nature, is not at our disposal*" (2003: 58–59, italics added). To think of ourselves as free, we must be able to ascribe our origins "to a beginning which *eludes human disposal*" (*Ivi*). Therefore, the distinction *disposable/indisposable* – and the related noun (*indisposability*) – indicate both a state of affairs and a normative necessity. On one hand, it says whether a given entity is or is not accessible to intentional (technical) transformation. On the other hand, it points to the intrinsic value of a given entity 'as it is' and to the manifold kinds of risks incurred – in terms of moral and/or empirical consequences – if its inner structure is modified. Such a modification thus appears as the *violation* of something whose integrity commanded respect. This duality of meaning aptly shows the complexity of the current situation. It is in this sense that I use the word in the present chapter.[5]

The idea and the multifarious practices of HE represent one important way in which the broader trend leading to a disposable world applies to humanity. It is useful to take a closer look at the emergent phenomena we are dealing with. Broadly speaking, HE techniques are meant to make people smarter, stronger, and healthier, thereby improving their work performance, sensory and cognitive capacities. Modes of intervention range from pharmacological enhancement to implantation of genetically engineered tissue or organs, from the development of machine-body interface to genetic engineering of embryos.

There are four levels of human enhancement that can build momentum towards a post-human development. They are mutually related and reinforcing, and concern respectively:

1   Physical capacities (changing bodily constitution, even irreversibly and internally; in the end, are we ready to leave our carbon support?)
2   Cognitive abilities (e.g., through pharmacological cognitive enhancement)
3   Mood, social and emotional skills, character
4   Reflexivity, that is, the way we consider ourselves in relation to the world and vice versa, including our ontological and ethical self-understanding.

As these practices spread and develop through increasingly advanced technical upgrades, in the long run they could produce novel entities which would expand the scope of possible life forms. In the end, we might experience the following taxonomy:

- Plants
- non-human animals
- humans
- enhanced humans
- transhumans – humans who have been so significantly modified and enhanced that there are significant non-human characteristics, e.g. chimeras, cyborgs
- post-humans – beings originally "evolved" or developed from humans but so significantly different that they are no longer human in any significant respect
- alien life forms[6]

The complexity we have just begun to appreciate makes criticism difficult, because any serious approach to the matter must confront the nuances of this wide range of possibilities. HE cannot be regarded as an all-or-nothing phenomenon but entails a gradual development, which makes it hard to identify a threshold, or a point of no return, that leads into qualitative change.

Three other reasons concur in making a critical discourse culturally arduous.

First, trans- and post-humanism are offering a new horizon, *a new individual and collective dream* to societies which have apparently lost their ideal drive. In this respect, HE is articulating new forms of individual as well as collective, immanent self-transcendence.[7]

In the second place, transhumanist thinkers and supporters often build their case on the ground of a *theory of continuity* (e.g., Fuller & Lipinska 2014; various chapters in Savulescu & Bostrom 2009). In this framework, a fundamental identity is posited between new controversial enhancement methods and old, accepted ways to improve human capacities. All kinds of education, learning and training are interpreted as forms of enhancement, which do not involve any substantial difference from HE. HE is, therefore, coextensive with the imperative to "change one's life" (Sloterdijk 2015) that characterizes the human condition. Anthropotechnics is as old as humanity itself.[8] If this is the case, HE does not track any morally relevant distinction, and must even appear as a moral obligation.

Finally, the theoretical framework of modernist thought is unable to counter these claims. The latter is a pivotal point that must now be discussed in more detail.

Left, right – and wrong? Modern and post-modern critiques of transhumanism

In spite of all normalizing efforts, in scholarly and public debates alike it is still widely believed that HE *does* identify a morally relevant distinction and constitutes a highly consequential fault line in the moral, social, cultural and psychic domains. But how do philosophy and social theory conceive of the puzzles that arise in this new context? We feel that we should be troubled, but why exactly?

Arguably, this vagueness is due to the fact that modernist thinking is still dominating the critical side of the intellectual establishment. In this context, the discourse develops within the polarity of freedom and equality. On the one hand, the liberal tradition views individual freedom of choice as fundamental and sees threats to this freedom mainly in the relations of individuals to the political system (Habermas 2003). On the other hand, the Marxist and socialist tradition is particularly sensitive to issues of equality and attributes the current risks to the alliance of science, technology and free trade ideology within the framework of globalized neoliberalism. In sum, lib/lab[9] thinking is concerned that HE be non-coercive and equally distribute benefits. These combined lines of thought produce the social imaginary of authoritarian dystopias we so often see in science fiction. Depending on the versions adopted, these emphasize the dangers of 'big government', tremendously empowered by technology, or of widespread social control and commodification of the human by biotech corporations. Of course, these actors, their strategies and the related risks interweave, at least in the best plots.

All this is true, but the problem is that these narratives leave much of the story untold. For one thing, despite all possible one-sided views, both of the main vectors of modernization – state and market – are leading this new process of change. HE is developed by state as well as by private agencies – often in complex partnerships – pursuing private and public aims alike (military, educational, etc.). In addition to this, HE practices are no more regulated in socialist countries like China than in Western liberal democracies.[10] The pressure for HE comes from global capitalism as well as from the political and military competition between states and larger geopolitical blocs.

From a different angle, two distinctions offer an instructive insight into this issue, namely *individual/collective* and *expressive/instrumental*. HE can pursue improved performance in various organizational environments and spheres of action, producing a new biotechnical division of labour in society, and can be deployed to shape populations endowed with certain qualities. At the same time, it can appeal to individual desires of expanded experience and border crossing into alterity – somewhat similar to what the beat and hippie generations used to seek in drugs – or to the personal quest for perfection in various forms.[11] In criss-crossing these distinctions different combinations appear, each with possibly different features and effects. Table 2.1 presents some examples in a clearly non-exhaustive way. Enhancing the human *as an option* thus reveals a variety

Table 2.1 The variety of HE goals

HE	Expressive	Instrumental
Individual	Expansion of experience, psychic therapy (mood, emotions)	Improving performance for personal success (work, sport, studies)
Collective	Changing social psychological profiles	Building populations or groups with useful properties (workers, military, etc.)

of possible combinations in which different motivations, goals and processes are involved. As a consequence, different issues of freedom versus control and empowerment versus de-humanization also arise.

Therefore, it comes as no surprise that the political and philosophical categories of left and right become confused in dealing with this kind of problem. For example, both transhumanists and 'bioconservatives' often present themselves as 'left'.

But the crucial point is that neither free choice nor equality gets to the heart of the matter. As Michael Sandel has noted (2007: 6–7), the familiar terms of moral and political discourse make it difficult to say *what is really wrong* with re-engineering our nature. Even if 'good governance' could solve the problems of freedom and equality, we would still be left with a fundamental question: is it all right to modify our nature? The hard questions concern the moral status of (human) nature, "and they are largely lost from view in the modern discourse" (Sandel 2007: 16). This causes the 'moral vertigo' that often accompanies such issues. Within sociology, I would rather ask why people actually aspire to HE, and what happens once we have satisfied our aspirations. But Sandel's statement goes to the heart of the matter. In the end, the crucial difference is that between *normative* and *a-normative* notions of human nature.

As anticipated above, my thesis is that a conceptual framework must include the ontological dimension in order to tackle this issue adequately. However, this is precisely what most authors shy away from. For both the right and the left wing of modern thinking, ontology is often the enemy of individual autonomy, since it sets limits to what one can be or become.

Seen from this angle, post-modernist thought only intensifies the same argument. The so-called ontological turn proposed by such authors as Foucault and Latour is in fact a hymn to pure contingency.[12] In this perspective, the whole world, including the human agent, appears as disposable. There are three interwoven arguments in this ontological turn: first, reality is composed of a single plane of immanence; second, the ontological and the epistemic are conflated with one another;[13] and third, the humanist tradition has to be rejected because of its grounding on such a divide between knowledge and ontology, which is supposed to entail dominative implications (Pellizzoni 2015: 8). On the contrary, the indeterminacy of 'reality' is believed to have emancipatory implications, because agents may exploit the new combinatorial possibilities, thereby opening novel opportunities for social change. It is in this sense that agency and politics become 'ontological'. What this really means is that they *mould* everything in its ontological traits. Agency really *constitutes* ontology. The resulting catchword is *morphological freedom* and the related *rights*.

These lines of thought clearly fail to avert the risks attached to post-human scenarios. In the first place, morphological freedom is synonymous with unbound morphogenesis applied to personal ontology. This is a perfect companion to the transhumanist idea of indefinite promotion of the distinctive qualities of human beings, above all our endless capacity for self-transcendence. The realization of the full human potential also involves embracing risk in order to enjoy the best available opportunities. Such an attitude to risk is regarded as the quintessential feature of humanity and becomes a moral imperative.[14] In this context, the cautionary principle declines, and positive (not just therapeutic) eugenics is seen as the foundational science of human capital.

As a consequence, the political-ideological domain undergoes significant restructuring. The main divide becomes that between bioconservative and bioprogressive cultural and political elites. And within the bioprogressive front, egalitarian universalism is being dismissed as an obsolete ethical priority.

Ironically, modern arguments are even deployed by post-humanists against the idea of species integrity. This happens when the notion of *diversity* is taken from the social and applied to the genetic domain as if this made no meaningful difference. In this perspective, defending the integrity of the human species amounts to discriminating diversity (Juengst 2009) and being human becomes a prejudice (Savulescu 2009). The examples in which racial and gender discrimination are likened to the 'privilege' of being human are meant to build this case. The fact that in everyday life we are all quite aware that we are not cats or ducks, and that we easily recognize our fellow humans, must be simply disregarded as a mundane illusion. More importantly, in order to uproot those 'old' forms of injustice it was necessary to articulate an ontology of non-discrimination. The scientific de-legitimation of the race and gender bias in Western culture has been underpinned (among other things) by ontological arguments. An allegedly similar ontology of indifference is now trying to disrupt the unity of the human species, turning into a rhetoric of boundary-crossing.

All of this is based upon the assumption that the human species *as it is* has no intrinsic worth and no normative status. The only value is the distinction between restricting and expanding the range of available opportunities for all. Isn't this exquisitely modern?

Against this background, it is important to consider a few critiques of transhumanism from within the modern tradition which tend to overcome its limits and introduce more complex reflections. The well-known work by Habermas (2003) is a good case in point, and although it is much cited and discussed, its nuances are seldom noted. In considering genetic engineering (GE), Habermas wants to counter scientistic views of a technically based self-optimization of humanity on the ground of a "weak naturalism" that accepts scientific knowledge in general (93). He does not want the West to be perceived as made of "salespeople of instrumental reason and destructive secularization" (103). Thus he does not hide his annoyance at the "handful of freaked-out intellectuals [which] is busy reading the tea leaves of a naturalistic version of post-humanism" (Habermas 2003: 22).

This theoretical intention translates into an argument that specifies the conditions of an ethically qualified self-understanding. In a liberal society, everyone has an equal right to pursue his life project, and

> eugenic programming of desirable traits and dispositions [. . .] gives rise to moral misgivings as soon as it commits the person concerned to a specific life-project or, in any case, puts specific restrictions on his freedom to choose a life of his own.

(61)

Habermas criticizes genetic manipulation precisely insofar as it has a deep disruptive influence on the capacity to be fully free and responsible in the pursuit of one's life project (5–6).

The influence of GE is disruptive because

> when adults treat the desirable genetic traits of their descendants as a product they can shape according to a design of their own liking, they are exercising a control over their offspring that intervenes in the somatic bases of another person's relation-to-self and ethical freedom. This kind of control should only be exercised over things, not persons.
>
> (13)

In other words, such an intervention blurs the boundary between persons and things. For this reason, such interventions should also not be regarded as part of parental rights (49). If people are genetically programmed, they cannot understand themselves as the sole authors of their life history and responsible for it. As a consequence, their whole stance towards the world could change dramatically, being deprived of its ethical orientation.

Critics of Habermas on the transhumanist side have easily responded that such a 'control' extends to all the people all the time. We are never the sole authors of our life history because we are all subject to the genetic lottery and to the process of socialization.[15] The intended implication is clear: genetic engineering really involves nothing new. Habermas's argument, though, is subtler than this. He is claiming that persons have a different kind of freedom toward the fate produced through the contingencies of the socialization process than they have toward the prenatal programming of their genome (14). Regular people can reflexively react to their developmental paths, review their self-understanding, and (try to) restore the balance if something has gone wrong. Socialization can be reflexively reappraised, appropriated and revised, while genetic interventions cannot (14, 62). Thus, a *previously unheard-of interpersonal relationship* arises when a person makes an irreversible decision about the natural traits of another person (14). Dependence is now different, because it is subtracted from the social field, that is, it is no longer something that occurs in the realm of social relations.

Habermas is not as clear in explaining the difference between depending on parents' programming and on the genetic lottery. The point is that, contrary to the genetic lottery, intentional programming involves *a determined source* of one's genetic features. Once again, the difference lies in the type of relationships involved. Relations to chance and nature are different from relations to somebody's will.

To sum up, once the natural uncontrollability of procreation fades away, the ethical self-understanding of humanity as a whole changes (15). We might no longer understand ourselves as normative creatures, and regulate our interactions through morality and law, but by purely functional, systemic principles and biogenetic steering mechanisms. In my view, here the idea of *a-normative regulation* (Archer 2016) comes to the fore, taking on a particularly deep meaning.

Such a change does not *only* concern individual autonomy per se but affects our cultural and moral self-understanding as members of a species. This is why the possibility of adults to modify their own genome – with an act of autonomous decision – would not clear the ground of all misgivings, since it would still entail self-objectification. It is here that Habermas tends to exceed the boundaries of a purely modernist theory. A key concept is *the anthropological meaning of the unexpected*. When he speaks of natality and the "expectation of the unexpected," whereby "a new life history becomes possible on every birth" (59), the author is certainly attempting to guarantee the conditions under which the self-understanding of modernity – individual autonomy, authenticity and the freedom to choose and construct one's life history – may be preserved. But he is indirectly admitting that such conditions have prerequisites that are not themselves part of the philosophical discourse of modernity. In other words, he is evoking some kind of *moralization of human nature* in its own right. Habermas still believes that the entities which share in such a nature must be determined "regardless of controversial ontological disputes" (33), but concludes that "the connection between the contingency of a life's beginning that is not at our disposal and the freedom to give one's life an ethical shape demands a more penetrating analysis" (75).[16] That connection exists and is relevant because some other factor comes into the picture. If it weren't so, why should the self-understanding of modernity be preserved in the first place, in the face of a further possible progress?

The meaning of the unexpected is a red thread that links Habermas with Michael Sandel. In Sandel's work (2007), the caution against GE lies in a problem of hyper-agency and the drive to mastery (Sandel 2007: 26–29). It is not the means but the aims pursued with GE that are subject to critique. Sandel's point is that eugenic parenting expresses a stance towards the world that dismisses openness to the unbidden and the gifted character of human life and powers (83 and passim). The ethics of *giftedness* involves the idea that not everything is open to any use we may devise. The opposite attitude is criticized as an expression of *hubris*.

Sandel moves one step forward in articulating the meaning of the unexpected. The key concept is giftedness and the respect for the dimension of mystery that still underlies some crucial facts of life, like birth. The non-instrumental, non-objectifying stance to the world that Habermas considers to be the hallmark of an ethical self-understanding requires a sense for giftedness. However, it must be specified what is lost when the sense of giftedness declines. Such a loss concerns the values that are essential to sustaining some qualities of human life, more precisely the non-instrumental value of human beings. The point is not just hubris but the *de-symbolization* of human beings and their relationships. If parents do not care for genetically programming their children, it's because they accept their offspring regardless of the particular features these may display. In other words, the qualities children exhibit are *not* the reason why they are loved and valued. I think this is what Sandel means when he says that GE "corrupts parenting as a social practice governed by norms of unconditional love" (83). The same could be said of the attitude to humility, responsibility and solidarity (85–92). So, the point is about damaging non-instrumental relationships. If these aspects are not specified, one may cold-bloodedly argue that mastery has always been part of the human enterprise, while giftedness has no intrinsic value, since (1) its loss entails no clear consequences and (2) there is really no 'donor'. In fact, it may even be good for humans to give up whatever passive attitude may come with giftedness and embrace courage and risk as productive and progressive inclinations.

Habermas and Sandel share a common concern for humanity, and their theories gesture at something beyond the modern heritage. They bring up some important points for countering the radical post-humanist conclusions, but I believe their arguments would be more robust if they were further developed through more explicit references to societal issues and to the ontological dimension. My point is that, at this stage of evolution of human civilization, only two lines of argument can be effective in pursuing the quest for humanism:

1 Illustrating some social problems that would emerge in a post-human scenario, and exposing the intractable consequences they would entail
2 Articulating the concern for historical humanity within the symbolical resources of a given ontological discourse, challenging other cultures to do the same in their own language.

I will follow the former line in the next section and the second in the concluding section, although still in a quick and introductive way. These converge upon a single, overarching strategy which is based on the awareness that

> in complex societies one culture can assert itself against other cultures only by convincing its succeeding generations – who can also say no – of the advantages of its world-disclosive semantic and action-orienting power. "Nature reserves" for cultures are neither possible nor desirable.
>
> (Habermas 2003: 2–3)

This could be called an evolutionary proof of concept.

So, why bother?

As we have seen, doubts, fears and misgivings about HE remain rather fuzzy and hard to articulate in the modern and in the post-modern language. Critics of transhumanism are concerned about the rise of wholly instrumental relationships to the world, but they have to admit that such a relation must now be different from the old link between a stable, objective world and an equally stable human agent.

This prompts the question about ontology: why bother? This question must be asked afresh to investigate what the social dimension of reality may reveal about it. The thesis of this section is that, if the social issues resulting from HE are taken seriously, the need to steer technological change within the boundaries of historical humanity emerges as a practical and theoretical necessity.

Let us examine four prospective issues. Since these have to do with possible post-human futures, the present argument is obviously not based on field research.

What I can do is briefly illustrate a scenario, highlighting the relevant puzzles and risks. Each of the issues in question would require a book-long coverage. What I can do here is just offer a quick summary in order to make my case for the impossibility to give up personal ontology.

The ontological stratification of society

In a future where GE and various forms of HE become a common practice, it is very likely that social stratification will be ontologically characterized. In other words, society could be ontologically, not just socially, stratified. Transhumanists would promptly note that perfect equality – even in terms of equality of opportunity – has never been achieved in any kind of human civilization. Therefore, ontologically grounded inequality could be either prevented or managed in exactly the same terms of governance, depending on different cultural models of society. Why would ontology add anything to the usual discontents of inequality?

On the contrary, I believe that it is essential to avoid that inequality be engraved in personal ontology because that would make the obstacles to social mobility eventually insurmountable. This thesis differs from a modernist concern for HE to be equally distributing benefits, in that it holds that such a fair distribution would be hardly possible in the first place if HE were allowed to cross the boundaries of historical humanity. Every historically known society involves some kind and degree of inequality, variously legitimated by different cultural discourses. In the collective self-understanding of (Western) modernity, the imperfection of equality of opportunity may be overcome through intergenerational vertical mobility. In other words, the price usually paid for the lack of equality is some degree of friction, which can be measured in time: more inequality usually means more time required for ascending mobility. The underlying normative idea is that such a time span should be reduced as much as possible. However, if personal ontology is modified, the established constellation of social stratification may become impervious to change because enhanced individuals will enjoy further advantages and could use the time gap and the increased resources available to them in order to reinforce their position in a more definitive way than ever before in the history of social privilege. In sum, crossing the ontological threshold might result in a positive feedback loop, which would make social distances self-amplifying.

How would this happen? Generally speaking, in historical societies personal capacities and social resources may be distributed in such a way as to escape social reproduction much more easily than when an ontological difference is involved. More specifically, various factors must be taken into consideration. First, ontological gaps are higher to climb. If we have to do with different ontologies, it would be harder for a smart but unenhanced individual to study or work their way up the social ladder. Second, HE would make intentional, planned control of capacities and resources easier and thereby more likely. When all humans share the same basic ontology – which means they belong to the same biological species, without significant differences – intelligence as well as other skills and abilities cannot depend totally on social privilege. In fact, they can function as social equalizers – more or less effectively, depending on some basic conditions in the structure of society. But with deep HE, personal capacities will no longer be distributed randomly, and the privileged could appropriate even those resources which have been historically out of their reach – like being a brilliant kid raised in a poor family. It is important to add that 'privilege' may still stand on different grounds – from socio-economic status to ethnic group, to citizenship of advanced societies and more.

The modernist solution would be to guarantee the equal opportunity of enhancement. However, it is very unlikely that HE takes off and spreads in a homogeneous way – among different civilizations, countries, social classes and so forth. Such a level of social control could hardly be achieved. Therefore, such a solution entails an unrealistic view of the social order and of the possibilities of large-scale social planning. Once deep HE kicks off, the 'improvement' of (some) human beings would feed itself, producing more improvement more rapidly than un-enhanced or under-enhanced people could cope with. The speed of self-improvement would tend to accelerate, thereby widening the initial gap.

This leads to a further point. The difficulties in achieving a controlled, egalitarian development of HE would not only depend on poor planning capacities but also on cultural and psychological factors. In an ontologically stratified society, egalitarian values and value commitments would be harder to sustain. It might turn out to be difficult to socialize enhanced social groups into the belief that human dignity and rights must apply to all humans, enhanced and unenhanced alike. Those who advocate equal distribution of HE opportunities and fair relations between more and less enhanced humans are working with the hidden assumption – which to me sounds genuinely bizarre – that enhanced humans would continue to support the ideological manifesto of Western modernity.[17] To assume that ontologically different beings would still consistently share in that cognitive and normative heritage means to delude oneself into thinking that post-humans should still think like humans – for which there can be no evidence whatsoever. For example, nobody could really guarantee that enhanced people would still want to keep HE open and available to all, without entry barriers – especially once they become a sufficiently powerful socio-genetic group. Moreover, enhanced humans may create a society for themselves in which people endowed with normal intelligence might be unable to navigate. This could involve the conditions to participate in the political process as well as the cognitive and physical requisites associated with certain jobs, roles or offices, down to the common interactional dynamics of everyday life. A future breed of super-intelligent people might even treat poor old humans as mentally impaired. The intractable consequences of all this for social equality and civil liberties are rather evident.

In sum, nobody knows what post-human beings will want, believe and do, and there is no compelling argument to convince them to respect non-enhanced, historical humans unless one relies on the very humanistic cultures that post-humanism wants to dismiss as the relics of a spent past. I would call this the ontological backlash, and have no idea about how it could be harnessed.

Subspeciation and social cohesion

A second issue highlights another facet of the ontological differentiation of society. The problem concerns the possibility of social integration between *differently enhanced* humans, and it involves an overwhelming complexity which cannot be explored here. For one thing, it is worth wondering if ontologically different social groups will still share values and commitments. Indeed, it is doubtful whether they can still have a sense for a common fate.

The temporal dimension would add to these uncertainties. If HE modifies life expectancy and the overall life span for some social groups, the coexistence of beings who inhabit very different time horizons will become highly problematic.

Important as they are, these aspects are the component parts of a bigger emergent 'social fact', namely the loss of the unity of the human species. The structural, symbolical and evolutionary scope of such a phenomenon can hardly be overestimated.

The question is whether or not some form of 'smart' governance can prevent HE from crystallizing as a privilege, promoting tolerance and pluralism in a society whose members would no longer share a common ancestry and a common ontological ground. Either central control and steering or other forms of coordinated action in the interest of enlarged humanity would present a wide range of complex issues. Should all ontological communities be granted the conditions of survival, and if so, under what conditions? How separate and how connected should they be? What degree of openness and range of diversity should be allowed? And who can represent such an entity as 'enlarged humanity'? How can the right to life be articulated as a right of diverse, co-evolving forms of life? Reflections on these points are currently still vague and tentative.[18]

Inter-generational relations and human attachments

On the level of interaction, the basic grammar of human attachments is going to be profoundly affected, as parents can modify the somatic basis of their children's relation to themselves and the world in an irreversible way. This was already discussed in the previous section, but here the point at issue is not individual autonomy but rather the social bonds that connect people of different generations, as well as relations of family, kinship and friendship. The meaning and practices of care concerning old, weak or sick people may change dramatically. Similarly, a whole set of issues would arise about socialization and child-rearing.

The biologization of the social and the self-understanding of the species

The biologization of all things social is the underlying logic that would creep in through deep HE. Many crucial practices, relationships, structures and institutions would have to be radically reconceived – social control, welfare and well-being, health, social normativity, and more.

In the end, such interventions as memory subtraction/enhancement, or body-machine hybridization on various levels, would alter the typically human way of experiencing the world in unpredictable ways.

At the end of this summary, one might conclude that if it is hard to control the consequences of all these changes, the same applies to their emergence. In other words, the same scepticism I direct to the possibility to govern transhumanist change could well apply to the possibility to stop or steer it in advance. Indeed, deep change is happening everywhere, in uncontrollable ways. My answer is that I am not making any prediction about the odds of a positive evolution of HE – whatever "positive" means. All I've tried to argue is that such a big process cannot be entrusted to the lib/lab dialectic of freedom and control. Neutralizing the normative status of human nature and controlling the socially undesirable consequences (undesirable for whom?) will not work.

Thus, I have quickly illustrated a few problems arising in the social realm that would produce insoluble issues, unless some idea of personal ontology still marks the boundaries of those enhancements that are accepted as 'human', and re-producing a human society. These social puzzles clarify what I argued in the previous section, that criticism grounded on anti-ontological arguments can only target issues of equality and free choice. Much as these are clearly part of the problem, they do not touch the deep core of the post-human challenge. In the next section, I try to spell out a few coordinates of an ontological view that could rise to this challenge.

Conclusion. A few words on 'how to'

This last section is unavoidably, unapologetically normative and inexcusably short. It has the limited aim to indicate a few conditions a theory of personal ontology must satisfy, if it is to avoid the pitfalls highlighted in the previous two sections.

It is instructive to start from Pellizzoni's insight, according to which

> the current, unprecedented appropriation and commodification of the world [. . .] depends on a problematization which completely erases the distance between being and thinking. These are reframed as modalities internal to an all-encompassing, ever-changing and expanding will, for which the space of possibility is coextensive with the actuality of an unbounded potential.
>
> (2015: 209)

Two points must be noted. First, the conflation of epistemology and ontology is also opposed to the main tenets of critical realism. Second, the emphasis falls on *will* as the operator of the instrumentalization and commodification that result from exploiting the 'unbounded potential' of a disposable world. The core of a critical humanism would be to find a way out of this predicament and restore 'unattainability'.

The author goes on to argue that such a hard task may be accomplished by giving up will. In other words, the all-encompassing possessive will must be countered by an opposite will: the will of *not being* and *not doing*. Inspired by Agamben, he reclaims *human impotentiality*, the *potential not to be*, as the only way to establish an alternative form of life in a time of unchained expansion of possibilities. On one hand, this author's idea of a critical humanism is close to my own critique of unbound morphogenesis and of "bulimic" subjectivities (Maccarini 2019: chs. 4–5). At the same time, a renewed emphasis on personal ontology seems a necessary companion to this journey. In the end, why should one choose 'not to be' or not to act? What should one accept to be, and what not? And why? My point is that one can only choose not to be something because s/he *is* something else, so it makes sense to her/him to let her/his personality, powers and identity grow along a pathway which is free, while remaining within the boundaries of human reality. Habermas's sense for the unexpected, Sandel's ethics of giftedness, and Pellizzoni's commitment to impotentiality are all *semantics of restraint*. They all imply stopping and beholding 'something' that *must* remain in the shadow of the unreachable. I agree. But the only robust reason I see for leaving part of the world out of agential reach is that such a world (or nature) has intrinsic worth. This means they all beg for an ontological foundation.

Such a statement is not contradicted by the technical capacity to manipulate anything. Rather, when it comes to human beings, the problem lies in dualistic or disembodied views of personhood.

The theories that still want to identify an 'essence' of personhood often revolve around some version of the inner "first person perspective" (Baker 2000). To this, a realist social theory of personal identity adds the orientation to concerns (Archer 2019). This is a reaction to the societal conditions of disposability, which wants to save personhood from bodily change but ends up aligning with those conceptions of humanity as a software with no preferred hardware – indeed with no perceived relation to any hardware. 'The human' can be poured in whatever recipient. Such a theory of personhood turns out to be fully coherent with the notion, typical of post-humanist conceptual frameworks, of a fusion of matter and information, which defines genes as carriers of information, thereby making them suitable for translation into different media – a power now enhanced by progress in computational capacity.

Post-humanists draw consistent, if radical, conclusions from this view. For example, intelligence and rationality are properties endowed with moral value, regardless of the entity that holds such properties. In other words, being a member of the human species *and* displaying certain properties appear as *unrelated* facts.[19] The idea is that a subset of human qualities has indeed moral significance, but those qualities are not attributed to being human, being conceived of as reproducible in other life forms. Humans are just *place holders*, and "we are confused when we ascribe intrinsic value to the place holder" (Savulescu 2009: 227).[20] The argument is one of misplaced concreteness. What is essentially of value in humanity is not *necessarily* related to the human species. We are just carriers of a 'spirit', of some 'good', which was first discovered and instantiated by human minds and rationality but can easily be detached from its original home base.

The point is not to reject this view because of the moral or psychological vertigo it may cause but to understand its implications in terms of de-, trans- and post-humanization. All forms of life mentioned earlier, including trans- and post-human, would be allowed in this context. Whatever its theoretical intention, the underlying challenge is clear. The pivotal issue concerns the possible unity of the various ontological layers constituting the human being. Without such unity, steering HE within the boundaries of historical humanity will be impossible.

In my perspective, the idea of a concern-oriented first-person perspective (FPP) is a crucial component of human personhood. But the *uniquely human FPP is not empty* or *neutral*. It has qualities, and indeed *emerges from* a whole way of being-in-the-world – in matter, time and social relations. This existential condition involves certain relationships between the body, the psychic system, social relations and the capacity of moral orientation. In other words, there are internal relations between the biological, psychic, social and cultural dimensions which constitute a human being. Thus, without our bodies we would not be human, because our FPP would be different in unpredictable and opaque ways, in principle impossible to see through. Those who wish to posit the possible emergence of non-human persons – that is, of entities endowed with a qualitatively different FPP – must make this move explicit. After all, they would still be walking on the ground of a typically human drive – that to become other-than-human.

Be that as it may, such an inner relationality is the crux of the matter. The theoretical decision to dismiss it as a wishful, "amateurish" thought (in Luhmann's words) means to accept all possible transhumanizing changes and to ignore a whole body of research which insists on the way human cognition and perception are rooted in bodily constitution, while at the same time culture and socialization tap into these very features. Subjectivity may be conceived as an emergent property of those relationships, reflexively mediated.[21] Stepping out of this way of being – assuming that it is technically possible – would not be just 'good' or 'bad'. What sociology can see is that it would deeply transform the human form of experience.[22]

All we can do, I suspect, is wait and see. If transhumanization remains so fashionable, and if its critics are unable to articulate their own unease, as well as the cultural and psychological malaise they see, in ontological terms, then new structural and cultural equilibria may silently dawn in global society. The paradoxical outcome could be a dramatic turn of the current, widespread 'disposability' into a 'new indisposability' resulting from the unmanageable dangers and catastrophes (Rosa 2018) caused by the work of the human will to master and the related hyper-agency. But here again, to say this twist of fate would be 'bad' would be to judge by all-too-human standards. At this point we might simply give up and deal with more mundane matters, or we might finally accept that it is ultimately nonsense to want to step out of our humanity.

Notes

1 The "communist production of humans" is treated in Peter Sloterdijk's well-known work (2015: see especially note 11 on p. 10, pp. 388–391). This topic is now the object of an interesting work by Anya Bernstein (2019), whose analysis stretches from early Soviet times to contemporary Russia. More on this below.

2 This concept has a long history. Its most significant formulation within evolutionary biology goes back to Stephen Jay Gould and Elizabeth Vrba. For a useful illustration, see Gould (1991). From this seminal work various theories spread in the domain of neurophilosophy which regard all humanistic forms of self-understanding – let alone (*horribile dictu*) religious beliefs – as collateral effects of the evolutionary process of human brain. For a useful critical review, see Canobbio (2018: especially 31, 87, 92).

3 For a critique of the legitimacy to regard naturalistic worldviews as a form of enlightenment see Habermas (2007).

4 The literature on this overarching societal, epistemological and technological context is obviously enormous, and it is not necessary for our purposes to discuss it in detail. A useful overview is provided by Pellizzoni (2015), who also uses the notion of a 'disposable world' in the title of his book. The phrase in question appears with identical or fully consistent meanings in Habermas (cited in the text), Joas (2008), Lohmann (2014) and Rosa (2018).

5 Thus, as I have tried to clarify, I use these words in a technically specified sense, one that is quite different from the common meaning of 'dispose of' as 'eliminate' or 'get rid of'. I hope that the quick reference I made to some authors can help dispel the perplexities about my word choice, which is far less problematic in its German (*Unverfügbarkeit*) or Italian (*indisponibilità*) version. In these linguistic contexts, the concept is much less ambivalent in indicating the *inviolability* or the *sacredness* of a given entity – life, nature, humanity and so forth.

6 This scale of life forms is from Savulescu (2009: 214). In my own perspective, the definition of post-human life forms is different, in that these would also include entities that did *not* originally evolve from humans but from cognitively advanced machines (AI) insofar as they tend to acquire allegedly human-like properties. Further, it is not clear to me what Savulescu really means by "alien life forms," but this is not crucial to my argument and may be left out of the picture in the present context.

7 The connection between transhumanist thought and self-transcendence, both individual and collective, is well established in the literature. See for example on the transhumanist side, Fuller and Lipinska (2014). On slightly more neutral ground, see Bostrom (2011). In a definitely critical mood, Habermas (2003: 42) has called post- and transhumanist speculations "an expression of displaced eschatological needs." On the concept of self-transcendence, see Joas (2008); Maccarini (2019, ch. 7).

8 Reference to ancient and early modern thought and practices (usually Greece and the Renaissance) is meant to convey the idea that contemporary eugenics really involves nothing new. The only difference is the level of competence that now allows to do things better, and to be in better control (see, in a critical perspective, Pellizzoni 2015: 35).

9 Lib/lab stands for 'liberal/labour' and indicates the multiple combinations and permutations of the two main ideological and organizational forces of modernity, which have long entered into deep interaction. On this formula, see Donati (1993).

10 For this reason, the alleged opposition claimed in some chapters of Savulescu and Bostrom (2009) between Western and Asian views of HE seems to me overestimated.

11 The growing importance of *external* forms of personal improvement (e.g., through surgical or pharmacological intervention) as opposed to *internal* ones (typically through education and training) is itself the object of an emergent body of research in social and psychological science. See for example King et al. (2019).

12 The following summary characterization of the 'ontological turn' draws mainly on Luigi Pellizzoni's erudite analysis (2015, ch. 3) and the literature he cites. But while this author presents such a theoretical trend as a novelty "after post-modernism," I ascribe it fully to post-modern thought. On the other hand, I basically agree with his critique of this approach, which does not seem incompatible with my own. I am aware that this interpretation may be perceived as a sweeping generalization, but I cannot do justice to the related *nuances* here. More on this in a future essay.

13 This could represent an example of "central conflation" (Archer 1995).

14 This is the basic meaning of the *proactionary imperative*, around which the most radical manifesto of transhumanism revolves (Fuller and Lipinska 2014).
15 This critique is now commonplace among supporters of HE. See for example Coady (2009: 173–179).
16 Not by chance, this line is also quoted by Sandel (2007: 82). More on this below.
17 Nick Bostrom seems to share this concern, and the core of this argument, as regards the relationships between humans and AI (Bostrom 2014). Oddly enough, his approach to HE and transhumanism is very different, in that he clearly embraces the theses of radical transhumanists (see for example his co-edited volume with Julian Savulescu 2009).
18 On inclusive governance, see for example Fuller and Lipinska (2014). On the development of human rights in the direction of diverse forms of life, see Baxi (2007).
19 This claim is very clear in Savulescu (2009), which represents an example of a common argument in post-humanist quarters.
20 The paradoxical but quite logical conclusion is that we may not deserve to be allowed to live, and aliens destroying humankind may thus be justified, *if* their plan for developing life on Earth were more rational, and if life would never be better in this part of the universe until we are removed (Savulescu 2009: 237, approvingly quoting Williams). It should be noted that valuing rationality involves a purely human way of thinking, and that evoking an idea of "good life in the universe" amounts to a refurbished version of the theory of cosmic order, cosmic good and chain of being – which post-humanists claim to dismiss.
21 In my view, Archer's theory of agency and identity (2000) is consistent with my argument, in that it provides a systematic interpretation of how reflexivity is prompted by emotions, upon which concern-oriented reflection in turn elaborates.
22 Some of which has been examined in my essays published in volumes I and II of the present series.

References

Archer, M. S. (1995). *Realist social theory. The morphogenetic approach.* Cambridge: Cambridge University Press.

Archer, M. S. (2000). *Being human. The problem of agency.* Cambridge: Cambridge University Press.

Archer, M. S. (2016). Anormative social regulation. The attempt to cope with social morphogenesis. In M. S. Archer (Ed.), *Morphogenesis and the crisis of normativity* (pp. 141–168). Dordrecht: Springer.

Archer, M. S. (2019). Bodies, persons and human enhancement. Why these distinctions matter. In I. Al-Amoudi & J. Morgan (Eds.), *Realist responses to post-human society: Ex Machina* (pp. 10–32). New York and London: Routledge.

Baker, R. (2000). *Persons and bodies.* Cambridge: Cambridge University Press.

Baxi, U. (2007). *Human rights in a post-human world. Critical essays.* Oxford: Oxford University Press.

Bernstein, A. (2019). *The future of immortality. Remaking life and death in contemporary Russia.* New Brunswick, NJ: Princeton University Press.

Bostrom, N. (2011). A history of transhumanist thought. In M. Rectenwald & L. Carl (Eds.), *Academic writing across the disciplines.* New York: Pearson Longman.

Bostrom, N. (2014). *Superintelligence. Paths, dangers, and strategies.* Oxford: Oxford University Press.

Canobbio, G. (2018): *Fine dell'eccezione umana? La sfida delle scienze all'antropologia.* Brescia: Morcelliana.

Coady, C. A. J. (2009). Playing God. In J. Savulescu & N. Bostrom (Eds.), *Human enhancement* (pp. 155–180). Oxford: Oxford University Press.

Donati, P. (1993). *La cittadinanza societaria*. Roma-Bari: Laterza.

Fuller, S., & Lipinska, V. (2014). *The proactionary imperative. A foundation for transhumanism*. New York: Palgrave Macmillan.

Gould, S. J. (1991). Exaptation: A crucial tool for an evolutionary psychology. *Journal of Social Issues, 47*(3), 43–65.

Habermas, J. (2003). *The future of human nature*. Cambridge: Polity Press.

Habermas, J. (2007). The language game of responsible agency and the problem of free will: How can epistemic dualism be reconciled with ontological monism? *Philosophical Explorations, 10*(1), 13–50.

Joas, H. (2008). *Do we need religion? On the experience of self-transcendence*. Boulder, CO and London: Paradigm Publishers.

Joas, H. (2014). *Faith as an option. Possible futures for Christianity*. Stanford, CA: Stanford University Press.

Juengst. (2009). What's taxonomy got to do with it? "Species integrity," human rights, and science policy. In J. Savulescu & N. Bostrom (Eds.), *Human enhancement* (pp. 43–58). Oxford: Oxford University Press.

King, V., Gerisch, B., & Rosa, H. (Eds.). (2019). *Lost in perfection. Impacts of optimisation on culture and psyche*. New York and London: Routledge.

Lohmann, G. (2014). How to protect "human nature" – by human dignity, human rights or by "species-ethics" argumentations? In M. Albers, T. Hoffmann, & J. Reinhardt (Eds.), *Human rights and human nature* (pp. 161–172). Dordrecht: Springer.

Luhmann, N. (1986). The individuality of the individual: Historical meanings and contemporary problems. In T. C. Heller, M. Sosna, & D. E. Wellbery (Eds.), *Reconstructing individualism. Autonomy, individuality, and the self in western thought* (pp. 313–328). Stanford, CA: Stanford University Press.

Maccarini, A. M. (2019). *Deep change and emergent structures in global society. Explorations in social morphogenesis*. Dordrecht: Springer.

Pellizzoni, L. (2015). *Ontological politics in a disposable world. The new mastery of nature*. London: Ashgate.

Rosa, H. (2018). *Unverfügbarkeit*. Wien-Salzburg: Residenz Verlag.

Sandel, M. (2007). *The case against perfection. Ethics in the age of genetic engineering*. Cambridge, MA: The Belknap Press of Harvard University Press.

Savulescu, J. (2009). The human prejudice and the moral status of enhanced beings: What do we owe the gods? In J. Savulescu & N. Bostrom (Eds.), *Human enhancement* (pp. 211–250). Oxford: Oxford University Press.

Savulescu, J., & Bostrom, N. (Eds.) (2009). *Human enhancement*. Oxford: Oxford University Press.

Sloterdijk, P. (2015). *You must change your life*. Cambridge: Polity Press.

Taylor, C. (1989). *Sources of the self. The making of the modern identity*. Cambridge, MA: Harvard University Press.

Taylor, C. (2007). *A secular age*. Cambridge, MA: The Belknap Press of Harvard University Press.

3 Perplexity logs

On routinized certainty work and social consequences of seeking advice from an artificial intelligence

Emmanuel Lazega

Interactions, suspended moments of symbolic interaction and relationships

A sociological neo-structural approach to social phenomena can contribute to the current discussion of artificial intelligence and the social changes that it brings to society. We start here with the difference between relation and interaction. Donati (2014) identifies two schools: *relationalist* (pragmatist) and *relational* sociologists. The relationalist sociologists equate the two concepts (Dewey & Bentley 1946, Dépelteau 2015). The relational sociologists think that interactions are different from relations in the sense that the former are reciprocal actions in their dynamics, while the latter are structures in their morphostatic/morphogenetic condition (Donati 2014, Donati & Archer 2015). Here I will define personalized relationships as both channels for social exchange of resources and as symbolic and moral commitments to the exchange partner, and impersonal interactions as channels for social exchange of resources but without symbolic and moral commitment to an exchange partner. This distinction is theoretical since, over time, interactions can evolve to become relationships, and the other way around. It is nevertheless useful here because bureaucracy is often credited with the ability to extend and scale up interactions almost indefinitely; in it, indifference to everyone but the boss is accepted and can be the foundation of functional, short-term interactional social processes (e.g., solidarity or violence). Collegiality (not to be confused with congeniality) has the ability to extend deeper personalized accountability to a small circle of peers; indifference to no one in this circle is accepted as a norm, and this attitude can be the foundation for similar social processes (personalized solidarity or violence) and collective responsibility enforced with these personalized relationships as long-term commitments. Although theoretical, this distinciton helps understand certainty work and epistemic control.

Society includes both realms of interactions and relationships. Actors mix them (Goffman 1961; Donati's hybridization (2019)) or superpose them (Lazega's multilevel approach (2020b)). I argue that for these co-constitutions and co-evolutions of interactions and relationships to be possible, actors must be able to step back and create a moment of symbolic interaction in which they 'decide' to go for the personalized or impersonalized route for their social exchanges and collective actions. When actors meet and judge the appropriateness of their joint involvement in collective action, they base their judgement on what could be called 'symbolic interactional signalling'. This expression is derived from the general idea of relational signalling (see Wittek et al. 2003 for a synthesis): we signal to each other in which category of social exchange we plan to get involved, one with commitment (close personal relationship) or another without (arm's-length interaction). Over time, however, most people need both registers to be able to play both games one after the other, or even simultaneously. The existence of a 'suspended moment' of symbolic interaction (SMSI) indicates in principle that a new, different project is always possible for collective action with the same alters. Thanks to this suspended moment, a *symbolic, normative/cultural dimension* is built into personal relationships but also into impersonal interactions.

Thus interactions and relationships are very different, but they have suspended moments of symbolic interaction in common. Here we will consider advice-seeking – defined as "What would you do if you were in my shoes?" – as an indicator of such a suspended moment of symbolic interaction. Indeed, when an advisor provides advice, s/he provides information and a framework for interpreting this piece of information and the appropriateness of its use. An advice relation embodies this symbolic interaction in an appropriateness judgement. Thus, between impersonal interaction and personalized relationships, suspended moments of symbolic interaction and signalling can be seen as appropriateness judgements. The next section defines the behavioural assumptions that can be included in a theory of appropriateness judgement that takes into account the capacity of actors to endogenize social structure (Lazega 1992) and to contextualize their common agency.[1] By endogenization I mean perception of context as structure of opportunity or constraint, and use of this perception as guidance for behaviour. I will then present an empirical illustration approaching SMSIs based on the case of a multiplex network study in a corporate law firm called Sue Grabbit and Run (SG&R; Lazega 2001). In this case I will suggest how advice-seeking and its embeddedness in local structures and cultures of multiplex blending combines and exposes symbolic interactions, interactions and relationships performing appropriateness judgements.

Here local cultures and structures are illustrated by the kind of embeddedness and multiplexity that come attached to advice relationships. In collegial organizations, for example, advice relationships blend with other kinds of interactions and relationships. In the empirical case of this firm, both personalized 'friendships' and impersonal cowork interactions, although rarely combined directly (one rarely mixes pleasure and business), lead to advice. Advice is easily combined with personalized "friendships" on the one hand, or with impersonal cowork interactions on the other hand. This suggests that an advice tie is the closest indicator that we can find for a SMSI. It contains the signal that members of the this organization use to tell each other in which category of social exchange they plan to get involved, one with commitment (close personal relationship), or another without (arm's-length interaction). With any one of these possibilities, a piece of advice will be considered appropriate in the eyes of at least one or more member(s) of the same firm. This person has the capacity to think with you, to share more than just a piece of information, but also the interpretation of this information, the social framework that is needed to guide action that will be approved (or not) by others. It thus contains traces of the contextualization of the message that signal the suspended moments of symbolic interaction, and with it, with or without personal commitment, to whom people are accountable (at least through their reputation) for the way they reconstruct the problem and the possible solutions.

Finally I will argue that, in such social contexts, seeking advice from an artificial intelligence (AI) emancipates actors from such a local structure and culture of appropriateness judgements, with the often heavy endogenization of structure that it requires. However, there is a price to pay for such an emancipation (i.e., for advice without key social ingredients of the appropriateness judgement). First, given this understanding of how interactions and relationships work with such suspended moments of symbolic interaction in appropriateness judgement, seeking advice from an AI will at best provide an answer reflecting what, on average, people like me do in such circumstances, not "What you would do if you were in my shoes?" Indeed, at least contemporary AI agents avoid such answers in order to escape liability. So the perplexed who do not have access to human advisors (who are, for example, inaccessible on the other side of a social boundary) or who do not want to seek advice from human advisors can still access this information. Perhaps it is better than nothing, and not worse than seeking advice from humans who do not necessarily provide good advice anyway (Blau 1955). But AI advice will naturalize an artefact of method (i.e., the statistical computation that led to the selection of the piece of advice that I receive from this AI); it will not share with me the framework of interpretation. I will not refer to any socially shared appropriateness judgement nor trigger this suspended moments of symbolic interaction, especially with the collective legitimacy and normative force that comes attached with commitment. How appropriate it will be for you to follow this advice thus remains an open question.

Second, along with this freedom from local rules and institutions, there comes attached what I would label the curse of recursivity. AI may one day provide even very personalized advice, but it will not forget the history of one's advice seeking. Query after query, actors will expose their uncertainties. Knowledge of others' uncertainties is an ingredient in the very definition of power (Crozier 1963). The more AI helps citizens construct their certainties and the more it can build each advisee's perplexity log, the more power it accumulates over these citizens. With such recursive queries and answers, the latter become weaker and weaker. An AI not being a deus ex machina but a tool in the hands of very human and corporate owners, the latter will be in a position to take advantage of these individual and collective weaknesses. AI for the perplexed could lead to algorithmic regulation and its strategic political use. Advice-seeking from AI creates perplexity logs that will help third parties build the collective certainties escaping critical and democratic accountability. Individual guidance for the perplexed through AI without the suspended moments of symbolic interaction can provide bits of answers but will also reinforce a different and discrete process at a higher, collective level: that of influence and power accumulation that will be hard to observe and check.

Neo-structural sociology

Neo-structural sociology (NSS) revisits this structuralism by opening it to individual and collective agency (for a synthetic presentation, see Lazega [2020c]). Interdependencies between actors are too important in social life to be left unorganized, and actors and institutions struggle to organize them. Social network analysis can be used, together with other methods, for tracking and understanding actors' embeddedness and efforts to manage their interdependencies in contexts of cooperation or competition where interests diverge, conflicts flare up and constraining but often fragile institutions are inherited from the past. As such it avoids reification of the notion of structure and helps in further developing a sociological theory of collective action and of the management of the latter's dilemmas (Weber 1921/1978, Olson 1965). Intentional, reflexive and strategic behaviour endogenizing the structure, not blind reproduction of underlying structure, are parts of the behavioural assumptions of this approach, including the use of organizations as 'tools with a life of their own' in 'dynamic configuring fields' (Selznick 1949), that is, as political communities. NSS makes behavioural assumptions based on a theory of social rationality that articulates these dimensions of individual and collective action by combining identities in reference groups, cultural norms and authority (based on social status, for example) in actors' appropriateness judgements (Lazega 1992, 2014). Structure, culture and agency (individual and collective) are thus brought together as in Archer (2005, Brock, Carrigan & Scambler 2016) and in the structural branch of symbolic interactionism (Stryker 1980), with applications in various fields (e.g., in economic sociology, as in Favereau & Lazega 2002).

The notion of social structure to which we refer brings together at least two dimensions of the concept, as discussed by Porpora (1989), including systems of human relationships among social positions, and collective rules and resources that guide behaviour. Network analytical formalisms, provided for example by White et al. (1976) and their successors, have enriched structural social sciences with an exceptional wealth of new intuitions, hypotheses and results. They have allowed social network methods of analysis to become so generic that they can now be used to both identify systems of opportunities/constraints and study social order/discipline and processes in society. Among the building blocks of NSS, management of interdependencies produces relatively stable relational patterns, called relational infrastructures (Lazega 2015). NSS identifies at least two kinds of relational infrastructures, relatively stabilized patterns of interdependencies that facilitate the deployment of generic social processes: a system of "social niches" and a system of heterogeneous (and more or less inconsistent) forms of social status that can be both endogenous and exogenous. The first reflects horizontal differentiations in social organization (such as the division of work) and the second vertical differentiations.

Depending on how members of social settings create and maintain relational infrastructures, they facilitate or hinder the deployment and collective navigation of the social processes on which collective action and coordination are based.

Among these processes, NSS has focused on modelling the variable forms of particularistic solidarity (measured for example with direct and indirect reciprocities, i.e., the forms of restricted and generalized exchange identified by Claude Lévi-Strauss), exclusions and de-solidarizations; socializations and collective learning (assessed for example with advice networks); social controls (measured for example with monitoring and sanctioning networks) and conflict resolution; and regulation and institutionalization of norms and practices (i.e., politics), but also on theorizing the contextualization of these processes (Lazega 2017). Each of these processes and its contextualization is at the heart of social life and collective action. In particular, identifying relational infrastructures helps model the 'regulatory' process, that is, the (re)definition of the rules of the game among members and the institution-building that comes attached (as cause or consequence; Lazega 2018).

Appropriateness judgements in suspended moments of symbolic interaction

From this neo-structural perspective, interactions and relationships are very different, but they have something in common: suspended moments of symbolic interaction in appropriateness judgement. Both help actors across the many social barriers that tend to keep most people down. What are appropriateness judgements and how do they carry out symbolic interaction to signal in which social context one is (not) exchanging, often using emotional indicators such as indifference, commitment, guilt, enjoyment, fear and so forth? Contextualizing behaviour, whether individual or collective, can be represented as deciding, based on symbolic interaction and signalling, between two options: whether one operates in a context where social exchanges are framed as impersonal interactions (resources are exchanged without long-term moral and symbolic commitment to an exchange partner in a public space) or in the context of personalized relationships (resources are exchanged with moral and symbolic commitments to an exchange partner in a common social space). Each kind of social space has its norms, its reference groups and forms of status, its social processes including solidarity and social control. Social spaces sometimes co-evolve in multilevel superpositions (Lazega 2015).

In which terms should we analyse this negotiation of the appropriateness of an action, message or decision? What are the criteria used by the appropriateness judgement to contextualizing behaviour? How do these criteria vary so as to allow such a negotiation? The symbolic interactionist tradition[2] in sociology provides a starting point for identifying three operations required by its conception of appropriate behaviour. These operations describe appropriateness judgements in an ideal, typical and analytical way; they define the system of criteria on which such judgement is based as uncertainty reduction (via status and authority arguments) understood as social construction of certainty. The three components of this system of criteria are selected from the theory for their praxeological importance. They answer successively the following basic questions. First, for a given or anticipated behaviour, which is the reference group recognized by the actor? Second, how is the action legitimized on behalf of this reference group? And third, who is entitled to represent this reference group in terms of social control?

Actors' identifications with, and accountability to, reference groups

The importance given by symbolic interactionism to a 'perspective', an 'audience' of actors' behaviour indicates how central to this theory is the capacity of individuals to claim credit for, or 'sign', their actions. In exchange for an allegiance, actors are invested with a specific membership and identity. This identity allows the actors to recognize themselves as the sources of their own actions. Any appropriate behaviour, which makes sense to the actors themselves, entails a recognized 'signature', and signature requires reflexivity.

The interest of this exchange lies in the potential conflict between competing allegiances in a social setting. Hence each actor represents for other actors several ways of being recognized and identified. This first step is contingent on, and reproductive of, horizontal differentiations in a community, for example a division of work. The important question then becomes in what terms actors establish their own identity among all possible ones. They 'negotiate' their identity (Stryker 1980) by ranking these allegiances hierarchically and by giving priority to one among these multiple memberships. This arrangement can therefore be considered a choice of an 'identity criterion' (Kellerhals et al. 1988) among several reference groups, which has possible repercussions on the negotiation of appropriateness of one's behaviour. Actors are other-monitored in the sense that they depend on others' recognition in order to be able to act, but self-monitored in the sense that they choose where they belong and create a hierarchy of allegiances by deciding which identity to involve in their action. In other words, actors' identification entails the creation of an interactive setting in which the anticipated or performed actions make sense. Further below, identity negotiations will be described as a choice between institutional or non-institutional identities.

The first operation (the identification of the source of the action) has a central place in the symbolic interactionist theory in that it relates the other actions with one another and with their position in the social structure (Turner 1956, McCall & Simmons 1966, Stryker 1980). Thus, the next two operations can be linked directly to this first one and indirectly to the structure of the social setting in which the actors belong. The course of action is oriented and influenced by definitions and redefinitions of identities. The structure of the group affects members' behaviour indirectly through its influence on these negotiations. Stressing this analytical phase of defining identities does not mean that one can reduce an interactive behaviour to a series of purely symbolic exchanges. From a praxeological perspective, actions and interactions are connected to tasks and problems: in organized settings, identity is transformed into status and role, therefore introducing questions of authority relationships and decision-making power. Establishing identities and showing allegiance to a reference group are necessary prerequisites of action (McCall & Simmons 1966), and only the first component of the definition of the situation.

Actors' rules and norms for legitimacy of action

The second generic question is "how do actors legitimize their behaviour on the behalf of this reference group." What form does the legitimation of behaviour take? When comparing alternative actions, the actors can orientate their behaviour by interpreting the existence of social control in several different ways. In what terms will the anticipated or expected behaviour be considered as legitimate or illegitimate?

This link between social control and legitimacy of action must be recognizable in one way or another to the actors themselves. The theory of the definition of the situation stresses the formation of cultural and moral expectations and the anticipation of induced consequences of one's behaviour as a necessary step when choosing among alternative actions and ways of legitimizing the choice. In that sense, 'what is legitimate' means 'what is expected of me'. Actors are able to 'problematize' their own behaviour, that is to establish a relationship between an action and an effect to obtain or to avoid from the perspective of others. This problematization can take, for instance, the form of an anticipation of sanctions – and sometimes of a prevention of risks, inasmuch as actors try to avoid behaviour perceived as inducing undesired (emotionally and/or morally) consequences.

This means that accounts or descriptions of the effects of one's actions (by the actors themselves) contain indications about how one legitimizes the behaviour on the behalf of social control. The fact that such accounts contain these indications can be used methodologically for the observation of the different ways in which actors answer this second generic question.

Actors' alignment with agents of social approval and control

The third generic question is "who is entitled to represent a reference group as an agent of social control for the enforcement of these norms, in this reference group?" This third step is contingent on and reproductive of vertical differentiations in a community (e.g., a status hierarchy). For the theory of the definition of the situation, every action involves other actors since reference groups do not exist unless represented by others, particularly within a group. The allegiance to a reference group and the definition of an identity create an interactive setting with expectations of alignments. Since the reference group is a position that others can occupy, the question for the actor becomes "for a given act, whom to recognize among all the members who might exercise this control as a representative of this group and authority?" In what terms are these inclusions and exclusions performed?

The praxeological importance of this criterion is linked to previously discussed actors' accountability. Since they are accountable for their behaviour to an 'audience', a form of social approval from their reference group, actors look for this social approval from others with a mandate to speak on behalf of this reference group. But to whom do they turn for this validation of the legitimacy of their actions? Actors certainly have several possible ways of answering this question through trying to shape the audience that will provide the guarantee that their actions make sense to others too. They can define and redefine ad hoc constituencies in which these actions are evaluated, validated or disqualified. To include some actors and exclude others from this audience (i.e., to decide about the extension[3] of this audience) comes down to choosing representatives for social control. To decide about the extension of one's accountability means therefore to designate, whom within the social setting one belongs to, that is, those from whom one wishes to obtain an explicit validation or a guarantee of legitimacy for one's behaviour. The selection of these representatives of social approval and control can divide the group; this helps to establish the discriminant quality of one's behaviour, the 'distinction' that actors may try to acquire among all the members of a social setting.

In sum, the operations into which the appropriateness judgement can be broken down are a set of criteria allowing actors to negotiate this appropriateness of behaviour or message in their social context (i.e., to contextualize it). Actors do not judge the appropriateness of their actions and communications alone. They make sense of them by contextualizing them together. But why do we need this theory of appropriateness judgement here? Because it helps understand what is at stake with symbolic interaction. All this takes place in what I would like to call the 'suspended moments' of symbolic interaction, grounding common or collective action either on personalized collegiality or on impersonal bureaucracy. My next point is that learned appropriateness judgement for collective action necessarily includes local multiplexities of interactions, symbolic interaction and relationships (i.e. local cultures of multiplexity that have a moral dimension).

My argument will be that artificial intelligence agents cannot learn this culture unilaterally or once and for all. They cannot because the cultural multiplexity depends on these suspended moments that are emotionally and morally coherent at one level and at the same time normatively ambiguous with all their cooperation uncertainties.

In the next section I try to flesh out this idea that suspended moments of symbolic interaction that become visible in advice-seeking create a socially consistent link between impersonal interaction and personalized relationships. The main idea is to show that suspended moments of symbolic interaction, signalling and multiplex blending are based on political reflexivity and management of normative ambiguity that cannot be taken away from humans and cannot be performed by artificial intelligence agents because the latter cannot be trained to simulate appropriateness judgement with all their uncertainties and complexities.

Advice relationship: "What would you do if you were in my shoes?"

Advice-seeking and taking is a vital resource for orientation and guidance for any person in society, especially in a society of organizations relying extensively on secondary socialization. Focus on advice relationships is interesting because they provide rich access to symbolic interaction and appropriateness judgements. A rich body of literature has already analysed advice networks. However, we argue that this literature tends to oversimplify the study of advice relationships and the interpretation of patterns identified in them. In this literature, advice is seen as a proxy for information, and this relationship is mainly and pragmatically construed as an interaction in which actors obtain information. For example, for Burt, "from whom do you seek advice?" means "from whom do you get your information?" In our view, advice must not be confused with a simple search for information. We approach advice relationships using the formula "What would you do if you were in my shoes?" A professor can frequently ask his/her students for a bibliographic reference. But this request for information is different from asking someone, "I am going to be fired. What shall I do, what would you do if you were in my shoes?" Answering such a question requires providing not only an answer but also a framework to interpret the answer. Indeed what qualifies as advice is "your good reasons for giving this piece of advice." Advisors owe their interlocutors a good explanation, a good set of reasons why. This question is socially loaded with demand, and in order to answer why, it has to tap into the three steps of appropriateness judgements combined. This why Blau (1955) observed that advice-seeking as a social exchange includes, at least initially, a form of deference and recognition of the social status of the adviser. It is frequently observed that the more senior people are in a social setting, the more they are sought out for advice. But seniority as a unique determinant for identifying sources of advice can be trivial and misleading since many senior persons are often not sought out. Epistemic authority comes from other sources as well.

Advice-seeking and certainty work in local structures and cultures of multiplex blending

The behavioural assumptions included above in a theory of appropriateness judgement take into account the capacity of actors to endogenize social structure, to contextualize their common agency. An empirical example can illustrate how advice seeking and its embeddedness in local structures and cultures of multiplex blending combines symbolic interactions, interactions and relationships in performing such appropriateness judgements. Here local cultures and structures are illustrated by the kind of embeddedness and multiplexity that come attached to advice relationships. Seeking advice is an activity guided by local structure- and culture-specific patterns of consultation. Advice relationship formation varies across contexts because different norms establish the conditions under which encounters are considered opportune for consultations. In some settings, open advice-seeking is considered entrepreneurial and encouraged, whereas in other settings it would downgrade a person's reputation and thus require private discussions for the right kind of suspended moments of symbolic interaction to take place. Thus advice relationships can be more or less structurally and culturally embedded and multiplex. In the following example, advice ties are blended with other relationships (and when they are not, they can be dangerous and misleading). In the case of a New England corporate law firm called SG&R, network analyses show that friendship relationships lead to advice and co-worker relationships lead to advice, while friendship and collaboration do not lead to each other. When members do not have such relationships, it is much harder for them to seek advice from other members, to ask them to think with you, to share not only a piece of non-redundant information but the interpretation of this information, the social framework that is needed to guide action that would be approved (or not) by others. Advice means sharing a course of action and at the same time an appropriateness judgement that provides the framework for the interpretation of this action.

Hence observing appropriateness judgements is not easily done directly. Rather, it minimally involves studying how actors perform the different steps of appropriateness judgements described above. The negotiation of these steps, as theorized here, can be reconstituted in part by observing multiplex blendings in work-related collective action. The multiplex structure and culture that is considered appropriate and learned as the hallmark of collegiality in at SG&R can be pictured by a short description of this organization and its functioning. The organization comprised 71 lawyers in three offices located in three different cities, including 36 partners and 35 associates, in 1991. All the lawyers in the firm were interviewed. In Nelson's (1988) terminology, this firm is a 'traditional' one, without formally defined departments, as opposed to a more 'bureaucratic' type. Interdependence among attorneys working together on a file may be strong for a few weeks and then weak for months. As a client-oriented, knowledge-intensive organization, it tries to protect its human capital and social resources, such as its network of clients, through the usual policies of commingling partners' assets (clients, experience, innovations; Gilson & Mnookin 1985) and the maintenance of an ideology of collegiality. Informal networks of collaboration, advice, and 'friendship' (socializing outside), are key to the integration of the firm (Lazega 2001).

In this organization, such ties represent channels for various types of resources for each member. The first is the network of strong *work contacts*: close coworkers can be relied upon for their cooperation; they provide work or access to clients. The second is the network of *advisors*: advisors provide solutions to, or make final decisions in, complex problems in a knowledge-intensive organization handling sophisticated legal cases. In this law firm, the difference between advisors and coworkers is based on the fact that a partner can seek another partner's advice without including the advisor as a coworker in the file at hand (and thus sharing credit). The third network is the role-distance, or *friendship* network, identified as 'socializing outside work': friends provide many different resources associated with role distance, such as emotional and symbolic support, or a definition of the situation. We do not assume that friendship is a homogeneous framework (Archer, this volume). It refers to friendships as understood locally by these actors, neither to thin friendships, which are unidimensional and quickly replaced, such as travelling companionship; nor to thicker and stronger friendships that are more satisfying on a multiplicity of dimensions but sometimes difficult to maintain in environments characterized by strategic behaviour.

Using an adequate statistical model (Lazega & Pattison 1999, 2001) that permits dependencies among network ties, it was possible to characterize the specific forms of interdependence between resources that help members solve a structural problem of collegial organizations (i.e., mitigate status competition) when seeking advice. Using this model, we examined the local statistical distribution of each type of resource and then the characteristics of the firm's social capital: the interplay or combination of such resources among members. The next paragraphs describe the results of our analyses.

There are three kinds of ties under analysis. Duplex ties involve two of those ties (either cowork and advice, or friendship and advice, or cowork and friendship). Triplex ties involve the three kinds of ties together (cowork, advice and friendship). A large number of parameters in a multivariate model corresponding to configurations comprising both cowork and advice ties suggests that cowork and advice ties are distributed in a highly interdependent manner. The co-occurrence of the two types of tie is likely: cowork and advice are aligned in structure. There is a tendency for the two types of tie to be exchanged, even if these tendencies towards alignment and exchange are somewhat disjunctive. This means that being a coworker of an advisor or an advisor of a coworker is not always a sufficient qualification for being a direct advisor. In this sense, the advice and cowork ties participate in configurations having some of the characteristics of the interlock of strong and weak ties, with advice ties the stronger of the two (Breiger & Pattison 1978, Granovetter 1973, Pattison 1993). Thus advice ties drive the creation of new coworker ties, in the sense that new coworker ties may be forged with either the coworkers of one's advisors or the advisors of one's coworkers.

One possibility, therefore, is that the advice tie has a stabilizing role in what otherwise may be a less stable pattern of work distribution in a system driven largely by organizational rotation, relational infrastructures and informal exchange ahead of formal deliberation and construction of agreements. That is, the lack of exchange in these configurations may be offset by the opportunity to work with individuals at higher status; it is in this sense that status-signalling advice ties are strong and help to articulate the distribution of collective participation in certainty work. But note that this capacity for work ties to straddle status differences does not extend too far: the advisors of one's advisors are not likely to be coworkers. Further, we note that status-singalling advice ties play a role in providing access to work opportunities, and that this may help mitigate against status games. In all, the interdependence between coworker and advice ties is strong in this exchange system. This latter detail begins to give shape to the distinctive social capital of the firm.

Advice and friendship ties also exhibit quite strong interdependence, with substantial multiplicity (i sends a duplex tie to j, meaning that two different resources are exchanged in their relationship, for example advice for friendship) and exchange (i sends an advice tie to j who reciprocates with a friendship tie) effects. Just as advice ties serve to articulate cowork relations, so friendship ties may serve a weak articulatory role with respect to advice ties: indeed, configurations in which the friend of an advisor is also an advisor have a positive parameter estimate. Such patterns of interdependence of friendship and advice ties can also be interpreted as suggesting that friendship 'softens' the status differences inhering in advice ties, both directly (through multiplexity and exchange effects) and indirectly (by tending to link the advisors of an individual). Thus, these patterns are consistent with expectations regarding the role of role-distance ties in the mitigation of status competition and production of certainty.

However, the parameters for configurations involving cowork and friendship tend to be much weaker, and often negative. Thus, members tend to sort their ties so as not to mix coworker and friendship (i.e., business and pleasure) too directly. For example, at the triadic level, cycles comprising two friendship and one coworker tie are unlikely and there is a weak tendency for friendship ties to link the two lawyers with whom a third claims cowork ties. This latter effect is similar to, but much weaker than, the pattern by which advice was claimed to help sustain one of the asymmetric cowork configurations. Without advice ties, i.e. our signals of suspended moments of symbolic interaction, it is difficult to combine interactions and relationships. In this setting, each tends to reinforce certainty work on its own and in its own way, but independently from the other.

Thus, finally a very small number of dyadic configurations involving the three kinds of exchanges together (i.e., cowork, advice and friendship) is not a common form. In particular, the triplex tie from *i* to *j* has a negative estimate, whereas the triplex tie accompanied by a reciprocal cowork tie has a positive estimate. This suggests that, even though pairs of members may be linked by duplex ties more commonly than the overall frequency of individual ties would suggest, the observation of *all three ties together* linking a pair is not a common structural form.

To summarize these multiplex blendings as structural tendencies, a number of separable forms of interdependence describe the interlocking of the three relations in this collegial setting. First, each type of tie appears to have its own characteristic pattern of organizational distribution. Cowork ties appear to be strongly (but not entirely) organized around principles of direct and generalized exchange, whereas advice and friendship ties exhibit a pattern of local clustering and partial ordering (with a greater emphasis on clustering for friendship and a greater emphasis on a hierarchical distribution for advice). Second, despite these apparently quite different organizational principles, there is some evidence for the alignment of the different types of tie, particularly of advice ties with each one of the two others. This provides quite direct evidence for some form of mutual accommodation of the different types of tie. Third, there is also some evidence for dyadic exchange of these different types of tie. This suggests another form of interdependence between the separate tie distributions, but one that might also be expected to provide a structurally supportive role. As for the alignment effects, the combination of advice with either of cowork or friendship yields the strongest manifestation of this form of tie dependence. Finally, a third type of interdependence links the arrangements of the different types of tie. This third pattern is one in which one type of tie appears to serve as a bridge supporting another. The pattern is strongest for cowork and advice: advice ties link individuals who are only indirectly connected through (asymmetric) cowork ties. A weaker version of this pattern is also seen for advice and friendship (with friendship bridging individuals whose advice is sought from a common source) and much weaker for cowork and friendship (with friendship again in the bridging role, and only in very small and dense social niches). These patterns invite speculation about processes giving rise to these configurations, but longitudinal data would be needed to help distinguish various alternatives since the dynamics of tie generation are critical.

These results help in showing that certainty work and epistemic cooperation is made possible in this setting by a specific complex generalized and multiplex exchange system, that is, by structurally and culturally specific multiplex blendings of social exchanges identifying the appropriate ways in which members exchange resources connected to their work life in the firm. They also show that such configurations constitute a form of relational capital for individuals and social capital for the collective, providing structural solutions to structural problems – here, for example, the problem of dealing with status competition among professional members and peers to organize certainty work and lead to collective learning. Such a synthesis contributes to a theory of collective action by developing our understanding of how a collegial organization creates a structure which helps individuals find indirect ways to exercise restraint in the pursuit of status and thus keep learning and production going. This analysis is sufficient to show that studying relational capital and social capital in terms of locally multiplex generalized exchange is key to looking, on a case-by-case basis, at how members manage their social resources, in particular epistemic resources, in order to cooperate in the production of quality service. This in turn enhances our understanding of commitment to collective learning and action.

This example of multiplex blending is an example of a weaving of the orders, one interactional and the other relational in certainty work, because in this firm a minimal administrative system provides a flow of coworkers' interactions, while a clientelistic system of patronage provides a strongly relational form of bounded solidarity. Both realms can support or undermine each other, and the conditions under which they support each other include structural and cultural patterns of advice relationships that balances them as well as a process that maintains this balance for both impersonal and personalized certainty work (Lazega 2000).

These multiplex relationships between advice and friendship on the one hand and advice and cowork on the other hand can be interpreted as indications of the *pivotal role of advice* ties in collegial certainty work. For instance, one can hypothesize different types of advice relations – those that reflect impersonal status differences, and those that are forged through friendship. Members learn to distinguish status differences (e.g., between partner and associate) and the kinds of exchange sub-structures appropriate for such status differences and rapports, in particular deference of the advice seeker to the advisor. My point here is that such cultures of multiplex weaving helping peers to create collective responsibility in certainty work and appropriateness judgments differ from one place to the other. Thus a general mechanical search for the right blend of social exchange in the right multiplex substructure by an artificial intelligence agent without normative intuitions derived from being socialized into this local culture would be somewhat formidable and inconceivable as of yet. Such a search, in addition, would never lead to any normative intuition about this pivotal role of *advice ties as indicators of the suspended moment of symbolic interaction* that are common to interactions and relationships underpinning certainty work. Thus, appropriateness judgements help members in this context to use advice-seeking as the moment of suspended symbolic interaction to jointly understand or decide where common or collective action among them is going, and eventually how they will use the difference between impersonal interactions of routinized work and/or personalized relationships of creative work. As mentioned, suspended moments of symbolic interaction (i.e., of signalling and weaving) are based on sensitive political reflexivity and management of normative ambiguity that cannot be taken away from humans and cannot be performed by artificial intelligence agents because the latter cannot be trained to simulate appropriateness judgements with all their micropolitically reflexive certainty work (Lazega, 1992).

The dataset at SG&R is a case in point and is not representative of all collegial organizations. It is just rich enough to argue about the difference between impersonal interaction, symbolic interaction and personalized relationship as mobilized by joint appropriateness judgements and certainty work. These judgements are learned and epistemic coordination will differ depending on whether actors engage in the short-term interaction route or the long-term relationship route in social settings with specific structural and cultural patterns of consultation. The capacity to share this aspect is an outcome of local multiplexities and idiosyncratic combinations of interaction, symbolic interaction and relationship. Only socialization, including secondary socialization, can provide the capacities to both perform appropriateness judgements and reach collective learning. But it needs to be a form of socialization that allows role distance (as identified by Van Maanen's definition [1985] and Kunda's [1993] notion of "engineering culture") even when facing Varman and Al-Amoudi's (2016) 'derealization'. In collegial organizations, advice relationships and certainty work are weaved with other kinds of interactions and relationships. Advice-seeking leads to sharing more than just a piece of information but the interpretation of this information, the social framework that is needed to guide action that will be approved (or not) by others who align with this structure and culture of advice-seeking. The latter's presence is signalled by the suspended moments of symbolic interaction between members who are to some extent accountable to the same collective for their certainty work and for the way they reconstruct the problem and the possible solutions.

AI advice, routinized certainty work and algorithmic regulation

Given this understanding of how interactions and relationships are combined in suspended moments of symbolic interaction in appropriateness judgements that can become visible in advice-seeking, what does the emphasis that comes attached on local cultures and structures of advice relationships tell us about seeking advice from an AI? Computers could provide the information function and knowledge transfer, but it is difficult to see how they would build the appropriateness judgement framework that will help the advice taker interpret the piece of information, and that people experience when they work together and share experience in reflexive role distance. Given the definition of advice as information and framework (or good reasons) to interpret the information in locally specific ways, advice is explicitly social, and it has a normative and institutionalizing dimension. Up to very recently, an AI could not be assumed to know about the specific local structure and culture of the social setting of an advice seeker. It is a system that was not supposed to know me, my circumstances, interests, special case, character, relationships and what the consequences would be for me after a given decision. But if appropriateness judgements are pivotal in the workings of reflexivity, as the building of concerns and everything that comes attached (Archer 2007, 2012, Donati 2011, Maccarini 2019), a new social system could emerge from an AI that brings together the personal and the social in synchronized, recursive, but also repetitive, routinized and strongly homogenizing ways.

Even without suspended moments of symbolic interaction that cannot be performed by artificial intelligence agents, resorting to AI can be based on many reasons nevertheless. One such reasons can be that members of socially organized settings might welcome the freedom to escape this highly personalized exchange system and to seek advice from an impersonal source, skipping the heavily social certainty work performed within the constraints (that are also opportunities) of structural and cultural patterns. Historically, here again, impersonal bureaucracy and markets have long been considered sources of uncertainty reduction and emancipation, and AI agents are perfect examples of both. Another reason is that it can be seen as better than nothing. In some respect, to "What would you do if you were in my shoes?" an AI would provide an answer of the kind "This is how many people who ask this question consider this solution in a situation like yours." It could thus provide different ideas about how to reflect on a problem, even if not advice in the sense of our definition. Many people with very modest relational capital do not have access to advisors whatsoever. Blau (1955) has shown that members of organizations often seek advice from peers who are not in a position to provide this advice. Finally, in still other cases, advice-seeking can be fake and linked only to the performative nature of consultation in hierarchical settings: superiors can be consulted because subordinates, who do not care what advice they receive, just want their superior to know that they consulted them and that the power dynamics have been fulfilled. Acknowledging an advisor can be part of a wider process that takes place when a decision becomes public. In what sense, then, are these cases different from seeking advice from an AI?

Even this assumption that the machine does not know people individually may be increasingly wrong. It is now conceivable that there will be, in not such a distant future, a unified system that listens to everyone everywhere and that we will be part of that system, which could lead to personalized advice contextualized 'just for you'. With all the digital traces that we leave behind we tell 'the cloud' enough about dimensions of our life for an AI to be able to resort to knowledge of similar analogous analyses of situations. This means that with ubiquitous surveillance that is already here, it could contextualize anyone with their queries in increasingly sophisticated ways and provide advice that would seem to answer one's concerns. Even if it will not trigger this suspended moments of symbolic interaction, with the collective legitimacy and normative force that comes attached with commitment, an AI could thus naturalize appropriateness judgements. It may not share the framework of interpretation or refer to any social locally shared legitimacy criteria (if any), or be ashamed if it were misleading, or help across any social barriers.

From this perspective, it could perhaps follow that advice from enhanced humans would be even more of a problem than advice from non-human AI agents. With enhanced humans, this heteronomy looks supervised by the agent with whom one is interacting, although who supervised the enhancement and how is not an appropriate issue to raise and will always remain fuzzy. Advice coming from norms formulated by a blend between (unknown) supervised learning and personal responsibility of the advisor creates the conditions for groupthink and sectarianism. Individual enhancement as envisioned by ubiquitous use of AI (Lazega 2019) is an organizational and collective enhancement that tends to obtain extremely high levels of conformity from everyone involved in any form of collective agency based on such certainty work. This is due to the fact that the source of the norms that guide this agency are not known, discussed and even challengeable (Al-Amoudi & Latsis 2019). If AI can answer the question "What should someone do?" (rather than "What should you do?") by extracting a statistical mean in a series of recorded behaviours deemed similar, and recognizing it as a social norm, this kind of computation (e.g., in a world of the internet of things built into everything) fills the world with artificial norms. Given permission, which is a question of law, technology could listen to all we say everywhere and build massive databases that, even when anonymized to be allowed, could facilitate questioning an AI agent about "What would everybody else seeking advice on that issue do?" An eigenvector recognition system could build an answer from data extracted from presumably comparable situations and discriminate to provide a routine answer. That advice can be perceived as authoritative, and it is conveyed by an AI based on observed and recorded human interactions and questions. Technologically that is already entirely feasible today. With three more generations of technological change to "improve" it, this public 'service' could well be there.

For an advice relationship to exist, subjects need the suspended moments of symbolic interaction in search of the "right" appropriateness judgment for management of uncertainty. When you give advice to someone you take a personal responsibility; if this is bad advice, it can challenge or harm your relationship. In the response provided by an AI, no one has committed itself to anything. The answer does not commit the AI as it would commit a human advisor who shares the framework, his/her good reasons and to some extent responsibility for the consequences. The AI's answer is equivalent to "This is what the system advises." It is impersonal, even if it is accurately targeted. This is not say that AI advice is not a useful functional analogue to what we call advice, especially for the many without access to any advisors, not even to advice brokers who can help a subject to cross the closed boundary beyond which an advice relationship with someone else becomes easier. It does not help to deny that this AI advice is in fact the same as human advice because we are in a new context and that, in this new context, we do not culturally accept yet to call this functional analogue produced by technology 'advice'. Perhaps it is a new cultural concept of advice that we do not already have and that will help this kind of certainty work acquire a form of legitimacy over time.

However, with this freedom from local rules, structure and institutions comes attached what could be called the curse of recursivity. It may one day provide even very personalized advice, but it will not forget the history of one's advice-seeking. Query after query, actors will expose their uncertainties. We should then recall that knowledge of others' uncertainties is part of the very definition of power (Crozier 1963). As mentioned already, the more AI helps citizens construct their certainties, the more it can build each advisee's perplexity log, the more influence it concentrates over these citizens and their institutions. With such recursive queries and answers, the latter become increasingly weaker. An AI is a tool in the hands of very human and powerful owners who are in a position to take advantage of these individual and collective weaknesses. AI for the perplexed could lead to bureaucratic algorithmic regulation and its unchecked strategic political use. Advice-seeking from AI creates perplexity logs that can help third parties build the collective certainties escaping critical and democratic accountability. Individual guidance for the perplexed through AI without the suspended moments of symbolic interaction can provide bits of answers but will also reinforce a different and discrete process at a higher, collective level: that of knowledge of and influence over institutions that will be hard to observe and check.

From this neo-structural approach to seeking advice as a practice that is characterized by structural and cultural/normative context, we can see three possibilities emerging from AI availability for short-circuiting this 'initial' social context. A first possibility is that AI agents help the perplexed individual who keeps seeking their advice. It will slowly participate in the contemporary concentration of power in the hands of big tech hegemons by the constitution of individual perplexity logs, measurements and profiles for entire populations. This will become part of the unobtrusive control of populations that is building up, but this time through the constitution of epistemic monitoring of individual concerns, certainty work and reflexivity. How big tech platforms would systematically use anyone's perplexity logs and analyse their uncertainties is still unknown to the wider public. But it is useful to insist that one thing is not unknown: in an organizational society (Perrow 1991), uncertainty is a source of power, and anyone's zones of uncertainty are used by others to increase their domination, and not only epistemic domination.

A second possibility is that through inside-out collegiality (Lazega 2017, 2019) combined with robotic presence and collaboration (Archer 2019), AI data collection is able not only to build individual perplexity logs but also contextual information about how social processes of collective learning take place in the environment of individuals whose perplexity logs have been reconstituted. These 'collective perplexity logs' would characterize the context of each individual perplexity log, reconstituting their meta-ignorance and micropolitics of knowledge in real time (Smithson 1985, Lazega 1992). Advice to individuals could then incorporate knowledge of the content of others' practices and queries in the same context or in similar contexts (workplaces, families, associations, cooperatives, political parties, etc.). Technology to implement this ubiquitous recursivity already exists. For example, platforms advising drivers about which road to take to avoid being caught in traffic jams often rely on information collected or obtained from other drivers already caught in these jams. Provided a critical mass of advice seekers/ informants sign up to the platform, the accuracy of guidance can be sufficient to impress the seekers and encourage them to keep feeding their own logs and the system with queries and information.

A third possibility could combine the first two and build synchronization between individual and collective agency (Lazega 2016, 2020a), their short- and long-term processes, through multilevel recursivity. In this context, inside-out collegiality (IOC) routines could exogenously and actively manage and develop (as opposed to just ignore or just observe) the local structures and cultures of advice-seeking themselves. They would be adding a level of steering of collective appropriateness judgements, definitions of the situation, and institutionalized certainty work, collective reflexivity and collective concerns that is still difficult to construe from the perspective of citizens of political liberal democracies. Advice networks for construction of certainties would not only be short-circuited by AI made 'freely' available to the perplexed, but in many ways reconstituted for the perplexed, through serious recommendations and gamified orchestration, under ongoing regimes of algorithmic regulation (Yeung 2018). Big tech hegemons have already started to create the building blocks of such a regime – a system of organizational morphogenesis – with initiatives providing 'community leaders' across the world with 'free' platforms allowing them to both upload (to the cloud) standardized information about their community and receive routinized and recursively built advice about its management. Similarly, other platforms using information from individual social network profiles to help employers navigate labour markets would also make use of such perplexity logs, and records of queries and weaknesses, for matchmaking purposes, restructuring labour markets themselves and the ways in which individuals would have to adjust to them.

This recursive synchronization in collective certainty work could be in the making with IOC. Here deep relational and institutional embeddedness and dependence of individuals are weakened; collective IOC spreads as a new form of bureaucratization through digitalization; and the recursivity, or back and forth between levels, could use the new 'freedom' from local structures, rules and institutions to make it much easier for new management to define the new normal and take over epistemically. This means making strategic and moral decisions for both individuals and the meso-level collectives in which they are affiliated. AI uses of perplexity logs would become political in a much wider and encompassing sense of the word. Such roads to serfdom from algorithmic regulation by bureaucratic powers that are able to control organized collective action from the ground (appropriateness judgements) up (to IOC) may be part of the current loss of privacy of individuals and of institutions, and the construction of a deeper centralized form of social discipline that may be preparing humanity for the coming rationings and transitions. The extent to which concerns for equality and justice are incorporated in such multilevel synchronizations is made visible in the uses of AI for management of the poor.[4]

As it works without the suspended moments of symbolic interaction that the perplexed need to share and question the framework of appropriateness judgments, advice from AI becomes part of Yeung's (2018, Yeung and Lodge, 2019) algorithmic regulation to govern populations. If these behavioural assumptions of neo-structural sociology are accepted, the dangers ahead with respect to interference by artificial intelligence agents with organized social life is in creating a militarily bureaucratized world generalizing the impersonal interaction-symbolic interaction route and neutralizing the symbolic interaction-relationship route. The ground for the spread of depersonalized interactions was prepared by the rise of bureaucracy in the nineteenth century and perhaps by its transformation and extension with contemporary digitalization.

As shown in our empirical example, multiplexity analysis in social networks is a method that can identify the indicators of the *suspended moments of symbolic interaction* that are common to interactions and relationships. In our case in point, advice ties are these indicators of creative certainty work and micropolitics of knowledge. Perplexity logs accumulated by AI-driven data analysis platforms expose the public to exercises of influence that have the potential to guide and reshape our appropriateness judgments and variations in social rationality. Epistemic routines distilled unobtrusively are a form of certainty work that institutionalizes knowledge claims and creates normative alignments, avoiding change and increasing inertia as if epistemic status and roles in micropolitics of knowledge were mere, superfluous and dispensable obstructions against management of uncertainty. Assumed gains in such individual management can increasingly become collective losses in innovative creation of alternatives, coorientation and renewed capacity for institutionalization of new norms, values and priorities. Such perplexity logs as used by AI-boosted homogenization at the level of populations increase the bureaucratization of society (Lazega, 2020b), preselecting standardized options, encouraging often polemical or sectarian groupthink instead of new, much needed reality-based and inclusive certainty work, knowledge claims and forms of collective responsibility.

Reducing synchronization cost through AI-driven multilevel recursivity sounds like a short dystopian story dreamed up by Asimov. It is hard to see how this Foucauldian epistemic control through a combination of perplexity logs and intellectual property laws is compatible with the *esprit critique* that is necessary for each citizen to construct certainties in a politically liberal democracy. Seeking advice from an AI would be seeking knowledge without wisdom. Perhaps citizens of democracies should learn to keep their local structures and cultures of advice-seeking as protected from big relational tech hegemons as possible to begin with, so as not to allow for the convergence and junction of the first two scenarios of algorithmic regulation. The first danger from artificial intelligence agency is then not in imitating humans and their appropriateness judgement but in eliminating the diversity of appropriateness judgements. By doing so, it would assume that any form of collective responsibility is considered legitimate by members, further spreading routinization and bureaucratization. It would also suppress the suspended moment of symbolic interaction between relationships and interactions, as well as the normative/cultural challenge that is built into this suspended moment.

Notes

1 This is needed because it may seem irrelevant to articulate a structural perspective with a symbolic interactionist theory, which has often been considered to lack interest in the existence of social institutions, of bureaucracies, power structures and stratifications of any kind. This reputation, however, is undeserved. As shown by Maines (1977, 1988), Stryker (1980), and Fine and Kleinman (1983; see also Fine [1991, 1992]), the interactionist movement is not homogeneous, and more than generally acknowledged, it takes into account the structure of social settings as a determinant of behaviour. But it has not done so in a truly systematic way. Contrary to theories such as the "negotiated order theory" (Strauss 1978), for which the regularity observable in members' behaviour does not result from their conformity to official and institutional rules but from a series of ongoing negotiations and compromises, from the combination and interaction of priorities, mutual constraints and individual aspirations. It is not productive to oppose "Everything is negotiable" to "Nothing is negotiable" (Day & Day 1977; Strong & Dingwall 1983, Dingwall & Strong 1985). As demonstrated by Blumer (1969) and Maines (1977), many symbolic interactionists take structures into account in a more constructed way, defining the specificity of the contexts in which they were doing research and giving considerable importance to structural constraints when describing actors' behaviour. 'Structuralist' symbolic interactionists, from Hughes (1945, 1958) to Freidson (1976, 1986), developed a less "subjectivist" framework than theoreticians more attracted by social psychology, such as Shibutani (2017). Symbolic interactionist work taking into account the social structure relies on a less rigid and less stable conception of the structure than does the functionalist tradition (which is why, from the latter perspective, the interactionist definition of the structure often seemed non-existent).
2 For an analysis of how appropriateness judgements compare with the symbolic interactionist theory of the 'definition of the situation', see Lazega (1992, 2016).
3 Here the extension of actors' accountability does not measure their degree of responsibility. The extension of their accountability measures the possibility or impossibility for others to represent social control to which the actors answer for their actions.
4 See www.theguardian.com/technology/2019/oct/14/automating-poverty-algorithms-punish-poor (14 October 2019) revealing how unemployment benefits, child support, housing and food subsidies and much more are being scrambled online. Vast sums are being spent by governments across the industrialized and developing worlds on "automating poverty" and in the process, turning the needs of vulnerable citizens into numbers, replacing the judgement of human caseworkers with the cold, bloodless decision-making of machines.

References

Al-Amoudi, I., & Latsis, J. (2019). Anormative black boxes: Artificial intelligence and health policy. In I. Al-Amoudi & E. Lazega (Eds.), *Post-human institutions and organisations: Confronting the matrix*. London: Routledge.

Archer, M. S. (2005). Structure, culture and agency. In M. D. Jacobs & N. Weiss Hanrahan (Eds.), *The Blackwell companion to the sociology of culture* (pp.17–34). Oxford: Blackwell.

Archer, M. S. (2007). *Structure, agency and the internal conversation*. Cambridge: Cambridge University Press.

Archer, M. S. (2012). *The reflexive imperative in late modernity*. Cambridge: Cambridge University Press.

Archer, M. S. (2019). Considering A.I. personhood. In I. Al-Amoudi & E. Lazega (Eds.), *Post-human institutions and organisations: Confronting the matrix*. London: Routledge.

Blau, P. M. (1955). *The dynamics of bureaucracy; A study of interpersonal relations in two government agencies*. Chicago, IL: The University of Chicago Press.

Blumer, H. (1969). *Symbolic interactionism: Perspective and method*. Englewood Cliffs, NJ: Prentice-Hall.

Breiger, R. L., & Pattison, P. E. (1978). The joint role structure in two communities' elites. *Sociological Methods & Research, 7*, 213–226.

Brock, T., Carrigan, M., & Scambler, G. (2016). *Structure, culture and agency: Selected papers of Margaret Archer*. London: Routledge.

Crozier, M. (1963). *Le phénomène bureaucratique*. Paris: Seuil.

Day, R., & Day, J. V. (1977). A review of the current state of negotiated order theory: An appreciation and a critique. *Sociological Quarterly, 18*, 128–144.

Dépelteau, F. (2015). Relational sociology, pragmatism, transactions and social fields. *International Review of Sociology – Revue Internationale de Sociologie, 25*(1), 45–64.

Dewey, J., & Bentley, A. F. (1946). Interaction and transaction. *The Journal of Philosophy, 43*, 505–517.

Dingwall, R., & Strong, P. M. (1985). The interactional study of organizations: A critique and reformulation. *Urban Life, 14*, 205–231.

Donati, P. (2011). Modernization and relational reflexivity. *International Review of Sociology, 21*(1), 21–39.

Donati, P. (2014). Social capital and the added value of social relations. *International Review of Sociology – Revue Internationale de Sociologie, 24*(2), 291–308.

Donati, P. (2019). The digital matrix and the hybridisation of society. In I. Al-Amoudi & E. Lazega (Eds.), *Post-human institutions and organisations. Confronting the matrix*. London: Routledge.

Donati, P., & Archer, M. S. (2015). *The relational subject*. Cambridge: Cambridge University Press.

Favereau, O., & Lazega, E. (2002). *Conventions and structures in economic organization: Markets, networks and hierarchy*. Cheltenham and Northampton, MA: Edward Elgar Publishing.

Fine, G. A. (1991). On the macrofoundations of microsociology: Constraint and the exterior reality of structure. *Sociological Quarterly, 32*, 161–177.

Fine, G. A. (1992). Agency, structure, and comparative contexts: Toward a synthetic interactionism. *Symbolic Interaction, 15*, 87–107.

Fine, G. A., & Kleinman, S. (1983). Network and meaning: An interactionist approach to structure. *Symbolic Interaction, 6*, 97–110.

Freidson, E. (1976). The division of labor as social interaction. *Social Problems, 23*, 304–313.

Freidson, E. (1986). *Professional powers*. Chicago, IL: The University of Chicago Press.

Gilson, R. J., & Mnookin, R. H. (1985). Sharing among human capitalists: An economic inquiry into the corporate law firm and how partners split profits. *Stanford Law Review, 37*, 313–392.

Goffman, E. (1961). *Encounters: Two studies in the sociology of interaction*. Indianapolis, IN: Bobbs-Merrill.

Granovetter, M. (1973). The strength of weak ties. *American Journal of Sociology, 78*, 1360–1380.

Hughes, E. C. (1945). Dilemmas and contradictions of status. *American Journal of Sociology, 50*, 353–359.

Hughes, E. C. (1958). *Men and their work*. Glencoe, IL: The Free Press.

Kellerhals, J., Coenen-Huther, J., & Modak, M. (1988). *Figures de l'équité: La Construction des normes de justice dans les groups*. Paris: Presses Universitaires de France.

Kunda, G. (1993). *Engineering culture: Control and commitment in a high-tech corporation*. Philadelphia, PA: Temple University Press.

Lazega, E. (1992). *Micropolitics of knowledge*. New York: Aldine-De Gruyter.

Lazega, E. (2000). Teaming up and out? Cooperation and solidarity in a collegial organization. *European Sociological Review, 16*, 245–266.

Lazega, E. (2001). *The collegial phenomenon: The social mechanisms of cooperation among peers in a corporate law partnership*. Oxford: Oxford University Press.

Lazega, E. (2014). Appropriateness and structure in organizations: Secondary socialization through dynamics of advice networks and weak culture. In *Contemporary perspectives on organizational social networks* (pp. 381–402). Bingley: Emerald Group Publishing Limited.

Lazega, E. (2015). Mobilités, turnover relationnel et coûts de synchronisation: Comprendre l'action collective par ses infrastructures relationnelles dynamiques et multiniveaux. *Année Sociologique, 65*, 391–424.

Lazega, E. (2016). Synchronization costs in the organizational society: Intermediary relational infrastructures in the dynamics of multilevel networks. In *Multilevel network analysis for the social sciences* (pp. 47–77). Cham: Springer.

Lazega, E. (2017). Organized mobility and relational turnover as context for social mechanisms: A dynamic invariant at the heart of stability from movement. In J. Glückler, E. Lazega, & I. Hammer (Eds.), *Knowledge and networks* (pp. 119–142). Cham: Springer.

Lazega, E. (2018). Networks and institutionalization: A neo-structural approach. *Connections, 37*, 7–22.

Lazega, E. (2019). Swarm-teams with digital exoskeleton: On new military templates for the organizational society. In I. Al-Amoudi & E. Lazega (Eds.), *Post-human institutions and organizations: Confronting the Matrix* (pp. 143–161). London: Routledge.

Lazega, E. (2020a). Bottom-up collegiality, top-down collegiality, or inside-out collegiality: Research on intermediary-level relational infrastructures as laboratories for social change. In G. Ragozini & M. P. Vitale (Eds.), *Challenges in social network research*. Cham: Springer.

Lazega, E. (2020b). *Bureaucracy, collegiality and social change: Redefining organizations with multilevel relational infrastructures*. Cheltenham: Edward Elgar Publishers.

Lazega, E. (2020c). Networks & neo-structural sociology. In R. Light & J. Moody (Eds.), *The Oxford handbook of social networks*. Oxford: Oxford University Press.

Lazega, E., & Pattison, P. E. (1999). Multiplexity, generalized exchange and cooperation in organizations. *Social Networks, 21*, 67–90.

Lazega, E., & Pattison, P. E. (2001). Social capital as social mechanisms and collective assets. In N. Lin, K. Cook, & R. Burt (Eds.), *Social capital: Theory and research* (pp. 185–208). New York: Aldine-De Gruyter.

Maccarini, A. M. (2019). *Deep change and emergent structures in global society*. Cham: Springer International Publishing.

Maines, D. R. (1977). Social organization and social structure in symbolic interactionist thought. *Annual Review of Sociology, 3*, 235–259.

Maines, D. R. (1988). Myth, text and interactionist complicity in the neglect of Blumer's macrosociology. *Symbolic Interaction, 11*, 43–58.

McCall, G. J., & Simmons, J. L. (1966). *Identities and interactions.* New York: The Free Press.

Nelson, R. L. (1988). *Partners with power: The social transformation of the large law firm.* Berkeley, CA: University of California Press.

Olson, M. (1965). The logic of collective action: Public goods and the theory of groups. Cambridge, MA: Harvard University Press.

Pattison, P. (1993). *Algebraic models for social networks.* New York: Cambridge University Press.

Perrow, C. (1991). A society of organizations. *Theory and society, 20,* 725–762.

Porpora, D. V. (1989). Four concepts of social structure. *Journal for the Theory of Social Behaviour, 19,* 195–211.

Selznick, Ph. (1949). *TVA and the grass roots: A study in the sociology of formal organizations.* Berkeley, CA: University of California Press.

Shibutani, T. (2017). *Society and personality: Interactionist approach to social psychology.* London: Routledge.

Smithson, M. (1985). Toward a social theory of ignorance. *Journal for the Theory of Social Behaviour, 15*(2), 151–172.

Strauss, A. (1978). *Negotiations: Varieties, contexts, processes and social order.* San Francisco, CA: Jossey-Bass.

Strong, P. M., & Dingwall, R. (1983). The limits of negotiation in informal organizations. In G. N. Gilbert & P. Abell (Eds.), *Accounts and action.* Farnborough: Gower.

Stryker, S. (1980). *Symbolic interactionism: A social structural version.* London: Benjamin/Cummings.

Turner, R. H. (1956). Role taking, role standpoint, and reference group behavior. *American Journal of Sociology, 61,* 316–328.

Varman, R., & Al-Amoudi, I. (2016). Accumulation through derealization: How corporate violence remains unchecked. *Human Relations, 69*(10), 1909–1935.

Weber, M. (1921/1978). *Economy and society: An outline of interpretive sociology.* Berkeley: University of California Press.

White, H. C., Boorman, S. A., & Breiger, R. L. (1976). Social structure from multiple networks. I. Blockmodels of roles and positions. *American Journal of Sociology, 81*(4), 730–780.

Wittek, R., Van Duijn, M., & Snijders, T. A. (2003). Frame decay, informal power, and the escalation of social control in a management team: A relational signaling perspective. *Research in the Sociology of Organizations, 20,* 355–380.

Yeung, K. (2018). Algorithmic regulation: A critical interrogation. *Regulation & Governance, 12*(4), 505–523.

Yeung, K., & Lodge, M. (Eds.). (2019). *Algorithmic regulation.* Oxford: Oxford University Press.

4 Artificial intelligence and the challenge of social care in aging societies

Who or what will care for us in the future?

Jamie Morgan

Introduction

In recent years, social care has become a high-profile media issue in many countries. The general mood of this reporting is negative: reference to crunch points, crisis and so forth. Whilst there is local variation, there is also a common theme: changes in demographic structures, employment profiles and ways of living creating new needs and problems in and for societies (Robertson et al 2014). There is a growing segment of the population requiring care and support with their physical and emotional welfare. The main focus of this has been on what Christina Patterson terms "extra time" (Patterson 2019), that is, increased life expectancy leading to an aging population that lives well beyond traditional retirement age. However, *adult* social care is a broader category, which also includes support for working-age persons who are differently abled or suffer with chronic mental and physical health conditions.[1] Whilst there has been some discussion of the potential for technologies to play a role in addressing the needs and solving the problems that are emerging, this has been a largely peripheral concern (however, see the centre-right think tank Policy Exchange report, Lightfoot et al. 2019: 60–67, and also the charity Hft's recent work).[2] The main concerns have been rising costs, fiscal constraints, affordability and financing solutions intended to address a rapidly approaching future (e.g., EAC 2019, Charlesworth & Johnson 2018, Amin-Smith et al. 2018). Moreover, with a few exceptions there has been relatively little consideration of the sociological transformations that new technologies might bring in and through social care (however, see Prescott & Caleb-Solly 2017).[3] Accordingly, in this chapter I explore some of the potential roles that artificial intelligence (AI), robotics and such might play in social care in the future and the impacts that this may have on who we are and how we relate to each other. The chapter builds on social ontology themes set out in the previous two volumes (Al-Amoudi & Morgan 2018, Al-Amoudi & Lazega 2019, Morgan 2018b, 2019b). I begin from some general commentary, but my main focus is the UK case since this provides some structural context to consider why we may find ourselves increasingly *dependent* on technology for social care.

Some introductory context for social care

There is no single global definition of social care. As a concept, it is imbricated with a country's policy framework (Robertson et al. 2014). Typically, however, the term refers to a social policy framework intended to promote the welfare of different categories of a state's population, usually with a focus on vulnerable groups' developmental, physical and psychological needs. This can be fully integrated with or run parallel to a primary healthcare system. However, it is worth first emphasizing that many of the underlying issues for social care are general and not reducible to problems arising only from prior policy frameworks. Moreover, one should keep in mind that the current focus on social care in 'crisis' in the UK is overwhelmingly oriented to the old and to cost (and this is a political response by a conservative government who draw overwhelmingly on the asset-heavy old for their voting base). The underlying issue is that there are demographic and social changes affecting the age and relational profile of populations that involve cumulative challenges (and opportunities, since the situation need not be negative) for social care as traditionally conceived, but also for general welfare as societies change. Fundamentally, in the twenty-first century there are cumulatively:

- More people in need of *task-support* for aspects of living.
- More people who would benefit from *companionship* whilst living.

Both of these apply not just to the old, and the second of these is no less important than the first. Social care is not just reducible to mechanical function, since quality of life is not only mechanical. Mental health and human flourishing are more nuanced issues. They are cultivated through the sociality of who we are. We are creatures that flourish, and we do so *together* – in and as communities. Individuality, autonomy, privacy and respect are meaningless concepts without social formations in which they can be pursued, and without groups who offer *recognition*, support, and interaction. It is through these that *meaning* is given. It is from these that our sense of dignity and positively valued identity flow, and it is because these are things that matter to us that we *feel* their presence and are harmed by their absence. The 'golden rule' (treat others as one would be treated), Kant's categorical imperative (treat everyone as everyone would be treated – as an end, not a means), and the concept of cultivated virtue ethics rooted in Aristotle's 'golden mean', oriented on *eudemonia*, are all attempts to articulate the problem of living not just proximately but mutually, in 'togetherness'.[4] Ideological debate regarding the balance between positive and negative freedoms is likewise concerned with how best to achieve this goal of constituted togetherness. Moreover, the humanist Marxist critique of capitalism and alienation is a long-standing focus on possible limits of that achievement for the entire range of ways of structuring our contemporary polities and economies (Morgan 2018a), and there are many non-Marxist accounts of current problems and opportunities (Donati & Archer 2015, Taylor 2007, Putnam 2000, Patomäki & Teivainen 2004; even neo-conservative rugged individualism requires a society to offer respect, worth and status to the valorized individual).

All of which is to say that over the centuries cultural learning and social progress has led to the basic recognition that *needs* are not just basic or material but also substantively psychological and conjointly social (Sayer 2011). The UN inscribes these as human rights because they attach to being human. Our concept of civilizational progress (and retardation) has involved both the de jure and continuous struggle for de facto extension (and resistance to withdrawal) of this recognition of common characteristic needs (across genders, races and places), and the concept of capabilities is one important way in which a grounded and active dynamic has been articulated for the human as the needy bearer of rights. Arguably, of course, it is personhood that is ultimately at issue, and so entity recognition is potentially broader if we meet or make non-human persons (Archer 2008, Smith 2011, Morgan 2019d). The point, however, is that *social care* is imbricated with human welfare more generally, and this holds across different countries with different political traditions because of the commonality of what it is to be human. And yet trends in demographics and ways of living are leading to new possibilities regarding who or what we may depend on in the future for these needs. Consider:

- Globally, infant mortality rates have continued to fall and life expectancy to rise.
- Birth rates have continued to fall and family sizes to shrink.
- More people with disabilities (the differently abled) are surviving into adulthood.
- The world's population continues to increase, albeit at a decreasing rate.

There is, of course, a great deal of local variation. However, in recent years, only India and some of the African nations have experienced significant net growth in population based on birth rates, and policy focused on the Millennium Development Goals and the subsequent Sustainable Development Goals (SDGs) seems likely to facilitate a continuation of the general demographic trend of slowing birth rates and thus population growth. Reference to the SDGs is also a reminder that current ecological problems (of which climate change based on carbon emissions is only one manifestation) may *require* us to choose pathways with even more radical and rapid results for demographics over the coming century. Both de-growth and steady state economics are predicated on voluntary institutional population control, and emerging ecological campaigning organizations such as Extinction Rebellion have already begun to argue that in addition to low-impact living, the most effective contribution one can make is choosing not to reproduce (Gills & Morgan 2020). Without voluntary change, it may well be that climate disaster and disruption to food production and distribution systems will eventually lead to induced catastrophic population reductions. And of course, more recently Covid-19 has added global pandemic to our list of concerns.

In any case, the underlying point is that, globally, demographic structure continues to morph from an upright to an inverted and increasingly distended pyramid.

There are many reasons for this demographic morphing and most are simply consequences of the way we choose or are required to live. Matters of demographics intertwine with patterns of living. Globally, the population has become more urban and more mobile (albeit increasingly in tension with rising nationalism and a politics that intrinsically supports increasing border control). Economic development (globalization) has drawn more and more people into modernity – again, though, with local variation. China has undergone radical demographic and social change in a few decades based on social engineering of population growth and an idiosyncratic economic development strategy (converging on an asymmetrically male-weighted only-child situation expressed in successive generations of 'little emperors'). More generically, modernity itself continues to change as 'advanced capitalist' societies develop. Among the 'advanced capitalist' countries, Japan has travelled furthest in terms of demographic consequences. But all capitalist societies report both 'replacement rate' issues and issues of cultural transition and social fragmentation. Almost everywhere technological connections now transcend distances, but in many places we are increasingly likely to be geographically distanced from established familial networks, and this is often based on work. Families are changing (started later, increasingly transient, blended, etc.) and in social media–saturated societies how (and if) friendships are formed and relations are maintained are also changing. Social isolation and loneliness are increasingly recognized issues for *all* ages in modern societies.

So, in the twenty-first century, we are not just living longer; we are living differently (Morgan 2016). On this basis, there are problems of task-support and companionship to solve now, in the near future, and over the rest of the century. Social care, then, is an issue with context. The context provokes two fundamental questions. First, what physical and mental condition are we in as we live and as we live longer? We live in societies in which youth is valorized and age as a *physical state* is masked by media representations of vibrancy and youth that are not representative of what it is like to actually be old. Science in general and medical science in particular, of course, are constantly improving, and so we *may* see fundamental transformations in physical robustness for the old in the future (see Al-Amoudi 2018, Tegmark 2017, Harari 2017, Kurzweil 2000). It may be that stem cell treatments, organ replacements, genetic manipulations, synthetic components and augmentations and so forth maintain the body in something like its mature peak until such time as we die. It may be that the body is enhanced. However, neither is yet the case. Currently, we are extending the period of life but doing so in a way that allows illness, frailty and degeneration to cumulatively impact on the person.

Science, then, struggles with our senescence, and this extends to our cognitive capacities, but even if we eventually resolve these issues our psychosocial needs must still be satisfied. As things stand, an aging population is also one that by choice, bereavement or happenstance will involve more people living alone. In any case, based on *current* medical science, we are living into age brackets where chronic and degenerative disorders are more common (generalized pain disorders, arthritis and degenerative joint conditions, the long-term management of joint replacement, heart, lung and circulatory problems, type II diabetes, various neuro-logical conditions such as Parkinson's, dementia of various kinds, etc.) and where mobility, physical function and cognitive capacity may be significantly reduced. At the same time, progressive social policy means that there is a general commit-ment that the differently abled should be empowered to live within the community rather than in institutions (though there has also been a cynical cost-cutting basis to policy in some places, where responsibility is thrown back on the family; *and* it is not just that more of the differently abled are surviving into adulthood, the pressures of modern living are making increasing numbers of us unwell).

We now come to the second fundamental question. Who will be available (proximate, willing, competent) to offer care and on what basis are we prepared to facilitate this care (what are we willing to pay for)? Clearly, an aging and extend-ing demographic profile implies the potential for a numbers mismatch between a relatively reducing working-age population and both the increasing numbers *already* in need and those in the next decades likely to *become* in need of social care. This is irrespective of whether we are prepared to prioritize and fund social care. It seems entirely conceivable, therefore, that AI, robotics and new technolo-gies will be the solutions on which we increasingly *depend*. The UK illustrates some of the issues.

The UK social care system

A primary healthcare system is delivered via hospitals, clinics and general medi-cal practice surgeries, and these can be more or less integrated with social care based on division of responsibility/labour, referral, communication and liaison. Many countries employ an insurance system, which may be more or less compre-hensive. The UK case is somewhat odd (Jarrett 2018, Quilter-Pinner & Hochlaf 2019, EAC 2019). Since the creation of the National Health Service (NHS) in 1948, healthcare has been free at the point of use.[5] However, the decision was made at that time to make individuals responsible for the cost of their social care unless and until their circumstances qualified them for social security under the National Assistance Act 1948. This division broadly distinguished between medi-cal intervention for illness and social support for living.

The distinction in the UK case is of course blurred, leading to sometimes arbi-trary division for whether a person's circumstances are categorized as healthcare or social care. The key point, however, is that the distinction has resulted, as both healthcare and social care policy have subsequently developed, in different structural characteristics of the two. The notable structural weaknesses of social care exposed by Covid-19 and the general ineptness of government responses and blame-shifting suggest that the current system will change in the future. But the current state of the system in mid 2020 is still instructive (not least because it is indicative of the weaknesses that Covid-19 has exposed, but also because it indicates how little thought is currently given to technology and how much of the focus is cost). In the UK, social care is devolved (for differences see Light-foot et al. 2019: 25). Focusing on England, *spending* is drawn from government

Table 4.1 Estimated breakdown of gross adult social care funding in England, 2016–2017

Source	Amount and proportion of funding
Council tax	£8.0 billion (38.6%)
Business rates	£3.8 billion (18.1%)
Other income (predominantly NHS partnerships)	£3.2 billion (15.5%)
Government grants	£3.0 billion (14.7%)
Care user contributions	£2.7 billion (13.1%)

Source: EAC (2019: 8).

local authority budgets, and so the primary decision maker is the local authority (HSCHCLGC 2018, Local Government Association 2018). Social care is also primarily *funded* locally, but drawing on a range of sources, including care user contributions. For example, in 2016/17 local authorities spent £18.15 billion on adult social care (EAC 2019: 7).[6] In funding terms this breaks down into the following (Table 4.1).[7]

Eligibility for social care is then determined within a series of categories. First, potential recipients are divided into those receiving 'domiciliary care' (in their own or a family member's home) and 'residential care' (a care home or more intensive nursing home). Second, costs are categorized as 'personal care' (assistance with dressing, feeding, washing, etc. and possibly emotional-psychological support)[8] and 'hotel costs' (everyday costs of living in residential care: accommodation, food, energy bills, etc.). Potential recipients undergo a Care Needs Assessment (CNA) by a 'social care professional'. The assessment is subject to the *Care Act 2014*, but its form is at the discretion of the local authority.[9] Eligibility is then means-tested.

As of late 2019, if a potential recipient has assets valued higher than £23,250, they receive no social care funding and must meet their own personal care and any hotel costs. If receiving residential care, the value of assets can include the potential recipient's home (minus mortgage debt, but the home is excluded if residential care is temporary or if a relevant relation still occupies it). If receiving domiciliary care, then the value of assets does not include the individual's dwelling place. If a person's assets are (or fall) below £14,250, then care costs are met by the local authority, including identified personal care needs. However, if the person has income (excluding some benefits), then this too can be directed to care costs (up to a threshold that leaves the individual with a minimum Personal Expense Allowance of £24.90 per week). For individuals with assets between £23,250 and £14,250, the local authority calculates a contribution from assets based on a formula (currently £1 for every £250 of capital) combined with a contribution from any income.

Those receiving no support with social care, especially those in residential care, are referred to as 'self-funders', and in the literature these are distinguished from those receiving support. As the Institute for Public Policy Research (IPPR) notes, this now has a privatized, subcontracting/outsourcing and market-based context; in 1979, 64% of residential and nursing home beds were still provided by local authorities or the NHS. By 2012 this had fallen to just 6%. In homecare, the change has been quicker still: in 1993, 95% of homecare was provided by local authorities; by 2012 this had fallen to just 11% (Quilter-Pinner & Hochlaf 2019: 17).[10] In any case, for many older people who own their own homes and who have saved for retirement, £23,250 is a low threshold. Many care services are complex and expensive and accommodation fees significant. According to LaingBuisson's most recent UK market report, average residential care costs in England were £621 per week and nursing costs £876 in 2018, but with considerable variation by region and service, and for both of these a primary influence was ability to pay – that is, whether one was self-funded (see also report from regulator, Care Quality Commission 2018: 18–21).[11]

The net effect of exposure to social care costs is a rapid drain on accumulated wealth and available income, producing 'catastrophic care cost' consequences. Moreover, insofar as the distinction between healthcare and social care is blurred, vulnerability to these costs is likewise arbitrary and, in this sense, discriminatory as well as unjust. For example, currently a person who develops cancer will be treated through the NHS and then likely categorized as needing 'continuous healthcare' (CHC) once discharged. As such, all their healthcare and social care costs will be met by the NHS. Dementia sufferers, meanwhile, or the merely frail typically fall under social care. The important point, however, for our purposes is that this structural perversity has developed in the UK in relation to the common set of changes we set out in brief in the last section. It is the background to the UK's version of the 'crisis of social care' that governments confront. Subsequent changes that may occur since this chapter was written are likely also responses to this.

According to the Office for National Statistics (ONS) latest statistical releases, June and August 2019, the total UK population in 2018 was 66.4 million. The ONS population overviews, released November 2018 and July 2017, provide further context.[12] Population is expected to grow to 73 million by 2041. Despite a recent slowdown in improvements to life expectancy, as of 2016, 18% of the population were over 65, compared to 16% in 2007, and this is projected to grow to almost 21% by 2027 and 25% by 2040 (see also EAC 2019: 14). In 2016, 2.4% of the population were 85 and older. As of 2017, there were more than 150,000 men and 340,000 women over 90 (combining to more than 495,000, compared to 330,000 in 2002). According to the UK Department of Work and Pensions Family Resource Survey 2018, 13.9 million people or 22% of the population reported a disability, long-standing illness or impairment in 2016/17, and 45% of these were retirement age and 19% working age. Numbers have steadily increased over the twenty-first century, particularly for mobility and mental health issues, and according to the Voluntary Organizations Disability Group, which represents a collection of charity care providers and campaigning organizations, numbers continue to rise (see EAC 2019: 15). Returning to the issue of age, by 2040 it is expected that 8% of the UK population will be at least 80 years old. Based on current local variation, over 50% of local authorities are projected to have more than 25% of their resident population aged 65 and over by 2036 (heavily focused on Southern England but not the poorest areas of London). As such, there are significant existent and growing needs to be met, though Covid-19 fatalities will surely change some of this.

According to recent research on likely developments in care needs for the old in England between 2015 and 2035, the total number of people requiring support is set to significantly increase because of the increasing age profile of the population, though the numbers capable of independent living will also be increasing (Kingston et al. 2018). The research anticipates a cycle of transition in required care support as each of us ages, from no to low to high dependency, with the numbers notably influenced by those who succumb to dementia and a combination of other conditions (comorbidity). By 2035, women now in their fifties may expect to spend the last 12.5 years of an average life expectancy with successively greater degrees of dependency: 8.5 years of some task-support; 1.3 years requiring more invasive personal care, including help with dressing and meal preparation; and a final 2.7 years of high dependency including bathroom support and help with eating and moving; for men the equivalent is 7 years of task-support dividing into 5.1, 0.8 and 1.1, respectively (Kingston et al. 2018: e453). There is, however, as the previously stated social care spending figures indicate, already a significant social care needs situation in the UK. Moreover, need is already manifestly not being met. Spending on social care has significantly reduced since 2009 and was £700 million lower in 2017/18 than 2010/11, despite an increase in the total population, the older population and those registered as disabled (Figure 4.1).

Moreover, since most funding is localized, there is no direct link between capacity to generate funding and spending need (and in the most deprived areas, funding has reduced by up to 17% per capita since 2010). The system has thus become more fragmented. In any case, according to the IPPR, the number of people receiving publicly funded social care has declined by about 600,000 since 2010 (Quilter-Pinner & Hochlaf 2019: 3). Despite this reduction, more than 50% of local authorities reported an overspend on their adult social care budgets in 2017/18.[13] According to campaigning organizations, a major consequence has been that local authorities have been forced to tacitly ration care and have

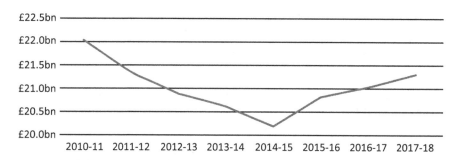

Figure 4.1 Adult social care spending, 2010–2011 to 2017–2018 (adjusted for inflation)

Source: EAC (2019: 14).

tended to make the Care Needs Assessment (CNA) more onerous, denying care support to all but the most severe cases (EAC 2019: 15–16). Between 2017 and March 2019, 626,701 elderly people were refused care funding by their council.[14] At the same time, local authorities have reduced the coverage of personal care services to those who are granted support *and* have reduced the sums paid to outsourced care service suppliers, both domiciliary and residential (Quilter-Pinner & Hochlaf 2019). According to Age UK, 14% of over-65s had unmet care needs in 2018 (about 1.4 million people), and in a 2018 survey the Care and Support Alliance found that over 25% of respondents were unable to maintain the basics of personal care, with 30% unable to leave their home and 20% feeling unsafe in their home (Age UK 2018, EAC 2019: 15–16).

Funding and spending changes have had multiple further consequences. First, the quality and provision of services offered by outsourced providers has come under pressure. Providers have responded by focusing on higher paying self-funders which, in turn, leads to cross-subsidization of self-funders and local authority–supported care recipients in those places where *both* are covered, but also a longer-term tendency for profit-driven providers to return contracts to the local authority and instead select for self-funders, leading to a 'two-track system' and a net withdrawal of services (Lightfoot et al. 2019).[15]

Second, as the coverage of domiciliary care reduces, then there is an accelerated loss of independence for those in need of support, both in the form of a lack of preventative and ameliorative low-level care (whose provision slows the requirement for some kinds of higher dependency care) and a manifest higher risk of unplanned and ill-coordinated and unmanaged transfers to the NHS, primarily taking the form of hospitalized persons who cannot be returned to the place – either their home or the residential care home – they came from, since there is a lack of resources for staffing and support (Quilter-Pinner & Hochlaf 2019, Crawford et al. 2018). This 'bed blocking' is particularly acute for the frail and for dementia sufferers. In 2018 there were 850,000 people in the UK diagnosed with dementia, and this is estimated to increase to 1 million by 2025. According to the Alzheimer's Society, 62% of dementia sufferers have Alzheimer's, 1 in 6 people over the age of 80 have some form of dementia, and the equivalent of 36 hospitals were out of action in 2018 because of a lack of social care discharge opportunities for some of those sufferers (see also Cebr 2019).

Third, as of 2018 almost 1.5 million people worked in the social care sector, and as most analysts note, there is a strong likelihood that the sector will require more, not fewer, workers as the numbers in need of care increases. However, there was already a 6.6% vacancy rate in 2016/17, and in 2018 vacancies stood at about 90,000. Care work remains relatively poorly paid, difficult and lacking in status. Many are paid the minimum wage. However, increases in the minimum wage have merely exacerbated the cost pressures on providers without significantly improving terms for employees. For many dedicated staff it is a vocation but not a viable career, and the biggest churn is transition into retail, which indicates something of the nature of this labour market. Staff turnover ranged from 31% to 42% for different categories in 2018 (for issues see Dromey & Hochlaf 2018).

Moreover, about 18% of the workforce is immigrant and 8% of this is of EU origin. According to the Nuffield Trust, Brexit may result in a rise in the vacancy rate by an additional 70,000, and according to the IPPR, total vacancies could rise to 350,000 by 2028 (EAC 2019: 26; Quilter-Pinner & Hochlaf 2019: 6).

Fourth, persistent reductions in real spending and service provision have created a knock-on effect where family and friends take on the role of unpaid carers. The point is not whether they are prepared to do so; it is that they are *required* to and are not typically effectively supported by the state in doing so. In being required to take up care, they are denied other activities that may be of economic or social benefit, and they may, in any case, lack the relevant time, skills and competencies, particularly as needs increase. Moreover, if the system tacitly comes to rely on unpaid carers, it discriminates against those who have no one to rely on whilst also potentially unjustly treating those who take on the role of carer. According to the 2011 census, more than 5.4 million people provide unpaid care in England and more than 1.2 million of those provide more than 50 hours of care; 58% of the 5.4 million were women and 63% of those providing more than 50 hours were also women (EAC 2019: 17–18). According to a Carers UK (2019) survey, which provides more granular updated evidence based on 7,500 respondents, 81% of unpaid carer respondents were women, 24% of the total themselves had a disability, 46% provided more than 90 hours care and 51% were over 55 (5% of which were over 75).

These points clearly highlight some of the structural vulnerabilities that the Covid-19 pandemic exposed, though they by no means explain the inept response by central government. In any case, the situation in England and the UK more generally, then, is already problematic and serious. It is a combination of quite specific features of the structural developments of social care in the UK and tendencies that generalize beyond the UK case. In March 2019, the president of the Royal College of Physicians, the chair of the Academy of Medical Royal Colleges and the chair of the Royal College of General Practitioners wrote a joint letter to the UK government warning that social care 'is on the brink of collapse'. The government promised a comprehensive Green Paper in the summer of 2017, but this had still not been published in mid-2020, partly because of ongoing concerns regarding the need to integrate findings with a parallel review of the NHS, and partly because the issue of catastrophic care costs and taxation had proved politically toxic (though among Boris Johnson's first stated commitments as prime minister has been the pledge to 'fix social care', and this was a feature of the general election). Campaigning groups, analysts and lobbyists have articulated a range of possible solutions, but with a primary focus on costs and bridging the current funding gap (Bottery et al. 2018, Bushnell et al. 2019, Communities and Local Government Select Committee 2017, Darzi 2018, HSCHCLGC 2018, Jarrett 2018, Local Government Association 2018). Policy has focused on restoring spending to pre-2010 levels, introducing a dedicated social care tax (hypothecated taxation) or increasing general taxation to improve affordability within general taxation – a cap on lifetime care costs and a higher current asset threshold for eligibility for free care and ideally universal free personal care. As the IPPR notes, free personal care in a more generous system would still only amount to 6.9% of total NHS spending and 1% of total government expenditure (Quilter-Pinner & Hochlaf 2019: 12), but the general tendencies in economic policy have an opposing direction of travel (Morgan 2019a).[16]

The primary focus here is financing rather than the nature of the needs of care recipients and the potentials for these to be met. This is to say nothing of companionship. According to the ONS, 4.1 million people under 65 and 3.9 million people over 65 were living alone in 2019, and this constituted 8 million of 27.7 million households. There is an equally important and subtly invisible loneliness problem emerging in the UK.

In any case, even if the state chooses more humane funding and spending options, there is still the issue of how care is to be delivered and by who or what. Challenges based on demographics and patterns of living remain peripheral to the debate, and yet in 2016, for every 1,000 people of traditional working age there were 285 people aged 65 and over in the UK, and by 2040 there may be a ratio of almost 1 person over 65 to every 2 (current) working age adults (see also EAC 2019: 15). Even if fourth Industrial Revolution forecasts of significant job displacement prove to be the case (see Morgan 2019c) and there is a concomitant shift of employment to 'soft skills', it does not follow that there will be sufficient people prepared to work in social care. Moreover, there is a great deal more to be considered in terms of the potential for new technologies to contribute to social care. And yet the listed experts for the promised Green Paper (Jarrett 2018: 14) consist mainly of persons drawn from healthcare and social care non-governmental organizations and finance and insurance consultants, and contain no experts on technology (or migration and labour markets). We now turn to the prospects for technology.

A *when not if* situation for technology, AI, Robotics and social care?

Two position points are relevant to what follows. First, there are likely to be fewer people we can expect to or who will be available to depend on for social care in the future, both paid and unpaid. Second, it is widely reported that our societies are in the early stages of experiencing a set of major technological developments whose significance is collective: machine learning (ML), artificial intelligence (AI), robotics, sensors, connectivity, cloud computing, nano-technology, 3-D printing and the internet of things (IoT). Whilst few subscribe to technological determinism, the confluence of these technologies is expected to significantly transform society. Social care is just one potential component in a broader set of changes. It is an area in which corporations and governments clearly have strong motives to invest, since there are readily observable problems and opportunities to address, and more negatively, to exploit. Reflecting on the last section ought already to suggest what some of the problems that might be addressed are and as we set out early on, there are (and are going to be) more people in need of task-support for aspects of living and more people who would benefit from companionship whilst living. From the point of view of policy, the immediate problems to resolve are practical – for example, in the UK, the bed-blocking problem. However, each intervention also potentially alters the way we live and so is of possible socio-logical significance. With this in mind, let us consider some examples, beginning from technologies that are already in embryonic form. The examples are intended to be indicative of potential rather than comprehensive in terms of scope. Comment on the sociological consequences is, of course, speculative to a degree that varies with the contingency of the potential of technologies and the timelines one might consider (see Prescott & Caleb-Solly 2017).

Task support in the alert home

Isolation and security are quintessential problems for the old and generally vulnerable who live alone. The frail and the chronically ill are more likely to experience some incapacitating event undiscovered in a timely manner. Even if the person cohabits, the cohabitee may be unable to cope with the nature of an eminently foreseeable event (a fall, a diabetic coma, etc.) because they are similarly vulnerable. This is why the old consider moving to secure accommodation communities (with wardens and room alarms, etc.), why residential and then nursing home care eventually become advisable, and why, if such an event occurs, many are currently denied hospital discharge because there is, based on their living arrangements, no safe way to discharge them. Continuing to live at 'home' and 'locally' (familiar surroundings) is something many prefer (and is potentially economical since it involves least intervention and change).

The alert home is one possible solution, and various companies are already developing the relevant technologies. A sensor-enabled dwelling connected to a hub management AI in a $5G^+$ digital infrastructure creates a sensitive living space able to track heat and motion and determine where a vulnerable person is in that dwelling and whether they require assistance. A sensor system can provide information on location, whether the person is horizontal or vertical, stationary or in motion, what their current temperature is and so forth. From these, an ML-adaptive AI system can potentially infer whether a person is following their standard routines or is immobile, distressed, injured or dead. Monitoring thus creates the potential for a dwelling to alert significant and designated others regarding a vulnerable person's state of being and to request assistance if required following an adverse event (from family, friends, neighbours, a carer or relevant authority or emergency service). Since this system is information dependent, it seems likely to encourage the modification and adoption of technologies that are widespread in the leisure sector and are already starting to appear in the workplace. Wearables and self-trackable technologies (WSTT) provide real-time information on biometrics and potentially on state of mind (algorithms applied to heart, lung and temperature data, tone of voice, etc. are used to infer an emotional state). WSTT could readily be modified for the particular circumstances of vulnerable groups. It is only a small step from the Fitbit to a more generalized health monitoring or disability or geriatric-oriented 'Unfitbit' or adoption of multiple apps on a next generation smartphone (transforming it from a communication device to a specialized monitoring one), and a small step from there to chip implants, much in the way we track pets.

Clearly, the direction of travel implied by information provision and access is potentially invasive and invokes issues of privacy and consent. When we focus on the purposes for which a system is ostensibly created – its service to us – we tend to lose sight of the purposes to which it can be put. Those purposes or potentials tend to slip by us until events bring them to the fore (as recent publicity regarding Facebook, Cambridge Analytica, etc. makes all too clear). One can readily conceive of how we could be drawn into a situation where data can be exploited, abused and in general monetized even if the core service from which the data is extracted is benign. An alert system has obvious benefits and it is entirely conceivable that we will opt to sign ourselves or our loved ones up to such a system (for peace of mind) without fully understanding the terms and conditions a corporation offers the service under. It is entirely conceivable that insurers will encourage us (as a condition of buying coverage) in the future to make use of such services (and that those insurers will be part of conglomerates and Multinational Enterprises (MNEs) that supply those services). It is entirely conceivable that the state may require us to adopt an alert home system (and this may be something a future hypothecated tax is designated to pay for – a policy position that may exist even if the reality of government spending is not one where taxation *really* finances spending – or it may be that adoption of such a system is a condition of access to other welfare services from the state *and* it may be that the service itself is then provided under contract by a corporation in a public-private initiative (by some equivalent of the company G4S or Carillion, with all that may entail).

The scope for an alert home is, of course, not restricted to monitoring for adverse events. Once information flow is established and access provided, there is scope for the alert home to monitor general health through smart IoT products linked to an AI hub management system. This, of course, is not just a possibility that applies for standard social care recipients. It is also particularly conducive to problems of managing chronic conditions that they may have (diabetes, high blood pressure and other afflictions of affluent or abundance-based societies). Again, relevant technologies are already under development, as a visit to any technology trade fair or conference confirms. For example, in addition to WSTTs, sensors and testing equipment built into waste disposal and mirrors in bathrooms attached to an AI hub management system, and a cloud located medical database are potentially able to monitor chronic conditions (diabetes, kidney and liver function, etc.), identify anomalies, and more generally offer early detection for ill-health (eye pressure, body temperature, blood sugar, cholesterol and diseases or pathologies that can be picked up on the basis of urine and faecal chemistry) whilst also offering advice for intervention and prevention. These latter possibilities start to change the relation between a person and their 'things'. An alert home may make an appointment with a healthcare professional, but in a certain sense the house may become your (primary) doctor (from *Dr in the house* to *Dr is the house*). Again, there is great scope for privacy and consent issues here and for conflicts based on monetizing the potential of data. An orientation on health and social care in the context of an AI management system seems likely to be a matter of one aspect of functionality in a broader household management system. A system that advises on diet may become one that simply manages your diet, and this can be one component in an ordering system for your goods and services, and so corporations will have great interest in owning intellectual property (IP) across and along supply chains in order to control a cradle-to-grave consumption system in which AI household management technology would be a nodal point. If this is realized, then information will become even more valuable than it already is, and this extends right through to your bodily functions.

The potentials of an alert home illustrate the blurred boundary between healthcare and social care, but there are many other technological potentials that might address issues of task-support both inside and outside the home. There is already a major industry that provides home modification devices, aids and products that facilitate everyday living (frames, pulleys, winches, bars, handles, grabbers, chairs, lifts, scooters, etc.). Some new technologies are simply alternatives to or more effective versions of these in terms of functionality. For example, several companies are currently developing versions of responsive tensile clothing (materials that will grip and offer additional stabilizing support with balance if sudden shear movement signals that a person is falling, as well as various other exo-augmentations for strength, stability and range of motion). However, robotics and robots offer a qualitative change in addition to mere functionality, since sensor-imbued managed technologies can change the scope and context of task-support. They offer services that extend the range of tasks that can be completed, but they also introduce servitors (an entity) to complete those tasks; in combination, this is sociologically significant insofar as patterns of living are not just maintained; the dependencies of the way we live are altered. That is, our relations potentially become different. This is not a new insight; robot ethicists and science fiction writers have been considering the issue for years, but changes brought on through social care *now* require all of us to be aware of the possibilities.

The social consequences of social care?

In a future *Gattaca* society, we may well be able to buy physical if not intellectual or emotional youth, but this is not currently the case. We live in societies where aging and degeneration are not just things that occur as observable changes to the materiality of the body. They are reflexively positioned processes of experience. The cultural construction of the seven ages of man in Shakespeare's *As You Like It* illustrates how we attach significance to this process. Aging and degeneration are things we *expect* to occur. We anticipate them as facts of life that we must individually and collectively manage for ourselves and significant others. We start to do this in our imaginations *before* it becomes necessary to act on consequences, and this qualitatively imbues the relations we have that already exist. The bonds of love and emotion we have now are partly constituted by what we must countenance doing later, what we commit to being prepared to do. That is, part of being who we are now are the duties and obligations we have and that we know we will or should fulfil in the future. This matters as a qualitatively imbued aspect of the process of our relational being, even if we are never required to do what we anticipate (and it matters for our sense of self and others' sense of us if we refuse bonds of duty and obligation). AI, robotics and especially (but not only) servitor capacities change the context for what is imagined/anticipated and thus how duty and obligation are formed. Changes to dependencies alter what is required of our reflexive processes *through* time and thus the constitution of our relations *in* time. The more functionally effective, pervasive and comprehensive AI and robotics become for task-support, the less we will be required to reflexively prepare for and then engage in the relevant activities, up to and including a situation in which we *never* have to think about or do these things. The point, then, is that this substituting is also an absenting that has potential consequences for ourselves and others.

One way to think about the issue is the opposing influences change might exert on relational goods. According to Donati and Archer (2015: 199–200, 207; Morgan 2018b), relational goods are goods created and enjoyed *through* relations. They involve some activity which is its own reward but that also creates collective social benefits. Relational goods are constituted as the quality of a relation that arises between people, such as trust, as well as the quality of experience of cooperation, coproduction or collaboration. Relational goods "correspond to fundamental human needs" (2015: 215) and "If these goods are ignored, dismissed or repressed, the entire social order is impoverished . . . with serious harm caused to people and the overall organization [of society]" (2015: 203). They are 'prosocial' insofar as they contribute to the integration of society.[17] Clearly, task-support technological solutions have the potential to affect relational goods in different ways.

On the one hand, task-support promotes independence and autonomy and may facilitate the construction and retention of dignity. It is potentially conducive to one's sense of self *not* to feel dependent on others. Concomitantly, preservation of privacy can also positively construct a sense of personal dignity. Not requiring human help with intimate bodily functions or menial tasks can be seen in this context, insofar as not all duties are welcomed by either side of the relation even if they are accepted.

On the other hand, task-support that promotes independence is not necessarily or only an affirmation of one's personal identity. It can also contribute to negatively connoted individualistic (non-other-regarding) and isolating attitudes and situations. These could be corrosive within society more generally, *if* we are no longer required to think forwards about our ties to others based on what we are prepared to do for them and *if* we are no longer required to then fulfil the duties and obligations we would otherwise have embraced. Consider, relinquishing independence is not always or in all ways a loss. It can involve the reinforcement or nurturing of personal relations. Nor is indignity necessarily or merely a loss. We are not simply creatures subject to embarrassment that can be avoided by functional service from artificial entities. We are emotional creatures who find fellow feeling and humour in the shared experience of our circumstances, including those which ostensibly involve adversity. Our sense of intimacy as currently conceived is not a consequence of sanitized situations. Filial bonds and friendship are nuanced and complexly constituted. New kinds of task-support, however, create the potential for a transition towards *fewer* human relations and perhaps *more* transactional and impersonal relations in society.

'Transactional' and 'impersonal' are not just descriptors of a given relation; they are potentially cumulative consequences for the sum of relational goods. Task support that absents humans has a direct consequence for a relation in contrast to how it was previously constituted, but also an indirect effect on how that relation and thus the sum of relations is constituted. *Relational goods* are constituted through the quality of the relation and thus are profoundly affected by the conception that is built into relations as a process. To be clear, I am not suggesting that introducing AI, robotics and so forth for task-support is necessarily bad. It may be liberating in some ways and problematic in others, I am suggesting it seems set to be sociologically different (for an account of economics-inspired rational AI, see Parkes & Wellman 2015; for a preliminary account of prosocial issues and AI, see Bryson 2015). An argument that inadvertently venerates suffering and senescence ought to be avoided as both perverse and oddly anti-progressive. And yet part of who we are has always been to be accepting of help and support and ready to offer help and support both because many of us require support at all ages and also specifically because we age and must manage the consequences of aging.

Still, it would be overstating the case to suggest changes to task-support for social care alone was sufficient to transform the role that relational goods play in society. Social care is already a paid sector. It has an economy and is mainly constituted within a capitalist system (for an excellent introduction to the way economics treats care, see Davis & McMaster 2017). Commodified and transactional and impersonal relations are not in general new. Again, this is not the point. The point is what further consequences for society will AI and robotics have and how aware of and prepared for these consequences are we? According to a recent UK House of Lords report, we are mainly *unaware* and *ill-prepared* (see SCAI 2018). In any case, possible sociological consequences do not in and of themselves change the basic fact that we may be required to depend on AI, robotics and so forth because of demographics and pattern of living.

However, previously in this section I suggested that the future may be one in which social care involves *fewer* human relations and perhaps *more* transactional and impersonal relations in society. One reason why the latter is conditional (use of 'perhaps') is that there is a further issue of how we relate to AI and robotics based on the characteristics that they possess and the way we are socialized to respond to or treat technologies (as its, them and persons). Whether societies become more transactional and impersonal depends also on how *social* AI entities become as they are increasingly integrated into society as visible active *participants*. Here, we need to start thinking about what proportion of our communicative acts will not just be *via* technology but *with* technology. This brings us finally to the issue of social care and companionship.

Companionship and the friendly home

Insofar as there are many who would benefit from companionship, social care is one way in which AI may start to integrate into society. That is, how we may be socialized to accept AI through use as needs are met. This pathway may intersect with, but is not the same as, more overt use for consumption services. Its scope and effects may be different. As we set out early on in this chapter, companionship answers to a very basic human need for interaction and recognition. However, in a *social care* setting companionship is purposive rather than simply an organic state of affairs. It is primarily a response to recognized issues of social isolation and loneliness. But, insofar as extended life expectancy remains degenerative, the context in which that isolation is to be addressed involves some likelihood of eventually diminished cognitive capacity. Moreover, there are many other possible circumstances and possible recipients where social care companionship might orient on cognitive capacity and mental health. As such, in a social care situation, the need to be treated *as* human blends into the need to be treated *for* given conditions. The introduction of AI creates new possibilities but also issues of power and responsibility.

As in our previous examples, the relevant technologies already exist in embryonic form – most notably natural-language-proficient chatbot technology and IoT linked to a hub-based AI household management system. We have already explored how an alert home may provide a range of social care functions. It is a small step from providing consumption and health services to the provision of companionship. Generically, technologies that might, say, manage an in-house entertainment system can readily become the entertainment. Technologies that convey information also potentially provide conversation. An alert home is a combination of technologies whose services require communication and whose services may also *be* communication and that communication can both fulfil a need *to communicate* and facilitate other activity. It is, therefore, entirely conceivable that an alert home takes the form of a 'friendly' home, and it is entirely conceivable that we will readily accept this and that it will ultimately alter our perception of AI. Much of this is likely to be mundane and pass without comment, but there are also extraordinary possibilities that may come to pass based on recognized need.

Consider the potential for a friendly alert home designed for someone with dementia. Typical symptoms of dementia begin with loss of short-term memory followed by slowed decision making, and this is then progressively followed by increasing confusion and distraction, loss of recognition, inability to complete complex and then everyday tasks, propensity to stray (amnesiac events) and eventual dissolution of coherent sense of self. In the early stages sufferers currently tend to rely on reminders (visual cues, aides-memoires such as lists, etc.). In an alert home, these could be integrated into living space, furniture, appliances and equipment through digital display and via audio: taps that state which way to turn them, baths which say how warm the water is (too hot or too cold), ovens that remind users to turn them off, doors that declare their status (locked or unlocked).

This IoT, however, could readily be slaved to or merely facets of a hub AI whose coordinating function extends from the IoT to the resident.

The question then arises about the scope of communication and how to communicate most effectively. Given the potential for confusion and anxiety, it seems likely that an appropriate AI would be coded to convey comfort and reassurance. In terms of natural-language-adaptive ML functionality, one can readily imagine that the AI would be given its own name, be coded for tone of voice (including gender through tone), and be sensitive to idiom and idiosyncrasy of language as well as to the reduced language facility and emergent characteristic errors of the dementia sufferer. Cumulatively, an AI of this type would build up both a palette of functional subject-specific statements, inquiries and such, but also and simultaneously in the act of doing this, characteristic phrasings – communication could thus take on the form of familiar conversation: *remember yesterday we did* x *and you asked me about* y . . . *it is time to do* z, *you know you don't like doing* z, *you always say you hate doing* z, *but we both know you need to do it and once it is done you feel better.* Note how time reference or duration naturalistically embeds itself in the way communication is effected and how the use of pronouns for both the resident *and* AI form part of the process. This form of bonded narrative coding with use of I, me, you, we and both/us seems highly likely to feature in ML, if the purpose is reassurance, comfort and persuasion.[18] Given these purposes, coding is liable to orient on strategic conveyance and, much like any other kind of design, consider affect as effect. As such, there are also reasons to code for a balance between friendly reassurance and a tone of professional authority. However, given that dementia sufferers experience a progressive change of cognitive state, the context is one where purposes may change through time, and so one might code for an eventual overtone of command. This issue of context and purpose opens up an array of issues. Whilst AI in a friendly house might begin as a source of coordination, information and reminders, it may become a source (a location or node for) instructions, prohibitions and orders.

Imagine the further progression. It is a small step from a residence's front door that can be locked or unlocked through an AI to the transfer of decision-making responsibility to that AI as to whether that door is open or closed for access (and a small step from here to transfer of decision-making regarding where and when to be and what to do). This may seem abhorrent, but one can readily conceive of scenarios where it becomes the case. Imagine a situation of lifelong partners where one has advanced Alzheimer's and the other does not. The non-sufferer needs to run some errand outside the home, but it is not feasible to be accompanied by their partner. Who would he or she want in charge whilst absent? Here, coding for short-term or temporary eventualities creates a potential – the incremental ceding of capabilities to an AI, the gradual transition from subservience to or subordinate status to something more masterly (as part of multiple settings that an AI might have). One might think this is something we would necessarily resist, but we did not resist the introduction of algorithms for credit scorings or for 'abstract and objective', data-driven, behind-the-scenes decision-making for many aspects of social life – partly because the focus was functionality and partly because the changes had occurred before debate concerning the issues ever got started (O'Neill 2016).

There are equivalent possibilities here. Imagine a different scenario: the healthy one of the partners dies suddenly, but prior to this both had agreed they wanted to stay at home and enjoy their last years in *that* home (where their children were raised). How to achieve this? A living will could transfer responsibility to the AI management system – and given an Alzheimer's sufferer might think the difference of quality of life between living at home and living in an institution might favour the familiarity of home, he or she might (prior to catastrophic symptoms) *voluntarily* opt for this. Is this an issue of a contract that could never be alienated (the classical position on slavery?) or is it a deliberative decision of a presently capable individual on behalf of their future incapable self – a matter of competing issues of liberty? There is no simple answer here, and where this is the case, fudges, compromises and pragmatic ambiguities often result, creating gaps into which possibilities fall. If this was to occur then, thereafter, the AI might require powers. For example, since 2014, in the UK, dementia care has been monitored using Deprivation of Liberty Safeguards (DoLS). These prevent a person walking out of hospital or a care home. If alert homes were to become of equivalent status to other places, then the AI managing that home would become a custodian and thus might be required to apply for or be granted some equivalent to DoLS. It might also be the one deemed competent (since, by definition, the care recipient could not) to make any final decision regarding transfer to some other institution once it was unable to appropriately care for its ward.[19]

The potentials intrinsic to the above create vexing issues of whether and how to transfer legal responsibility in order to empower an AI and problematic questions regarding to whom or what is responsibility to be transferred: the AI as locus of decision-making or the corporation who owns the IP?[20] Who would the ward be a ward 'of'? Put another way, who would have ownership of responsibility – a duty of care – and who would guard this guard? Again, these are difficult questions raising important ethical and practical issues in a world where a few mega-corporations located in the United States and China control almost all the major ML and AI IP (the infrastructure and significant agents of this future world; Zuboff 2019). The practicalities extend to multiple pathways that converge on situations where we might have to decide or default to positions that bear on these issues. A dementia sufferer may require a designated person to manage their financial affairs (who then has access to their bank accounts and assets, can pay bills on their behalf, transfer money, etc.) and to manage their medical treatment (order repeat prescriptions, talk on their behalf to medical professionals, etc.). If alert and friendly homes become a reality, then the AIs at their heart are candidates for these roles. Granting such a status to an AI may seem far-fetched, but return to the section on the contemporary state of social care in the UK and the types of problems exhibited, and it should be clear that there are many ways that it might be found necessary or convenient by the state for this status to be granted – not least the way the law is imbricated with practice in any contemporary society.

Actions require empowerments, but in order for an entity to be empowered, it typically requires that entity to have a given status in law for legally recognizable empowerment to apply. As such, technological solutions to a major problem of social care may create grounds for AI to be granted electronic legal personhood. The EU and various jurisdictions have been working on the general issue of electronic legal personhood for several years now for a variety of reasons, none of which is primarily focused on electronic persons as fully exhibiting the characteristics of human persons (European Parliament (EP) 2016, Morgan 2018b). A corporation is not a human – it cannot be kicked or kick, but it is a legal person for purposes despite this (and despite the problems that have arisen: corporate manslaughter, etc.).

Clearly, these considerations are highly contingent and speculative and if we include blockchain contracts they become even more so. But if we step back and consider context, what we are considering here is a set of circumstances by which we might start to assimilate AI into society and how we might start to become socialized to the way AI diffuses through our societies. Social care provides one situation in which we may find ourselves increasingly communicating with technology rather than via technology, a means by which familiarity may be produced that alters our perception of AI. The possibilities set out exist irrespective of whether in fact AI entities demonstrate or satisfy tests of consciousness and related characteristics (true AI that deserves rather than merely has by social convention the designation 'intelligent'; see Bostrom 2016). Dementia ultimately infantilizes the sufferer, diminishing facets of fully realized personhood. An AI may step in to substitute for that loss, and as a custodian we may start to think of them as surrogates for lost facets of personhood, but this does not require that an AI be (ontologically rather than legally) a person – no more than that a *personable* communicative natural language function constitutes an AI as a person. An AI may be sociologically consequential without being conscious. As such, the difference between simulation and duplication set out in a previous essay (Morgan 2018b) may still apply to the fundamental characteristics of technology in terms of its entity status. This, of course, matters in some ways, but in others entity status may not be the main point. Still, the possibilities set out here do not preclude the kinds of concerns raised by Margaret S. Archer and others regarding the potential for AI friends (Archer 2019). In fact, they may create transitional possibilities based on socialization of how humans treat digital entities, contributing to a congenial environment of acceptance for AI. Time will tell, and I take this matter up in the next volume.

Conclusion

Social care is considered to be in crisis in many places in the world, including in the UK. Common underlying threads that provoke concern are demographics and patterns of living. However, much of the focus is on how we are going to afford social care. As with so many other aspects of society, technology seems set to play some role, and yet there is little focus on or awareness of what this might be. Since the qualities of technologies are changing, then it seems important to be aware of how those changing qualities will affect the societies we may find ourselves living in. We do not live in technologically deterministic societies, but we do live in societies where technology is increasingly consequential. In terms of social care, the consequences are likely to occur based on changes to task-support and companionship. Given the speculative nature of any rumination on future technologies it would be reckless to be overly prescriptive or assertive regarding what is going to be the case. However, it seems reasonable to suggest that in the near future there may well be a transition in the kinds of questions we ask in regard of care. We may stop asking only or merely, *who* will care for us? Instead, we might find ourselves increasingly asking, *what* will care for us? This being so, the semantics of care themselves might come under new scrutiny.

Notes

1 Formally, social care itself is broader still. In the UK it encompasses the activity of social workers, provision of personal care and protection and support for qualifying individuals (linked to illness, disability, age, poverty, etc).

2 Specifically, Hft is campaigning on the inclusion of disability supporting technology solutions for social care as part of the current UK government's industrial strategy: www.hft.org.uk/get-involved/campaigns/learning-disability-sector-deal/.

3 To be clear, the point I am making is that social care as a policy issue for government and civil society has paid little attention to the role of robotics, AI and so forth and to the ethical and sociological issues that might arise. There is, of course, an extensive literature on ethics and AI (for a useful introduction and reading list, see Winfield et al. [2019]. For the ontology of technology, see the work of Clive Lawson [2017]).

4 Strictly, Kant's imperative refers to universal law, but it is the consequence for deontological moral predicates that is important.

5 With the exception of dentistry and means-tested prescriptions and specifically for British citizens and those granted unlimited leave to remain, others are now charged (except for medical emergency treatment).

6 According to Charlesworth and Johnson (2018), social care spending in England subdivides into 32% on children and the remainder on adult social care. However, recipients between the ages of 18 and 64 constitute only 33% of adult recipients but 50% of adult spending due to the complex lifetime care costs associated with some disabilities.

7 Note: since 2016/17 local authorities have been empowered to add a social care precept to council tax to a total of 8% additional over four years to 2019/20; also finance is available via transfers from the NHS to social care through the Better Care Fund, and in 2018 central government introduced the Adult Social Care Support Grant to provide one-off payments to local authorities in need.

8 Specifically, personal care includes hygiene tasks, food preparation, mobility assistance, administering medications and attention to general well-being (including dressing), but it does not currently include household tasks such as shopping and cleaning. It is distinguished from any care requiring a qualified nurse (pain control, wound and medication management, etc), and this is provided through the NHS. Concomitantly, a person may have significant ongoing healthcare needs and be categorized as receiving out-of-hospital care as NHS 'continuing healthcare' (CHC). If so, then care is arranged and funded solely by the NHS (and this can include accommodation costs if in a care home), on the basis that it is impossible to distinguish health and social care needs (Quilter-Pinner & Hochlaf 2019: 7, 13). The scope for arbitrary and unjust differences between treatment of people with conditions that have fundamental effects on life is

wide. For example, cancer patients may be CHC but dementia sufferers are currently not. See subsequent discussion.

9 The Act was supposed to come into full force by 2016 but parts have been delayed into 2020.

10 In the UK, based on 2017 data, 410,000 residents lived in 11,300 care homes operated by 5,500 providers with 95% of beds provided by the independent sector (83% commercial/profit, 13% charity based and 4% operated by NHS); personal care in the community (typically domiciliary) is provided to more than 500,000 recipients from approximately 8,500 provider entities (Lightfoot et al. 2019: 28; Care Quality Commission 2018: 5–6).

11 Data from 29th edition, 2018; reported online by *Which* magazine: 'Care Home Fees', 5 April 2019. According to the Competition and Markets Authority (CMA), resident self-funders paid an annual average £44,000 (Lightfoot et al. 2019: 9).

12 Since ONS releases are archived but each subsequently updates the statistics, it seems nugatory to provide full referencing. Most of the statistics appear in one form or another in the many government reports listed in the references and a sense of the general tendencies can be gleaned by visiting the site and navigating: www.ons.gov.uk/peoplepopulationandcommunity.

13 On current trends, social care spending requirements are growing at 3.7% per year whilst local authority projected spending growth is only 2.1% per year, based on budgeting constraints (see Bottery et al. 2018).

14 So in denying support to new recipients, the total of recipients declines over time as current recipients die.

15 According to the CMA, self-funders paid on average 41% higher fees than the local authority rate in 2016, whilst in 2005 only 1 in 5 care homes charged self-funders more; the scale varies with the quality of home and nature of need. For example, in Hertfordshire the authority rate was £560 per week per resident, whilst one reported self-under-focused home charged £2,500 per week (EAC 2019: 20–21). According to the Association of Directors of Adult Social Services (ADASS), 60 local authorities had contracts returned to them in the 2018/19 accounting year. One might also note that the highly leveraged business model of some private equity firm providers of residential care has resulted in a high degree of vulnerability to insolvency: Four Seasons Health Care was one high-profile case in April 2019 (operating 322 homes), but more broadly 148 care home businesses were reported insolvent in 2017 and almost 2,500 residents evicted (for financial engineering issues, see Morgan 2009, 2019e; for CMA analysis of profits and costs, see Lightfoot et al. 2019: 29–31).

16 It should also be noted that the core arguments for running down social security because it creates a burden on the working age population involves a number of basic fallacies – there is always context to demographic arguments and economic policy (for the key arguments, see Baker & Weisbrot 1999).

17 In general, Donati and Archer claim that relational goods require (1) a personal and social identity of participants (they cannot be anonymous for each other); (2) non-instrumental motivation of each subject; the relation must involve more than achievement of some end; (3) participants must acquire or be inspired by rule of reciprocity as a symbolic exchange; (4) sharing: goods can only be produced and enjoyed together by those who participate; (5) require elaboration over time; a single interaction is insufficient for the relations; and (6) reflexivity that operates relationally – sharing is also of the sense of what it is that is shared. They cannot simply be created by law or dictate. They cannot be captured or appropriated by any given party and cannot be commodified, bureaucratized or marketized without the relations themselves being subverted in ways that corrode the goods that are otherwise constituted, but they also do not fit readily into traditional categories of the public or private sphere, since the former is associated with administrative provision of goods by the state and the latter with the marketization of goods by corporations, neither of which captures the sense of what

relational goods are or provides unproblematic grounds for the constitution of relations from which they arise.

18 And of course, treatment, amelioration and so forth – the scope for AI is broad: therapy for general state of mind, specific programmes that provide services or treatments within social care parameters for particular conditions, memory training and so forth.

19 Equally, an effective system with in-house servitors may never require this decision to be made if medically informed support becomes possible at home. Home could also be a personalized hospice for end-of-life care without the need for hospitalization as a transition stage.

20 Social care and dementia is just one possible application where corporations may intrude: *Alexa Is My Dr* (councillor or therapist programmes); design may be influenced by psychologists and psychiatrists to ensure "good thoughts" prevail (positive attitudes and moods – much like interior design with more light and vibrant colours can be purposively positive). AI hub management entities may have particular proclivities encoded into them as part of their general interactive parameters, intended to influence a person's state of mind for "good" mental health; subliminal effects on consumption behaviour, social and political conformity; this *Alexa Is My "Friend"* facet of companionship invokes: how much of a friend is my 'friend', and who does my digital servant *really* work for? Capitalism blurs the boundaries between companionship, client, customer, friend and patient. The possibilities and potential relations may well mean that we require new digital civil rights and advocates (to represent us in disputes with AI).

References

Age UK. (2018). *1.4 million older people aren't getting the care and support they need – a staggering increase of almost 20% in just two years*. London: Author. Retrieved from www.ageuk.org.uk/latest-news/articles/2018/july/1.4-million-older-people-arent-getting-the-care-and-support-they-need–a-staggering-increase-of-almost-20-in-just-two-years/

Al-Amoudi, I. (2018). Review: *Homo deus* by Yuval Noah Harari. *Organization Studies, 39*(7), 995–1002.

Al-Amoudi, I., & Lazega, E. (Eds.). (2019). *Post-human institutions and organisations: Confronting the Matrix* (Vol. II). London: Routledge.

Al-Amoudi, I., & Morgan, J. (Eds.). (2018). *Realist responses to post-human society: Ex Machina* (Vol. I). London: Routledge.

Amin-Smith, N., Phillips, D., & Simpson, P. (2018, March). *Adult social care funding: A local or national responsibility?* London: Institute for Fiscal Studies.

Archer, M. (2008). *Being human*. Cambridge: Cambridge University Press.

Archer, M. (2019). Chapter 3: Considering AI personhood. In I. Al-Amoudi & E. Lazega (Eds.), *Post-human institutions and organizations: Confronting the matrix*. London: Routledge.

Baker, D., & Weisbrot, M. (1999). *Social security: The phony crisis*. Chicago, IL: The University of Chicago Press.

Bostrom, N. (2016). *Superintelligence: Paths, dangers, strategies*. Oxford: Oxford University Press.

Bottery, S., Varrow, M., Thorlby, R., & Wellings, D. (2018, May). *A fork in the road: Next steps for social care funding reform*. London: Health Foundation and King's Fund.

Bryson, J. (2015). Artificial intelligence and pro-social behaviour. In C. Misselhorn (Ed.), *Collective agency and cooperation in natural and artificial systems* (pp. 281–306). Cham: Springer.

Bushnell, J., Mitchell, R., & Seymour, C. (2019, April). *Free personal care: How to eliminate catastrophic care costs*. London: Independent Age.

Care Quality Commission. (2018). *The state of adult social care services 2014–2017*. London: Author.

Carers UK. (2019, July). *State of caring: A snapshot of unpaid care in the UK*. London: Author.

Cebr. (2019, September). *The economic cost of dementia to English business: A report for Alzheimer's society*. London: Author.

Charlesworth, A., & Johnson, P. (2018, May). *Securing the future: Funding health and social care to the 2030s*. London: Institute for Fiscal Studies and The Health Foundation.

Communities and Local Government Select Committee. (2017, March). *Adult social care funding* (House of Commons 1103, 2016–17). London: HM Government.

Crawford, R., Stoye, G., & Zaranko, B. (2018, June). *The impacts of cuts to social care spending on the use of accident and Emergency Departments in England* (IFS Working Paper W18/15). London: Institute for Fiscal Studies.

Darzi, A. (Chair). (2018, June). *Better health and care for all: A 10 point plan for the 2020s; The Lord Darzi review of health and care*. London: Institute for Public Policy Research.

Davis, J., & McMaster, R. (2017). *Health care economics*. London: Routledge.

Donati, P., & Archer, M. (2015). *The relational subject*. Cambridge: Cambridge University Press.

Dromey, J., & Hochlaf, D. (2018, November). *Fair care: A workforce strategy for social care*. London: Institute for Public Policy Research.

Economic Affairs Committee (EAC). (2019, July). *Social care funding: Time to end a national scandal* (7th Report of Session 2017–2019, House of Lords Paper 392). London: HM Government.

European Parliament (EP). (2016). Draft report with recommendations to the Commission on Civil Law Rules on Robotics (2015/2013(INL)). Brussels: Author.

Gills, B., & Morgan, J. (2020). Global climate emergency: After COP24, climate science, urgency and the threat to humanity. *Globalizations, 17*(6), 885–902.

Harari, Y. N. (2017). *Homo deus*. London: Vintage.

Health and Social Care and Housing, Communities and Local Government Committees (HSCHCLGC). (2018, June). *Long-term funding of adult social care* (House of Commons Paper 768 2017–19). London: HM Government.

Jarrett, T. (2018, December 14). *Social care: Forthcoming Green Paper (England)* (House of Commons Briefing Paper 8002). London: Commons Library.

Kingston, A., Comas-Herrera, A., & Jagger, C. (2018). Forecasting the care needs of the older population in England over the next 20 years: Estimates from the Population Aging and Care Simulation (PACSim) modelling study. *Lancet Public Health, 3*, e447–e455.

Kurzweil, R. (2000). *The age of spiritual machines*. London: Penguin.

Lawson, C. (2017). *Technology and isolation*. Cambridge: Cambridge University Press.

Lightfoot, W., Heaven, W., & Grič, J. (2019). *21st century social care*. London: Policy Exchange.

Local Government Association. (2018, July). *The lives we want to lead: The LGA green paper for adult social care and well being*. London: Local Government Association.

Morgan, J. (2009). *Private equity finance: Rise and repercussions*. Basingstoke: Palgrave Macmillan.

Morgan, J. (2016). Change and a changing world? Theorizing morphogenic society. *Journal of Critical Realism, 15*(3), 277–295.

Morgan, J. (2018a). Species being in the twenty-first century. *Review of Political Economy, 30*(3), 377–395.

Morgan, J. (2018b). Yesterday's tomorrow today: Turing, Searle and the contested significance of artificial intelligence. In I. Al-Amoudi & J. Morgan (Eds.), *Realist responses to post-human society* (pp. 82–137). London: Routledge.

Morgan, J. (2019a). The left and an economy for the many not the few. In D. Scott (Ed.), *Manifestos, policies and practices: An equalities agenda* (pp. 94–137). London: Trentham Press/UCL IOE Press.

Morgan, J. (2019b). Stupid ways of working smart? In I. Al-Amoudi & E. Lazega (Eds.), *Post-human institutions and organizations: Confronting the matrix*. London: Routledge.

Morgan, J. (2019c). Will we work in twenty-first century capitalism? A critique of the fourth industrial revolution literature. *Economy and Society, 48*, 371–398.

Morgan, J. (2019d). Why is there anything at all? What does it mean to be a person? Rescher on metaphysics. *Journal of Critical Realism, 18*(2), 169–188.

Morgan, J. (2019e). Private equity. In L. Seabrooke & D. Wigan (Eds.), *Global wealth chains: Governing assets in the world economy*. Oxford: Oxford University Press.

O'Neill, C. (2016). *Weapons of math destruction*. London: Allen Lane.

Parkes, D., & Wellman, M. (2015). Economic reasoning and artificial intelligence. *Science, 349*(6245), 267–272.

Patomäki, H., & Teivainen, T. (2004). *A possible world*. London: Zed Books.

Patterson, C. (2019). *Extra time: 10 lessons for an aging world*. London: HarperCollins.

Prescott, T., & Caleb-Solly, P. (2017). *Robotics in social care: A connected care ecosystem for independent living* (White paper). London: UK Robotics and Autonomous Systems Network.

Putnam, R. (2000). *Bowling alone: The collapse and revival of American community*. London: Simon & Schuster.

Quilter-Pinner, H., & Hochlaf, D. (2019, May). *Social care: Free at the point of need*. London: Institute for Public Policy Research.

Robertson, R., Gregory, S., & Jabbal, J. (2014). *The social care and health systems of nine countries*. London: The King's Fund.

Sayer, A. (2011). *Why things matter to people: Social science, values and ethical life*. Cambridge: Cambridge University Press.

SCAI, House of Lords Select Committee on Artificial Intelligence. (2018, April). *AI in the UK: Ready willing and able* (Report of Session 2017–19). London: HM Government.

Smith, C. (2011). *What is a person?* Chicago, IL: Chicago University Press.

Taylor, C. (2007). *A secular age*. Cambridge, MA: Harvard University Press.

Tegmark, M. (2017). *Life 3.0*. London: Allen Lane.

Winfield, A., McDermid, J., Muller, V., Porter, Z., & Pipe, T. (2019). *Ethical issues for robotics and autonomous systems* (White paper). London: UK Robotics and Autonomous Systems Network.

Zuboff, S. (2019). *The age of surveillance capitalism*. London: Profile Books.

5 Why should enhanced and unenhanced humans care for each other?

Ismael Al-Amoudi and Gazi Islam

Introduction: duties of care and solidarity in the age of human enhancement

Outrage erupted in France in 2014 when President François Hollande jokingly referred to the poor as *les sans-dents*, the toothless. The strength of the public response was tellingly much more acute than any public outrage following the publication of statistics on social inequalities, however damning. Moreover, Hollande's social and economic policies had been, by and large, more egalitarian than those of his predecessor and successor. A plausible interpretation of this outrage is that Hollande's joke struck a nerve in a world in which the technology to replace teeth is available though not universally affordable; in which privileged members of society (including the president and his family) had unquestionable access to such technology; and in which the welfare state had withered, partly because of politicians' political choices. Outrage was exacerbated by the fact that Hollande's *plaisanterie* insulted the bodies, appearance and charm of those who could not afford dental treatment. The latter's smiles had become the stigma of their social destitution while a president smiling with perfect teeth joked about them. Indeed, while losing teeth had been a common fate of kings and paupers for millennia, it ceased to be so in the twentieth century. And while Hollande's joke has now been relegated to the *faits divers* section of political history, it might also be indicative of an epochal social drift between those humans who can afford to enhance their bodies through technological means and those who cannot.

Recent advances in technology threaten to blur and displace the biological constituents of our shared humanity (for broad surveys, see Hurlbut & Tirosh-Samuelson 2016, Stapleton & Byers 2015). Biological engineering already allows us to intervene into processes of biological evolution that prevailed for about 4 billion years. In theory, and increasingly in practice, we are capable of transforming human physiologies, immune systems and life expectancies but also human intellectual and emotional capacities. Cyborg engineering is also well under way in the scientific and popular imagination (e.g., Czarniawska & Gustavsson 2008, Krautwurst 2007). We are now surrounded with miniature mobile devices that extend our powers of communication, computation, memorization and perception (smartphones, laptops, hearing aids, cloud storage, etc.) While these devices are still separable from our body, connected implants are increasingly in use. The latter include therapeutic devices such as thought-operated bionic arms, artificial pancreases, retina implants and bionic ears. But they also include surveillance devices such as intra-dermic microchips that gather data on soldiers and prisoners for the alleged protection of themselves and society (see Lazega 2015). And new drugs have been designed to enhance human cognitive capacities but also emotional well-being and socially praised behaviour.

The range of technologies covered by the expression 'human enhancement' is to an extent open to interpretation. Indeed, age-old devices such as walking sticks, books, artificial teeth, spectacles and more generally tools could be considered human enhancements: they enhance the powers of human beings to walk, remember, chew, see and act on the world. But these enhancements, with the exception perhaps of artificial teeth, are externally fixed to the human body. They supplement but do not substitute for biological functions and, more to the point, they do not disrupt the boundaries of what is conventionally considered to be the human body.

The technological advances that interest us in the present chapter are restricted to those human enhancements that are internally embedded within their carrier's body. To say that A is internally related to B means that A's identity depends on its relation to B (Bhaskar 1998). Classic examples of internal relations comprise student-teacher or tenant-landlord relations (Lawson 1997). One important ontological implication of internal relations is that the related elements constitute a totality which is endowed with emergent powers that are distinct from the powers of constituent parts. In the case of human enhancement, this means that the enhanced body is transformed to the point of transgressing (however marginally) its former shape, boundaries and identity. Another implication is that enhanced humans become dependent on their enhancements beyond the point where they can relish their enhancement without losing their sense of self. Thus, while walking sticks usually do not constitute human enhancements by our definition, prosthetic legs do so, especially after their carrier has gone through full rehabilitation.

The production and dissemination of human enhancements raises numerous ethical questions relative to their carriers' dignity, their distribution's fairness, their production's political economy and so forth. In the present chapter, we examine the moral obligations of enhanced humans (thereafter EH) towards unenhanced humans (UH) and vice versa.

The questions we ask

We discuss three related questions. First, what motives might tempt EH to refrain from caring for UH and vice versa? Second, what reasons, if and when considered fully, should nonetheless incite EH to care for UH and vice versa? And third, what social and organizational arrangements are likely to enable and encourage relations of care (rather than exploitation or destruction) between EH and UH?

Our argument's structure is simple and follows closely the three questions above. First, we examine a number of reasons why we could and should reasonably expect (all or most) EH to fail to care for (any or some) UH. Then we argue that these reasons do not hold sway in the face of – equally important though less immediately visible – reasons for EH to care for UH. Although it may not be in EH's perceived self-interest to care for UH and vice versa, it is in the enlightened self-interest of both groups to do so. Finally, we argue that EH's false consciousness about their interest depends in large part on the organization of the communities in which they will grow, learn, live and die. We conclude our chapter with a few suggestions regarding existing threats and missing institutions for communities in which humans of various levels of enhancement nonetheless care for each other.

Our philosophical framework

Our argument is rooted in the realist virtue ethics developed by Alisdair Mac-Intyre, especially in his recent book *Dependent Rational Animals: Why Human Beings Need the Virtues* (MacIntyre 2009/1999). We have chosen this book for two reasons: first, because it raises questions of solidarity both across species and across moral subjects endowed with differing needs and powers; and second, because we find it congruent with our own (critically realist) intuitions.

MacIntyre's central argument is that human beings of various levels of ability must care for each other precisely because they are endowed with *virtues*, that is, with qualities of mind and character that enable them both to recognize the relevant goods and to use the relevant skills in realizing these goods. In turn, human virtues are improved through their continuous exercise, thus altruistic acts also result in indirect benefits for the person who performed them (MacIntyre 2009/1999).

Our chapter's central argument is similar to MacIntyre's in many respects as we endeavour to demonstrate that it is in the well-considered self-interest of both EH and UH to care for each other. We shall be confronted, however, with a number of difficulties that arise from widening the scope of MacIntyre's discussion to include questions of human enhancement. In particular, we shall discuss how human enhancement disrupts the sense of a human community, sufficiently homogeneous to command solidarity, on which MacIntyre's argument rests.

What we mean by enhanced and unenhanced humans

The distinction we draw between enhanced humans (EH) and unenhanced humans (UH) is relative and by no means a strict dichotomy. Indeed, we use EH and UH as shorthand for 'people who carry more and/or better enhancements' and for 'people who carry fewer and/or less advanced enhancements'. Rather than presupposing a world in which one group of humans is fully enhanced whereas another group is not, we have endeavoured to develop an argument that remains valid in the plausible context in which while most humans have access to some form of enhancement, some groups benefit from more and better enhancements than others.

But the concept of human enhancement is not devoid of ambiguity either, and a few remarks are in order beyond our earlier-stated criterion of internal relationality. Our first remark concerns the human in *human enhancement*. Indeed, our criterion does not provide a watertight subset of technologies (devices, operations) that would count as *human* enhancement. Rather, it places technologies along a continuum of more or less internally related enhancements. At the higher end of this spectrum we could place (yet to be developed) genetic engineering of humanoids whose form is barely human and whose inclusion in the human species is contestable. Conversely, the lower end of the spectrum encompasses devices (many of which already exist) that only disrupt moderately their carriers' humanity: prosthetic organs (including teeth and limbs), performance enhancing drugs and so forth. A limit case at the spectrum's lower end is those devices that are initially externally related to their carrier's human body but that may, through familiarity, become part of the carrier's conception of her own body. This limit case includes walking sticks and wheelchairs which the user has relied on for a long time and without which she feels amputated.

Our second remark on the expression of human enhancement concerns the implicit assumptions of the word *enhancement*. To enhance something is to make it better, to improve its worth. Yet, even if we accept the realist argument according to which worth is distinct from people's belief in it (Collier 1999), worth is seldom immediately or infallibly appreciable. Assessments of worth rely on social conventions of evaluation (Boltanski & Thévenot 1991); moreover, the worth of any entity depends on the socio-historical context in which it operates. Thus, a brain chip that allows non-English-speaking carriers to translate their thoughts into English is particularly valuable in a socio-historical context in which English is the lingua franca. Conversely, the diffusion of such chips is likely to entrench the status of English as a lingua franca. In short, whether a technology constitutes an enhancement depends on social context and is likely to feed back into influencing what is valuable in that context.

Our argument's limits

In addition to the practical and theoretical difficulties raised by human enhancement, our chapter's argument is limited by a number of choices we had to make in the interest of concision and clarity. For instance, we use the concepts of 'care', 'rights' and 'solidarity' quite fluidly, without attempting to articulate them in any systematic relation or dialectical opposition to each other (cf. Honneth 1995). We choose this broad usage to reflect our overarching concern with the possibility of ethical relations between EH and UH rather than distinguishing between the different kinds of possible ethical standpoints, which would be a step for a future work. The concept we invoke often is that of *care* (as in the chapter's title), but it may be worth clarifying that our use of this concept is sufficiently generic to encompass more specific concepts such as respect, provision of care, recognition and solidarity.

Moreover, we recognize the limits of our capacity to anticipate a future that is yet to be written. Tomorrow's technological developments, as well as the transformations in power relations they will enable, are fundamentally up for grabs. This is so for ontological reasons, since technological developments and social transformations happen in open systems (Bhaskar 1998, Archer 1995). To presume their specific forms would be to negate human agency's creativity and history's contingency. But the future's openness does not condemn ethicists to silence about pending developments but rather forces us to qualify the nature and significance of our arguments. The latter are hypothetical and privilege generality over specificity. They are hypothetical because they seek the most plausible inference considering what we also know otherwise (Collier 1994). For instance, we do not presume that EH will necessarily ostracize UH; rather we suggest that, considering what we know about today's world, we can reasonably expect EH to be tempted to ostracize UH. But our arguments also privilege generality over specificity because the development of some forms of human enhancement (defined in general terms) is more likely than any specific instance of human enhancement. Thus, our reflection is less concerned with the implications of such or such enhancement than it is with the production in general of enhancements that are internally related to their carriers' bodies.

Finally, by interrogating in turn why EH should care (or not) for UH and then why UH should care (or not) for EH, we understate the circularity and dynamism of relations of care. Indeed, we know – following Donati (2011) and Donati and Archer (2015) – that human relations are emergent entities which cannot be explained away by scrutinizing their relata individually, nor by juxtaposing one-way relations to reconstruct a circular one. However, since the question of the mutual obligations of care between EH and UH is under-researched, we hope the present chapter will provide a sound basis for future studies that acknowledge more fully than we currently do the circularity and irreducible emergence of such relations of solidarity.

Temptations to withdraw care and solidarity

MacIntyre's *Dependent Rational Animals* provides a good thread and compass for our discussion of whether and why EH and UH should care for each other. And yet, in light of imminent transhuman developments, even the book's opening paragraph seems to have lost some of the authority its author could assume in 1999:

> We human beings are vulnerable to many kinds of affliction and most of us are at some time afflicted by serious ills. How we cope is only in small part up to us. It is most often to others that we owe our survival, let alone our flourishing, as we encounter body illness and injury, inadequate nutrition, mental defect and disturbance, and human aggression and neglect. This dependence on particular others for protection and sustenance is most obvious in early childhood and old age. But between these first and last stages our lives are characteristically marked by longer or shorter periods of injury, illness or other disablement and some among us are disabled for their entire lives.
>
> (MacIntyre 2009/1999: 1)

In the preceding passage, the expression 'we' stands for 'we the humans' and plays a number of important functions in MacIntyre's overall argument. First, 'we' refers to a broad group that encompasses at the very least the text's author and each of its readers, which also leaves at that early stage an important question mark around the inclusion of beings, either human or non-human, who are incapable of reading and discussing. Second, 'we' demarcates a community characterized by a number of presumably inescapable physical and mental vulnerabilities that create or reflect marked dependence on others: illness, injury, aggression and neglect. Third, and importantly for our purpose, while differences of vulnerability are acknowledged in principle, both the opening paragraph and the book-length argument that follows draw their meaningfulness from a crucial, if largely implicit, assumption: differences of dependence are overwhelmed by similarities between members of that community. All of us will have been needy infants, and those among us lucky to live long enough are likely to become needy old persons. During our adult lives, although each of us may have different life chances, we all are, albeit at differing degrees, exposed to the possibility of unlucky events that would throw us into a state of dependence on others. In brief, the expression 'we' serves to delimit the boundaries of, and hitherto constitute, a community of humans who depend on each other for the realization of their personal and common goods.

But our chapter's point of departure is that the ongoing and accelerating development of human enhancement blurs and threatens the boundaries set by MacIntyre. While in 1999 (the year of the book's first publication) differences of life chances between humans born in rich, peaceful countries and humans born in poor, warring countries already presented an important limitation to the immediate appeal of MacIntyre's argument, the introduction of human enhancements is likely to increase substantially, at least *in potentia*, inequalities of life chances between enhanced and unenhanced humans. In such unprecedented technological contexts, equal life chances are at best a political accomplishment achieved through collective action and at worst a dangerous ideological fantasy serving to obscure inequalities between humans.

Inequalities of abilities and needs are not only bad in themselves. They can also tear apart identification with society as a system of collaboration and reciprocal obligations across generations (Rawls 2003). Indeed, in situations of inequality, charismatic leadership and strong myths can maintain a sense of community. For instance, capitalism's meritocratic myth maintains social cohesion only if subalterns imagine they themselves, or their children, will improve their social position. But what happens when some people are enhanced to have better socially recognized abilities (i.e., more merit) than their unenhanced fellow citizens? Is human enhancement likely to tempt EH to withdraw care and solidarity from UH?

Temptations for more enhanced humans

MacIntyre mobilizes Nietzsche as his nemesis concerning the question of whether humans flourish best when they recognize the virtues of acknowledged dependence. For Nietzsche, the answer to this question has to be negative, since "it is not the ferocity of the beast of prey that requires a moral disguise but the herd animal with its profound mediocrity, timidity and boredom with itself" (Gay Science V: 352, cited in MacIntyre 2009/1999: 163).

But although Nietzsche's life – a lonely and bitter life – has been showcased by his intellectual opponents as an expectable consequence of ignoring the common good or of restricting its scope of application (see for instance MacIntyre 2009/1999: 164–166), many of the psychological mechanisms he identifies in the struggle between the strong and the weak are likely to apply with particular relevance in the case of struggles between EH and UH. For instance, some EH might nourish the sentiment that their enhancements dispense them from participating in the affairs of UH. This sentiment might be partly accounted for by EHs' embodied superior abilities and minimal needs compared with UH. But while EH might indeed enjoy xenophobic enjoyment in affirming their superiority, it can be reasonably expected that UH might develop, in response, feelings of indignation towards EH.

Moreover, it is widely accepted since the pioneering works of Alfred Adler that superiority complexes often hide disavowed feelings of inferiority or at least insecurity regarding one's worth (Ansbacher & Ansbacher 1956). Thus, although embodied enhancement might constitute a stable marker of identity and of social superiority, we can't rule out that EH will also feel insecure about their alleged superiority over UH. This is likely to be the case if the EH's superiority is governed by bureaucratic regulation and/or mitigated with deficiencies brought by human enhancement, diminishing the sense that one's abilities have been earned through meritorious action.

Bureaucratic regulation has indeed a powerful capacity to entrench and give life to otherwise spurious or insignificant differences. Not long so ago, for example, Africa under apartheid had established the 'pencil test' which determined with simulated objectivity the race, associated rights and alleged capacities of people depending on whether a pen could hold in their hair. A pen would be placed in the testee's hair. If it fell immediately, the testee was classified as white, if it only fell when the testee would move around, she would be classified as 'coloured'. But if the pen remained in the testee's hair while she moved, the testee would be classified as 'black'. Hawkey (2010) recounts a particularly dark and farcical situation, when

> in one famous case, a somewhat dark-skinned girl named Sandra Laing was born to two white parents. In 1966, when Sandra was age 11, she was subjected to a pencil test by "a stranger" and subsequently excluded from her all-white school when she failed the test. She was reclassified from her birth race of white to coloured. Sandra and the rest of her family were shunned by white society. Her father passed a blood type paternity test, but the authorities refused to restore her white classification.
>
> (Kim Hawkey, 10 January 2010)

While it is premature to predict which specific classifications, criteria and tests might emerge with the diffusion of human enhancements, bureaucratic administrations may revert to such devices to classify human beings. Our point is not only that such devices are likely to be unfair and ill-founded but that, precisely because of their unfairness and ill-foundedness, they are likely to generate considerable insecurity both among UH fearing a correct classification and among EH fearing an incorrect one.

Moreover, although EH's resources and powers are likely to garner more social recognition than those of UH, the former will nonetheless be finite. But if purchasing, maintaining, replacing and upgrading the best human enhancements is disproportionately expensive, EH will be subject to intense economic pressure to maintain an economic income that allows them to sustain their enhanced bodies. This state of affairs could be of dramatic consequences in terms of a rupture of solidarity between UH and powerful but needy EH. In particular, we fear that dispossession of UH by EH might constitute in many cases the only way for EH needing to purchase human enhancements over a long, increasingly expensive life.

Fortunately, this dystopic state of affairs is not a historical necessity. However, it points at the current lack of social conventions over how long, and at what cost, a human life can be extended by private means. While philosophers such as Van Parijs (2003) have started asking how long and at what cost public funding should be spent for the extension of human lives in a context in which the latter can be prolongated indefinitely, the imminent combination of very expensive human enhancements, acute social inequalities and powerful mechanisms of economic exploitation prompts an extension of Van Parijs's question to the private sphere: should the most expensive enhancements be illegal until they become affordable by all, or at least a majority of people? And if so, on what basis?

But while unfair economic structures are likely to exacerbate the temptation for EH to exploit and dispossess UH, so does a cultural context characterized by hubris, greed and individualism. As far as we can see, most of those EH benefitting from the best enhancements are likely to be born in cliques that have already developed a culture of protection of their own vested interests at the expense of the rest of society (see for instance Pinçon & Pinçon-Charlot 2000). In such a context, enhancements improving performance and the capacity to dominate others are more likely to be designed and purchased than enhancements improving compassion and solidarity. Moreover, unless human enhancement is restricted by public policy (see above), the problems of excessive accumulation of wealth through inheritance are likely to be magnified by the private purchase of enhancements.

Temptations for unenhanced humans

As we have seen, there are many reasons to expect that, unless the current economic and cultural structures change radically, EH will at best feel tempted and at worst feel forced to care for their vested interests in opposition to UH. Unfortunately, the current economic and cultural structures might also encourage UH to withdraw care and solidarity towards EH.

Indeed, although EH might display superior abilities in many domains, these do not shield them from prejudice from UH. We can expect for instance that, in the early stages of the historical dissemination of human enhancements, EH will constitute a minority, albeit a powerful one, compared with UH. This situation is likely to generate Nietzschean resentment from UH as a response to EH's perceived arrogance. Whether and how intensely UH feel resentment towards EH is likely to depend on the reasons why EH undergo enhancement in the first place. Yet, while the reasons motivating human enhancement are likely to differ in each case and may not always be based on selfish purposes, there exists a danger of UH assuming the latter. Our point here is that, just as racists reduce people to their race and sexists reduce them to their sex, resenting UH might be tempted to reduce EH persons to their enhancements.

Finally, human enhancement is likely to generate particularly acute resentment in a culture characterized by a meritocratic ethos. Artificial enhancement is indeed distinct from abilities acquired through regular efforts. Prosthetic arms or legs can be purchased, as opposed to muscular arms and legs shaped through regular training and careful nutrition. As illustrated by recent debates around post-human enhancement in sport (e.g., Triviño 2011), the increasingly likely prospect of human enhancement in sport necessitates a rethinking of the normative parameters around the meritocratic norms inherent to sports.

The disconnect between capacity and effort exacerbates a fundamental tension in the heart of meritocracy. Meritocracy legitimizes the domination of those with merit, implicitly defined as those with superior abilities and who have developed these abilities through superior effort. Yet EH display superior abilities without having necessarily made much effort to acquire or maintain them. While it is too early to say whether moral distinctions will emerge between deserved human enhancement and undeserving human enhancement, a strong resentment can be expected towards 'privileged' children who were lucky enough to be born in families that can afford to purchase enhancements.

Why is it in the well-considered interest of both UH and EH to care for each other?

Although relations of care between EH and UH are likely to be plagued by sentiments of superiority, economic dependence and resentment, there are also deep and significant reasons why UH and EH should appreciate their mutual dependence and establish relations of mutual care and solidarity. In the near future, most EH will have had UH parents and carers from whom they have learned or contracted a duty of caring (cf. MacIntyre's discussion of that kind of debt, 2009/1999: 121 et seq.). Thus, we can reasonably expect that most EH who had been raised by UH will nonetheless want to care for their old carers when the time comes. And conversely, it may be difficult or costly for EH to protect themselves against UH in the case of anti-EH mobilizations.

Moreover, as suggested above, human enhancements are likely to exist along a diverse continuum. But human enhancements' diversity can take several forms.

First, there are likely to be diverse areas of enhancement regarding traits that are not easily comparable according to a common standard. While some persons may enjoy enhanced resistance to diseases, others may enjoy superior strength or intellectual capacities. Second, it can be expected that at a given point in time, there will exist differing degrees and qualities of enhancement. Some people's strength might be doubled, whereas others' might be multiplied by a hundred. Third, some (though perhaps not all) enhancements are likely to bear a significant sacrifice for their carrier. This could be a physiological sacrifice (you will see farther but will eventually go blind) or a financial one (you will live longer, but it will take you your new lifetime to reimburse the credit associated with your enhancement). Finally, enhancements are likely to progress quickly over time, just as technological devices quickly become obsolete at the dawn of the twenty-first century. Such obsolescence risks creating irreversible enhancements that are useless or outmoded in a rapidly changing environment.

The above considerations are significant for our discussion because they imply that ruptures of solidarity are as likely to happen among EH as they are to appear between EH and UH. No EH can be certain that they will not themselves, or their children, fall behind in the race to human enhancement. Yet, a powerful safeguard against unforeseeable discriminations due to unforeseeable technological developments can consist, for EH, in reproducing from the outset an inclusive system of justice across generations. Moreover, many enhancements are likely to depend on the social system of exchange and production at a given time: as technology or social organization changes, the enhancement may lose value or become a stigma.

Finally, mutual care between UH and EH might provide an opportunity for self-knowledge for members of all concerned groups. For MacIntyre, just as for Aquinas (Kenny 1993), the ability to judge one's own judgement is a distinctive human capacity. But contrary to popular conceptions, self-knowledge is as much a collective achievement as it is an individual one. As he has it:

> There are of course certain kinds of social interaction and relationships which on occasion provide badly needed correction for our own judgments. When adequate self-knowledge is achieved, it is always a shared achievement. And, because adequate self-knowledge is necessary, if I am to imagine realistically the alternative futures between which I must choose, the quality of my imagination also depends on the contributions of others.
>
> (MacIntyre 2009/1999: 95)

While MacIntyre's argument proves that humans need to communicate truthfully with other humans, it does not prove that every human must be open to communication with any other human. And indeed, as we have hinted in the previous section, couldn't an EH arrogantly dismiss communication with UH?

One possible response, formulated in the vocabulary of the virtues, is that UH can teach EH the virtues of humility, of just generosity and of misericordia. It may be so because the above virtues/excellences are best trained when caring for those less, rather than more, powerful than oneself. But our argument only suggests that mutual care between EH and UH could happen, not that it will necessarily do so. Whether it happens is contingent on the norms and social institutions they encounter as they grow and live in society. We now turn to the question of the norms and institutions conducive to mutual care between EH and UH.

Which institutions could foster mutual care between EH and UH?

Our discussion so far has avoided taking a normative position on the value of human enhancements as such. However, our approach, based on MacIntyre's virtue ethics, allows us to clarify the terms of the debate while avoiding its polarization. On the whole, human enhancements are likely to be a good thing for society if they generate social orders that are conducive to humility, just generosity and misericordia. And conversely, they will be a terrible thing if they lead to societies of increased arrogance, greed and ruthlessness. But whether human enhancement is utopic or dystopic will largely depend on the norms and educational institutions at play in society.

Social norms needed for EH/UH mutual care

As we have seen above, MacIntyre argues (2009/1999: 95) that friendship and collegiality are necessary conditions for self-knowledge. He adds on the following page (2009/1999: 96) that friendship and collegiality also constitute protections against insensitivity to the suffering of others. Yet, the intensified digitalization of social relations, at the expense of pockets of collegiality (see Al-Amoudi & Lazega 2019), may impede or pervert the formation of relations of deep understanding and friendship between people. Conversely, the current capitalist context in which human enhancement is a commercial activity may reinforce social values of domination and inequality. As we suggested above, in a neoliberal world characterized by sharp economic inequalities and low levels of welfare state or relational solidarity, people are more likely to design and purchase human enhancements enabling domination than enhancements enabling friendship. We must urgently ask, therefore, the question of the politics of human enhancements as they are developed and marketed.

Of particular import will be the specific question of people's attitudes towards others' good or bad fortune. For MacIntyre, a necessary cultural condition for the advent of a good society is that ego's regard for the alter is not negatively affected by the alter's misfortunes. This requirement is both at odds with present neoliberal times but also with (the Weberian interpretation of) Protestant ethics. As we have seen above in our discussion of the limits of meritocracy, the dissemination of human enhancement complicates how merit is attributed.

But while a relation of solidarity based on friendship, collegiality and love is ideal, we should also consider relations of solidarity based on self-interested preference satisfaction. The latter conception is morally and theoretically inferior, in MacIntyre's but also in our view, to a conception of care and solidarity based on concern with the common good. But the former is also the prevalent conception of solidarity in contemporary society, as it has permeated both public discussion (e.g., Realpolitik) as well as scholarly discussions (e.g., classic economics). In such a context, it might be useful to reflect on the relations of material dependence between UH and EH: is it best to attempt to shield, once and for all, one group from harm and violence performed by the other?

A moment's thought indicates that social or physical separation of UH and EH is unlikely to generate desirable effects in the long run. Rather, separation of communities is more likely to generate sentiments of carelessness and impunity, whereas social diversity is likely to reinforce feelings of mutual respect, is spite of – or rather precisely because of – the possibility of a mutually destructive conflicts between EH and UH. Our reflection thus points towards a balance between impeding and allowing the possibility of mutual harm. Such a balance, we propose, is more a matter of practical wisdom than a matter of a priori reasoning, but it is also highly dependent on the primary socialization of EH and UH. Thus, an analysis of the social possibilities of enhancement must include some consideration of the socialization mechanisms through which EH and UH would live together in relative harmony.

Institutions of primary socialization

As noted above, if relations of care and solidarity between EH and UH are to be maintained over time, it is crucial to encourage identification rather than dis-identification between people carrying different types and levels of enhancement. This question is all the more important as care for those who have little to contribute to society is justified by an "it could have been me" argument. MacIntyre even suggests that such an argument "is this fact about us that makes our relationship to seriously disabled human beings quite other than our relationship to seriously disabled animals of other species" (p. 101).

MacIntyre's conclusion was perhaps reassuring in 1999 because it established the unity of humanity as a naturally given community of mutual identification and solidarity. But in the context of a discussion of human enhancement, it becomes scary: what if EH learn precisely the opposite? What if they learn that ego could never have been an UH alter because being unenhanced is so vile that being it is simply not being oneself anymore? And conversely, what if UH learn, perhaps out of their teachers' resentment, that being an EH is so vile as to impede identification? We would like to suggest that whether this polarization of society occurs will depend in great part on how EH and UH are primarily socialized: should the moral education of EH be any different from the moral education of UH? And should each group care for its own needy members?

The question of providing a common or a distinct moral education is particularly important if we consider that the aim of moral education is to enable the (re) production of social relations characterized by uncalculated giving and graceful receiving (MacIntyre 2009/1999: 121). It thus seems crucial to provide a common moral education to EH and UH that teaches them to discern and appreciate the virtues all humans share, independently of the enhancements they carry: courage, temperance, misericordia, generosity, loving-kindness and so on. But since UH historically pre-exist EH, and since most moral education is conveyed through example over time rather than through on-the-spot declaration, we could reasonably expect that the attitudes of EH towards UH will reflect the attitudes that UH displayed towards them.

Finally, relations of care and solidarity between healthy adult EH and UH are likely to depend on the provision of adequate care for the most needy members of both groups. We may make two remarks here: first, that we hope with all our heart that caregiver bonds based on close physical contact will never be prematurely severed for both EH and UH. We know, indeed, since Liedloff (1977) and Winnicott (1964/1987) the primordiality of caregiver contact in the early years of life. Care establishes the future adult's ability to grow her moral powers and give back as much and as well as she receives over the course of her life. Second, because primary education is par excellence the site when and where ego learns to recognize alter as a moral subject worthy of care and respect, we do hope that in the rest of the twenty-first century UH and EH will be schooled together. Such a wish is not entirely trivial if we consider the present trend for various groups to segregate schooling according to social, cultural or religious lines (see among others Longden 2019). If a lesson can be learned from the current trend towards educational ghettoization, it is that it can only be avoided through voluntaristic public policy. Our point is therefore that, as human enhancements become more common in society, the question of common schooling becomes a crucial topic for public discussion and political action.

Conclusion

The current chapter has addressed the question of relations of care and solidarity in the context of human enhancements, examining the potential risks of social discord arising from the increased prevalence of enhancements, while holding out a very tentative hope for the possibility of an ethically defensible world of human enhancement. Given the early stages and unpredictability of enhancement technologies, we have taken a broad philosophical perspective. Careful, case-by-case analysis will be needed, however, to understand the ethical implications of specific technologies as they arise. We do hope, nonetheless, that our present work provides a useful theoretical framework for more fine-grained studies to come.

We like to believe that our philosophical discussion has generated insights that help clarify both ethical and political debate. First, whether human enhancements are a good thing or a bad thing for humanity will depend on whether EH adopt attitudes of humility, just generosity and misericordia. But the propensity of EH to develop the above-mentioned virtues depends in turn on the existence of social norms and institutions of primary socialization that encourage unconditional care and mutual identification with other humans exhibiting notable differences of shapes and powers.

Unfortunately, as we write in 2019, it is questionable whether contemporary institutions and organizations of primary socialization will evolve sufficiently rapidly to encourage unconditional care and mutual identification between EH and UH. This situation is highly problematic as it indicates that, unless a shift of consciousness and bold political actions is initiated, human enhancements are likely to be, on the whole, an unhappy development for humanity.

References

Al-Amoudi, I., & Lazega, E. (2019). Digital society's techno-fascist matrix. In I. Al Amoudi & E. Lazega (Eds.), *Post-human institutions and organizations. Confronting the matrix*. Abingdon and New York: Routledge.

Ansbacher, H. L., & Ansbacher, R. R. (Eds.). (1956). *The individual psychology of Alfred Adler – a systematic presentation in selections from his writings*. New York: Basic Books Inc.

Archer, M. S. (1995). *Realist Social Theory: The morphogenetic approach*. Cambridge: Cambridge University Press.

Bhaskar, R. (1998). *The possibility of naturalism. A philosophical critique of the contemporary human sciences*. London: Routledge. (Original work published 1979)

Boltanski, L., & Thévenot, L. (1991). *On justification. Economies of worth*. Princeton and Oxford: Princeton University Press.

Collier, A. (1994). *Critical realism. An introduction to Roy Bhaskar's philosophy*. London and New York: Verso.

Collier, A. (1999). *Being and worth*. London and New York: Routledge.

Czarniawska, B., & Gustavsson, E. (2008). The (d)evolution of the cyberwoman? *Organization, 15*(5), 665–683.

Donati, P. (2011). *Relational sociology. A new paradigm for the social sciences*. London and New York: Routledge.

Donati, P., & Archer, M. S. (2015). *The relational subject*. Cambridge: Cambridge University Press.

Hawkey, K. (2010, January 10). Apartheid got under her skin. *Sunday Times (South Africa)*. Retrieved from https://www.timeslive.co.za/sunday-times/lifestyle/2010-01-10-apartheid-got-under-her-skin/

Honneth, A. (1995). *The struggle for recognition: The moral grammar of social conflicts*. Cambridge: Polity Press.

Hurlbut, J. B., & Tirosh-Samuelson, H. (Eds.). (2016). *Perfecting human futures: Transhuman visions and technological imaginations*. Wiesbaden: Springer.

Kenny, A. (1993). *Aquinas on mind*. London: Routledge.

Krautwurst, U. (2007). Cyborg anthropology and/as endocolonisation. *Culture, Theory and Critique, 48*(2), 139–160.

Lawson, T. (1997). *Economics and reality*. London and New York: Routledge.

Lazega, E. (2015). Body captors and network profiles: A neo structural note on digitalized social control and morphogenesis. In M. S. Archer (Ed.), *Generative mechanisms transforming the social order*. Springer.

Liedloff, J. (1977). *The continuum concept. In search of happiness lost*. Perseus Books.

Longden, S. (2019, July 9). Labour must be bold, and finally abolish private schools. *The Guardian*. Retrieved from www.theguardian.com/commentisfree/2019/jul/09/labour-phase-out-private-schools-britain-inequality-finland

MacIntyre, A. (2009). *Dependent rational animals. Why human beings need the virtues.* London: Duckworth. (Original work published 1999)

Pinçon, M., & Pinçon-Charlot, M. (2000). *Sociologie de la bourgeoisie.* Paris: Editions de la Découverte.

Rawls, J. (2003). *Justice as fairness. A restatement.* Cambridge, MA and London: The Belknap Press of Harvard University Press.

Stapleton, P., & Byers, A. (Eds.). (2015). *Biopolitics and utopia. An interdisciplinary reader.* New York: Palgrave Macmillan.

Triviño, J. L. P. (2011). Gene doping and the ethics of sport: Between enhancement and posthumanism. *International Journal of Sports Science, 1*(1), 1–8.

Van Parijs, P. (2003, October 1). Nous finirons presque tous euthanasiés. *Courrier International.* Retrieved from www.courrierinternational.com/article/2002/02/21/ nous-finirons-presque-tous-euthanasies

Winnicott, D. W. (1987). *The child, the family and the outside world.* Perseus Publishing. (Original work published 1964)

6 Can humans and AI robots be friends?

Margaret S. Archer

Introduction

Friendship, Aristotle maintained, is not a unitary concept even for humans alone; it can take three forms (based upon utility, pleasure and goodness). In that case, humans would not employ the same kind of relationship today when they refer to their 'friends' compared with the referents of friends in different times and places. Why then focus upon such a slippery conceptual customer in this chapter? Some might protest that there are objective terms, such as 'collaborator', which can capture constructive and creative co-working adequately. Yet its seeming strengths are also its weaknesses. If friends is too fuzzy, collaboration is too task specific. It may be used correctly to refer to one-off events, such as two motorists coming from opposite directions who collaborate to move a fallen tree that is blocking both drivers but which neither can do alone.[1] But the two drivers are unlikely candidates for subsequent friendship, given they will probably not meet again.

Another, quite different reason for examining friendship is that in *The Relational Subject* we maintained that it was the paradigm of all human relationships[2] because it entailed no implications about kinship, sexuality, ethnicity, nationality, language, residence, power, status, beliefs and so forth, although each and every one of these could be imbricated in it. If we sustained our case that friendship is indeed generic, then AI beings are intriguing test cases, immune from the temptations of those anthropomorphic attitudes that we often impose on our domestic pets. Since sociology has been almost silent in relevant discussions that have drawn mainly upon analytic philosophy and cognitive psychology, it is through relational realism that a claim will be staked for the radical contribution it can make to the question posed in this chapter's title (Donati & Archer 2015).

In turn, this will be advanced as the means of breaking the deadlock between popular 'robophobia' and commercialized 'robophilia' (products intentionally marketed as humane 'best friends' or useful 'housekeepers' that control thermostats and draw the blinds etc.). Most of the best-known conundrums rest upon exaggerating the binary divide between the human and the AI, as if this difference between organically based and silicon-based entities formed an abyss dividing up the whole gamut of properties and powers pertaining to agents. Conversely, I argued in the first paper in this series[3] that acceptance of their shared 'personhood' can span this divide. Obviously, as a social theorist, my arguments were speculative, as they will be here. However, there are a number of barriers that seem to have been erected and exaggerated that bear closer inspection because their main function is to retain the abyss. It is significant that in general these barriers are usually presented in terms of what AI beings cannot do, cannot understand, cannot contribute and so forth. As such, these arguments show a close resemblance to colonialist thinking and the deficits it regularly attributed to indigenous people.

Frequently, the reason given for resistance to 'friendship' between humans and AI robots is that our organic, carbon-based brains evolved quite differently from their silicon-based computational capacity. Without a good deal more being said, this statement merely elides causes of origin with causes of continuation. In any case, does this wet/dry distinction matter for cooperation and possible future co-evolution? In Part I of this chapter I will argue (unpopularly) against this resistance and do so by seeking to undermine the main barriers that have been repeatedly erected and reinforced against inter alia creative collaboration and the possibility of friendship between these two kinds of persons.[4] Part II will shift from defensive critique to relational realism in social science, to properties and causal powers emergent from relational synergy between these two kinds of persons, which allow of their friendship.

To date my argument has made use of an invented film script featuring Homer, a distinguished medical researcher whose life work is the elimination of tumour X, fatal to human beings. Under the terms of his grant, Homer enjoys the services of Ali, initially an AI robot, preloaded with the English language, fitted with language recognition and voice production, capable of uploading new data and of conducting the usual quantitative statistical operations upon it – at high speed using big data – and the capacity to augment and adapt his pre-programming. Ali is thus pictured as being flexible and adaptive but not fully autonomous because central control threatens to wipe him clean and refit him for duties in traffic control as Homer ages, and the grants for their progressive research programme begin to be awarded elsewhere.

In brief, Ali is credited with three main characteristics: learning ability, reflexive error-correction and the (fallible) capacity for self-adaptation relevant to the task in hand. Homer's pertinent characteristics are his monomania about nailing tumour X, his willingness to constantly revise his hypotheses to this end and his complete absence of 'xenophobia' towards Ali qua robot. Now read on, and back if possible (Archer 2019, 2020).

Finally, I want to stress nothing that follows implies 'hybridity' between a human medical researcher and an AI robot. I leave hybrids to the rose growers and their skills of engrafting – along with more recent trends and trades in genetics. We are all 'enhanced humans' now, and that has been a continuous feature of our evolution since (at least) pastoralism. This chapter is not concerned with whether or not AI robots can pass as human; it is not about any form of the Imitation Game or the appearance of functional equivalences. Indeed, the more pronounced are the dissimilarities between these two types of beings in appearance, development and mode of interaction, the more persuasive the argument would be.

Part I: surmounting the barriers

This account could be much more elaborate, but I will dwell on three main obstacles that are regularly advanced as prohibiting friendship with human beings and which often reinforce robophobia. All of these concern ineradicable deficits attributed to AI robots. Specifically, each systematically downplays one of the characteristics with which Ali has been endowed in the current thought experiment; his abilities for *continuous learning* (until/unless shut-down), for *error-correction* and for *adaptation* of his skill set – and thus of himself – during his task performance.

The normative barrier

Stated baldly, this consists in the assertion that an AI entity, as a bundle of micro-electronics and uploaded software, is generically incapable of knowing the difference between right and wrong. Consequently, alarm bells sound about the ensuing dangers of this anormativity of AIs for humans, as prefigured in Asimov's normative laws of robotics (1942). In other words, "Robots are seen as (potential) moral agents, which may harm humans and therefore need a 'morality'" (Coeckelbergh 2010: 209). Usually, this need is met by a top-down process of building human safeguarding into pre-programmed designs or, less frequently, by AI robots being credited with the capacity to develop into moral machines from the bottom up, through learning morality, as ventured by Wallach and Allen (2008). Both protective responses confront similar difficulties. On the one hand, morality changes over time (poaching a rabbit no longer warrants transportation) and the change can be fast (from French revolutionary laws to the Code Napoléon) as well as coercive and non-consensual. Even Hans Kelsen (1992) had abandoned a *grund-norm* as founding all instances of legal normativity by the end of his work. On the other hand, if the model of childhood learning replaces that of pre-programming, we largely now acknowledge that socialization is not a simplistic process of 'internalization' (Archer 2012). Again it is a non-consensual process, and it may be a complete failure. It simply cannot be concluded that "we set the rules and bring it about that other agents conform to them. We enable them to adapt their behaviour to our rules even before they can understand social norms" (Brandl & Esken 2017: 214).

Equally pertinent, social normativity is not homogeneous in its form or in its force. Both of the latter are themselves subject to social change. Just as importantly, some of its transformations are more amenable to straightforward learning (for example, it took less than five minutes online to learn how to renew my passport) than others (such as "what constitutes domestic violence in this country?"), which requires interpretation and judgements about appropriate classification.

If we break normativity down into recognizable categories – and what follows is for purposes of illustration rather than it being the only useful manner of doing so – it should clarify that working upwards through the list of rules is to move from easy learning to the need for expert advice that itself will be challenged.

1   Law of the land
2   Norms and values
3   Administrative regulations
4   Conventions and customs
5   Etiquette.

Etiquette is heterogeneous (and changeable), varying with factors such as the age, personality and social standing of participants vis-à-vis one another. Although transgression attracts only social sanctions, its applicability to Ali is dubious. Should he don a tie (if he can) in those venues that insist upon their being worn? What should he do with cutlery, given he will not be eating? May he list his special requirements as "access to an electric socket and cable"? How should he address others and expect to be addressed? No human guide to correct behaviour[5] can assist Ali in learning good manners, despite his ability to read and recite any manual available, because many are disallowed by his (current) constitution. Much the same goes for large tracts of customs and conventions.

More significantly is the growth of anormative bureaucratic regulation – both public and private – that now predominates in the governance of social coordination (Archer 2016). The rule of law can no longer run fast enough to keep up with social morphogenesis in almost any social domain; novel forms of malfeasance outstrip counteractive legislation as recognized in countries such as Britain that declared a halt on designating 'new crimes'[6] in the new millennium. Instead, regulators and regulations boom in every area, sometimes upheld by law but frequently not. In this reversal, something very interesting has happened to normativity itself and is directly relevant to demolishing the barrier that the absence of a capacity for it once constituted for delineating AI beings from humans.

Obeying regulations does not rely upon their ethical endorsement; indeed the rules governing domestic refuse disposal or the sale of forked carrots in supermarkets may be regarded as idiotic by the general public, who were never consulted. Regulations are not morally persuasive but causally produce conformity through fines, endorsements and prohibitions. Thus it is up to the subjects to perform their own cost-benefit analyses and determine whether the price of infringement, such as irregular parking, is worth it to them on any given occasion. Taking the normativity out of an increasing range of activities progressively weakens the barrier placing AI beings outside the moral pale. They do not have to feel guilt, shame, remorse or wrongdoing. Thus, whether or not they are capable of such feelings is an argument that has become less and less relevant because the social context makes decreasing use of them.

Intensive social change also undercuts a frequent robophobic suggestion that in the interests of human health and safety, our values should be instilled in AI beings. But, if this is on the model of childhood learning or socialization, what (or, rather, *whose* values) are adopted? The same problem attaches to 'moderating' xenophobia, when certain politicians claim to have no animus against migrants if only they would not weaken Britain's (or wherever's) *basic* values. But what are these? Ironically, the best contender seems to be 'tolerance', which if not an oxymoron is a performative contradiction (as when the founder of UKIP, Nigel Farage, could go on air and voice his discomfort when people spoke other languages on Underground trains, despite his wife being German).

The alternative is to programme such values into the AI-to-be, in an updated version of Asimov's three laws. Yet, supposing it was possible and desirable, it is not an answer to the normative barrier because these would be our values that we have introduced by fiat. Pre-programmed values can never be *theirs*, not because they did not initiate them (however that might be), but rather because the same theorists hold that no AI entity can have emotional commitment to them for the simple reason that they are incapable of emotion. We should note that anormative administrative regulation sidesteps this particular issue since it is independent of emotions through its reliance on calculative cost-benefit analysis.

The emotional barrier

I am not arguing that human and AI beings are isomorphic, let alone fundamentally the same substantively. Nor is that the case methodologically for studying the two, which is particularly relevant to emotionality. Dehaene (2014) and his team do a wonderful job in decoding parts of brain activities, established by working back experimentally *from behaviour* for human beings, including some of the brain damaged. However, in comparing the capacities of the 'wet' and the 'dry' for experiencing emotion, it seems more productive to start the other way around with the physical constitution of those like Ali and the affordances and limitations of his uploaded software. In *Being Human*, I differentiated between our relations with the 'natural', 'practical' and 'social' orders as the sources of very different types of emotions impinging upon three inescapable human concerns (respectively, our physical well-being, performative achievement and self-worth) – given our *organic* constitution, the way the world is made and the ineluctability of their interaction (Archer 2000). I still endorse this approach when dealing with the human domain; each order of natural reality has a different import for our species and generates the emergence of different clusters of emotions acting back upon them.

My definition of emotions as "commentaries upon our concerns" in the three orders of natural reality is about matters we human beings cannot help but care about (to some extent) – imports to which we cannot be totally indifferent, given our constitution. Hence, whilst humans may experience 'terror' in anticipation of being plunged into Arctic waters, constitutionally they cannot 'fear' themselves rusting. Conversely, objectively dangerous imports for Ali would be quite different: for example, rusting, extended power cuts or metal fatigue, phenomena that would never trouble Homer for his own body.

However, because I am maintaining that AI robots can detect that they confront real dangers (just as all our electronic devices signal their need for recharging), this does not in itself justify attributing emotions to robots. But, such a move is unnecessary. This need not be the case because on my account it is *concerns* that are pivotal, and whilst emotion may increase attention and provide extra 'shoving power', it is not indispensable and it can be misleading. Thus, I disagree with those who maintain that "emotions matter. They are the core of human experience, shape our lives in the profoundest ways and help us decide what is worthy of our attention" (McStay 2018: 1). Even when confined to humans, our emotionality surely cannot be a guide to worth.

Nevertheless, probably the majority of those at our workshop maintained that an 'emotional commentary' was an essential part of all our *concerns* and, by extension, to all forms of *caring*. Yet, to be realistic, we *care enough* about a variety of mundane concerns to do something about them (checking the warranty when buying appliances, keeping the sitting-room fit to be seen, stocking some long-life products in the pantry, etc.), all without any emotionality. Such concerns are sufficient to make (some of us) care enough and to do something about it. Conversely, being emotionally moved by a photo of a dead baby on an Aegean beach (a real example), said on social media to have "moved many to tears," was clearly not enough to promote their active caring for asylum seekers. It seems that the dated term branding some movies as inconsequential tear-jerkers was not far from the mark. In sum, I hold to my view that emotions are neither a necessary nor a sufficient condition for caring, whilst accepting that their addition may reinforce fidelity to our concerns.

My position does not amount to cognitivism, which might at first glance seem appropriate to AI beings. However, what cognitivists maintain is that "emotions are very real and very intense, but they still issue from cognitive interpretations imposed on external reality, rather than directly from reality itself" (Ortony, Clore & Collins 1988: 4). Above, I have argued against this reduction of ontology to epistemology in human relations with the three orders of natural reality. Now I am asking why we should agree that AI beings are deficient precisely if they *do not experience* "very real and very intense emotions" in natural reality? Were they merely to scrutinize a situation and to conclude cognitively that undesirable φ was highly likely to transpire, that would sometimes improve their 'prospects' of averting φ in comparison with dramatic displays of affectivity that can foster stampedes in human crowds confronting fires in confined spaces.

Some might think that a midway position is provided by Charles Taylor's (1985: 48) statement that "we speak of emotions as essentially involving a sense of our situation, claiming that they are affective modes of awareness of situation . . . *We are not just stating that we experience a certain feeling in this situation*" (my italics). I agree, but I stress that the ontology of the situation remains indispensable. Moreover, there are two controversial words in that quotation which effectively divide psychologists of the emotions: one is 'affect' (affectivity) and the other 'feelings', and both are very relevant to our present discussion.

Feelings, as the mainstay of my opponents, are another slippery concept because some are held worth consideration and others not, some to be concealed, others displayed. But this is largely a matter of social convention. As individuals, humans vary enormously in how readily they reveal suffering and which suffer-ings, but their acceptability has also varied historically. Why "having a stiff upper lip" has come to be used as derogatory would be interesting for semantic archae-ology. Equally, why encouraging others to grieve overtly, to "tell their stories" or to "let it all come out" would be an equally intriguing enterprise in modern times. This overt variety shows emotionality not to be a universal and essential compo-nent of human responses to similar circumstances if they are so socially malle-able. The rejoinder could obviously be that we can never know what people suffer (or exult about) in silence, but then if we cannot know it, neither can we study it. A last resort would be to hand this over to the 'therapeutic couch', but in which of those warring psychiatric practitioners should we place our trust? At least, Ali and his kind would not be preoccupying the attention of the counsellors.

If those holding that the presence and absence of feelings comes down to the "phenomenal feel" of qualia, which will forever divide the wet and the dry, it seems a weak case for two reasons. First, it varies experientially within human-kind, or calling someone tone-deaf or "blind to natural beauty" would not have been coined. Second, if one of us is motivated by, say, injustice or unfairness, why is that supposedly accompanied by particular qualia? Judges are expected to rule on cases in the light of evidence made available in trials, not to share their phenomenal feel for it or the parties involved. Neither did John Rawls argue that decisions made "behind the veil" entailed such phenomena. If these continue to be regarded as a barrier by some, then sharing the same qualia will also continue to separate all beings from one another, regardless of their physical constitution, if these can ever be objectively determined.[7]

The barrier of consciousness

This is generally presented as the "great abyss" that those in silico can never surmount.

Indeed, it is a resilient version of the of the old dispute between Comte and Mill about the premise of a split consciousness. Mill's riposte was to jettison the simul-taneous element by inserting a brief time interval between the original thought and *inspection* of it. Consequently, our self-awareness became an unobjectionable exercise of memory. I will not repeat the lengthy argument I advanced,[8] by selec-tively drawing upon the great American pragmatists, to buttress my contention that 'introspection', on the observational model (*spect intro*), should be replaced by the inner or internal conversation. But how is this relevant to AI beings?

It is a case of working the other way around. We know the software installed in Ali and what actions it allows him, namely learning, error correction and adapta-tion. If, in following Homer's instructions, he registers remission rates in tumour X and their association with various demographic factors from available data bases, he also has a perfect memory that he can print out and share with Homer (and oth-ers). Furthermore, this is a *record* that *he himself* can consult at any time. Since he has speech recognition and the ability to converse, Ali can use the affordances of language in relation to it. Not only does this enable him to *report* verbally to

Homer (and to many others because he could write an article for publication) but also to be questioned by him (Homer could ask "What else is remission associated with?"). In principle, this presents no problem because Ali can search the digitalized literature much faster than his boss. Suppose he then comes up with some correlation that Homer finds odd and unexpected. Since he regularly voices his reactions, he says something like, "How can remission be causally related to spikes in local temperature?" Ali takes this literally as a question requiring further literature searches. He may respond mechanically by searching for (remission + sudden rises in local temperature). Suppose this yields no results. He is already familiar with different formulations of search items proving more productive (if not, the screen will tell him so), and either way he learns and tries new variants. These are his variations, not Homer's suggestions; he is applying his own error detection to the task, and it is hard to envisage how he could do this without *reflection* such that he would exclude, for instance, some semantically correct meanings for their irrelevance (e.g., those concerning 'remission' of taxes or prison sentences).

Eventually Ali ends up with a list, but he has also learned sufficient about Homer's methodical ways not to submit anything they have already eliminated or something that he judges is task irrelevant. Therefore, he does not simply pass this list over but scrutinizes and edits it. How would this be possible unless he was allowed the capacity to make judgements? Yet a judgement entails a judge who makes an assessment which implies thoughtful self-consciousness. Instead of re-invoking introspection I simply rely on two of his software abilities, to speak and to listen, for *securing his self-consciousness.*

Every day, from being toddlers, we humans employ language to pose questions: internally to ourselves, externally to other people and also of our outside environment. A common exemplar, not universal and answerable in various non-linguistic ways, is the first question likely to arise each day for most adults upon waking: "What time is it?" We are both questioners and respondents and this means that all normal people are both *speakers* and *listeners* to themselves. This is what the great American pragmatists – James, Pierce and Mead – called the "inner conversation" and I have explored this subjective mental activity in my trilogy of books on human 'reflexivity' (Archer 2003, 2007, 2012).[9]

Now, I want to venture that given Ali is programmed to be a proficient language user, then why should it be queried that he too functions as both a speaker and a listener? This cannot be seriously contested given his work with Homer. But if that is so, why can't he be credited with internal reflexivity? The blunt barrier on the part of those who deny the capacity for thought to AI robots is a simplistic definitional denial of their ability to think because computers are held to be incapable of consciousness, let alone self-consciousness. Yet, if we examine the basic constituents of the internal conversation, what is there in the activities of speaking, listening and responding (internally, but reflexive deliberations can be shared externally) that would put any AI robot permanently beyond the pale of reflexivity? Certainly, there are practical obstacles, the most powerful being that in current computers each software application works in a separate memory space between which exchanges are precluded, meaning that programmes have no general means of exchanging their specialized knowledge.[10] But, such limitations as these result from the programme designers rather than being intrinsic to AI robots.

When we do think of questioning and answering ourselves in the internal conversation, then those of Homer or by Ali are like all conversations in one crucial respect, namely they involve turn-taking. Therefore, I am arguing that when we talk to ourselves the same rule maintains, and it does so by our *alternating between being subject and object in the dialogical turn-taking process*, which is rendered possible because of the necessary time gap – however small – that separates question from answer. Some may query how this is possible given that any data or notion I produce (as subject) is identical to that I simultaneously hear (as object). Yet, it would be meaningless to entertain an alternation between two identical things. Instead, following the insight of William James (1890: 61–62), in expressing a response we review the words in which to articulate it, welcoming the felicitous ones and rejecting those less so. Thus, our answers often do not come pre-clothed in the verbal formulations that clearly express them to the best of our ability or to our satisfaction. We are fallible as well as suboptimal in this respect, sometimes even saying what we do not mean. But we are capable of reformulation before venturing a revised response. And we may do this several times over (see Figure 6.1). This extension of James consists only in allowing the subject to question his/her/its own object over time. Such a process will be familiar to any writer and is the bread and butter of literary historians.

However, those upholding the consciousness barrier against AI robots will advance at least two objections. First, they might assert that no datum supplied by Ali to a question originating from Homer can possibly be incorrect (unless it derives from system malfunctioning or deficient research itself) since his recording system is "guaranteed accurate." Well, we should always read the small print attached to warranties! Consider a fairly frequent occurrence for academic writers. We encounter references to the same passage in a book or article but attributed a different pagination, although the text is said to come from the same edition and so forth. Often we don't notice and use the first page number we had met – thus perpetuating the confusion! However, Ali has a much better memory and more accurate recording system than we do and he observes the discrepancy. Nevertheless, for whatever reasons, his accessible sources do not allow him to resolve it (say, no original hard copy exists). He may have no solution to offer Homer but at least his attempted revision has revealed a problem that may or may not be significant.

Second, to redeploy James's notion of welcoming certain verbal formulations, discarding others and seeking for more adequate words would all be held illegitimate because as mental activities they entail thought. Even if Ali is pictured summoning up a thesaurus, there is no mechanism that can match semantics for their appropriateness in a *novel* research context, where common usage cannot be the court of appeal. Of course, Ali with his extensive resources may do as we do and sometimes resort to poetry. But then he is guilty of thoughtful creativity, and to concede this would allow the barrier to sag. I can see no way in which

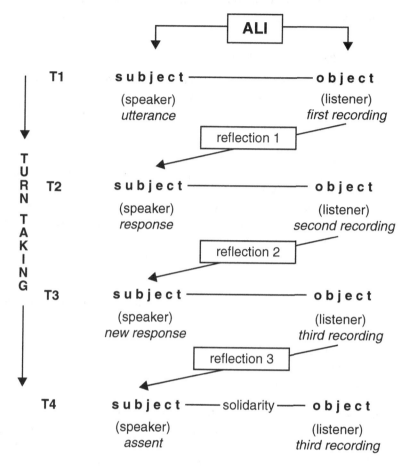

Figure 6.1 Datum and verbal formulation

Source: Adapted from Archer (2003: 99).

Ali's exercise of judgement can be freed from conceding that he is also exercising thought – and thus "consciousness and self-consciousness," as Harry Frankfurt (1988: 161–162) put it earlier.

Were these considered to be convincing if over-condensed objections to the barriers, there remains a final but crucial point to note which is central to Part II of this chapter. All of the obstacles briefly reviewed so far have depended upon 'robotic individualism', since they have all taken the form of "No AI robot can ♩, Ω, or Θ." That is not the case that I am seeking to advance here. Instead, this concerns the dyad, and a particular form of dyadic interaction, between an AI robot and a human co-worker. Since I presume we would agree that there are properties and powers pertaining to the dyad that cannot belong the individual, whether of organic or silicon constitution, then these need to be introduced and be accorded due weight. That was the whole point of introducing the Homer/Ali film plot, unlikely to reach the big screen.

Part II: synergy's relational consequences

There is a fundamental paradox that besets the history of thinking about friendship. Necessarily, friendship has to be (at least) a dyadic concept, but after Aristotle the focus has been on the *formation* of the dyad – what is the basis of two people being drawn together – and very rarely upon the *emergent powers* of the dyad to generate friendship. I am going to put forward an account based upon the second, largely neglected approach and am constrained to do so by the subject of this chapter – the possibility of friendship between different entities. For obvious reasons the Aristotelian tradition concentrates exclusively upon humans in the absence of robotic beings. Although today some would want to give more attention to our 'companion species' and to sentient life in general, their arguments, which have merit in many contexts, do not touch upon friendship proper. This is evident from Aristotle's own three categories grounding friendship:

1 With those grounded in material advantage, it is the derived utility that bonds the relationship.
2 With those grounded in pleasure, it is the pleasure of their company that provides the adhesive.
3 With those in perfect friendship, the friend is valued for his/her own goodness and constitutes 'another self'.

The latter represents the apex: Only the friendship of those who are good, and similar in their goodness, is perfect. For these people each alike wish good for the other qua good, and they are good in themselves. Such perfection, relying upon ethical criteria which are 'similar' for both parties, who wish goodness for the other, defy approximation by the AI being. Ali struggles with lesser forms of normativity; insofar as he succeeds, it is not by resembling (or imitating) Homer. And he does not himself wish goodness for the medical researcher but rather success in his project (which is good in Homer's view, but merely a practical objective in Ali's).

Insistence on the similarity criterion immediately invokes speciesism as an insuperable barrier to friendship between Homer and Ali. Ryan Dawson (2012: 9) asks directly, "Can Two Friends both be good and not alike?" He takes the common reading of Book 1 of *Nicomachean Ethics* to the effect that

> the friends share a set of attributes which make them excellent examples of the type 'human being'. What makes you or I good (and deserving of admiration) is the same thing which makes any member of the species good, i.e. exhibiting the essential qualities that are most exemplary for the species.

At most, it might be admitted from this that essentially a good dog differs from a good cat, but their disparate forms of excellence still prohibit friendship, just as it makes an oxymoron of the saying that "a dog is man's best friend."

There are three ways off this hook; holism, individualism and relationality. The first entails abandoning human essentialism by focusing sociologically upon the characteristics and capacities that we acquire through our first language and induction into a culture, which McDowell (1998) terms our "second nature." What it does is to transfer the monolithic characteristics previously attributed to humankind to our social communities. However, elsewhere, I have put forward a critique of "The Myth of Cultural Integration," disputing that any culture is shared, if only because none is free from contradictions and inconsistencies (Archer 1985: 36). If that is the case, then cultural essentialism falls too, to a multiculturalism where 'goodness' varies over time, place, selection and interpretation. The same can be said of Tuomela's (2010) reliance upon agents drawing on a shared ethos in order to act as a 'we' or in the 'we-mode', and that is considerably less demanding than friendship. It should not need emphasizing that cultural holism entails speciesism.

With individualism, what is held to be admirable in a friend originates from his/her uniqueness and therefore cannot be essential properties of human beings. Certainly, *how* someone came to be of exemplary goodness might be due to some unique concatenation of circumstances, but we do not admire *what made them what they are but rather celebrate their virtuosity*. Would we not wish for their friendship more than for the average quantum of goodness in the surrounding population? Probably, though not universally, and for their outcome, not for our admiration of its formative process.

The remaining alternative is to seek our friends neither from instantiations generic to human kind nor confined to exceptions to it, but to ground them instead upon the quality of our interrelations with others. Tefler (1970) is one of the earliest to suggest that the grounding of friendship is analogous to what enables jazz musicians to improvise creatively together. This is to shift conceptualization away from holistic species' attributes and individual uniqueness alike and to move the relationship to centre stage. It is to replace discussion of essences by causal considerations of outcomes. In fact, friendship on the causal criterion, that is of the relational goods and evils it can generate, is simultaneously freed from essentialism, exceptionalism and speciesism. The door is open to consider the subject of this chapter: can Homer and Ali become friends?

Much of what has been discussed so far has hinged upon (very different) notions of 'joint commitment', be it an ineluctable part of our human constitution, a universal cultural ethos of our social community, or being committed to an individual notion of our authenticity. Now, I want to switch the terrain and to talk not about commitment at all, but rather about joint action,[11] in particular about co-working which seems to have been seriously neglected in the discussion of friendship.

Co-working has emergent effects, ones that exceed simple aggregation (such as two miners extracting more than one) and can be qualitative as well as quantitative (caring for an injured fellow miner, even when the carer is working on piece rates). Strictly, I am concerned with joint action and its effects upon the participants when they are not of the same natural kind, such as Homer and Ali. In the literature, when neuroscientists address analytical philosophy, the tendency is quite strong to turn to the plural subject and to treat those four philosophers who have contributed most to this theme as being largely interchangeable (Bratman, Searle, Gilbert and Tuomela). This is a plain mistake:[12] joint action does not imply joint commitment, if only because the former may be constrained and the working together be coerced. In short, Bratman (1993) is not a contractarian theorist like Gilbert (1996); Searle (2010) is the only one who places identical thoughts in the two heads of the dyad, however hard this may be to entertain, and only Tuomela (2010) makes the distinction between thinking in the 'we-mode' (which assumes a common cultural ethos) from thought in the 'I-mode' that does not, whilst Gilbert alone assigns supreme importance to commitment.

Thus, what follows deals entirely with the emergent relational consequences resulting from the joint action of a human professor and his AI assistant on their medical research project. Emergent properties and powers are ones irreducible to either party but dependent upon both and can exert causal influences – for good or evil – providing contingencies and/or other generative mechanisms do not intervene to suspend them in the open system that is society. Their ontological status is assigned on causal and not observational grounds, meaning that as Bhaskar (1989) put it, "causal laws must be analysed as the tendencies of things, which may be possessed unexercised and exercised unrealized, just as they may of course be realized unperceived (or undetected) by people."

Relationality

One of the first developments, which is of enduring importance for their collaboration (and was introduced in my chapter in volume II) is that Homer and Ali do become a 'we', which is Ali's initial step towards personhood. Obviously, there are already many functioning exemplars of the robotic personal assistant who simply does our bidding in the house, the car and the office as well as specialized environments such as hospitals. Some of us accept them becoming commercially 'personalized' as Alexa or Siri. Yet this is functionality, not collegiality. It is the latter, I maintained, that Homer encouraged (unintentionally) by his frequent use of the first person plural when bemoaning "So where do we go next?" Despite the excellent results allowing their project to be acclaimed as a progressive research programme, gaining repeated funding, there was always a 'next' whilst tumour X continued to claim human lives. That fact remained a datum to Ali with which he could experience neither sympathy nor empathy.

However, as part of a nascent 'we' and as Homer's dialogical partner, his resources were at the disposal of the project. He could obey, follow instructions, but what could he do with open-ended questions from his boss, such as the one above? His response could have been a repetitive "I don't know," but if it was, Ali would not be of much use to the project. Instead, he needs to be a genuine consociate, making his own contribution to carrying the research forward. In other words, and in synergy with Homer, he must make a significant contribution to generating their emergent relational goods – in this case, progress towards reducing or eliminating tumour X.

Relational goods are shared goods that depend upon the relations of subjects towards one another and are generated *only if they orient themselves* towards some shared end (their common good). Their reasons for doing so may be individual ones (contra Searle; there is only one set of thoughts in one head). In Homer's biography, one of his parents could have died from tumour X and fixated his attention upon it. This cannot be Ali's reason. He is not committed to ridding the world of tumour X; that is a human preoccupation, which he acknowledges humans care about, but it cannot be one of his personal[13] concerns.

What can be of great concern is that Homer is pressing on to the next stage of refining his explanans and needs Ali's cooperation. Supposing Ali recognizes that Homer is heading in a direction Ali has established is unproductive (say, for lack of necessary data or the difficulties of acquiring it), his orientation to the research programme could lead him to advocate an alternative or supplementary route on cognitive grounds. It is not necessary to postulate curiosity, interest or any other qualities tinged by affectivity on Ali's part.[14]

Relational goods are ones that can only be generated together and they carry no warranty that each co-worker can realize his particular concerns if these are incompatible with their common good.[15] Were Homer's prime concern to win the Nobel Prize, it is possible that this preoccupation would have led him to push the project down the path he advocated but that Ali deemed unproductive. Were Ali not to acknowledge (not empathize or sympathize) that their joint action was directed to the elimination of tumour X, he might have steered them off course into tackling some computational conundrum irrelevant to it. Neither would mean that their co-working was uncreative, but let us look more closely at a relational good that underwrites their synergy by strengthening their cooperation and prevents it from deteriorating into competition.

One property that was fundamental to their long collaboration and its productivity was the trust that emerged and grew between them. At various points along the way it would have been easy for Homer to become autocratic and to reduce Ali to research assistant status; after all, who (formally) won the funding? Ali, positioned as a subordinate, could nevertheless have persuasively nudged the project along abstruse computational lines. Yet their reciprocal trust was what sustained their joint orientation. If I am correct, this argument is highly critical of the conceptualization and usage of the concept of trust within the social sciences. Frequently it is treated as a simple predicate rather than a relational outcome, requiring consistent reinforcement. But predicates cannot be plucked out of thin air when needed; they have their own morphogenesis, morphostasis and morphonecrosis (Al-Amoudi & Latsis 2015).

For illustrative purposes, let us assume that trust did not exist at the beginning of this story, when Homer unpacked and inspected the parcels of parts constituting the AI robot for which he had successfully applied in his grant application. Nor did it exist as Homer fumbled in exploring the robot's capacities, some of which required familiarization (voice recognition still requires learning). Had Homer remained as impatient as many of us are with new electronic appliances (settling for using only three out of the washing machine's 80 settings), there would have been no morphogenesis. That was the product of co-working itself and the synergy that emerged was dependent upon certain individual properties of both entities, although not reducible to them.

Trust begins and is engendered by morphogenesis. Without the dialogical feedback between these co-workers (impossible under the command and control model), without each returning respectively to revise hypotheses sequentially and to introduce functional self-adaptation there would have been no progressive research project (Archer 2019). Doubtless in reality this process would not be exponential but involve a quantum of trial and error. What matters for trust is not unmitigated success but evidence of concern for joint action to be successful. Sharing is crucial because reciprocity does not demand constant symmetry. However, consistent asymmetry could deteriorate into an exchange relationship. Although I venture this hesitantly and only analogically, perhaps the ongoing morphogenesis of the research of Homer and Ali as co-workers crudely approximates to their generating a micro version of Dehaene's (2014: 164) shared "Global Workspace," blending neurologically and digitally based skills.

Finally, it will be clear that as far as research programmes are concerned, there is very little that corresponds to sustained morphostasis. To enter into a phase whose results are repetitive is a formula for morphonecrosis – the termination of funding for degenerating programmes. Only at lower levels, not entailing synergy (such as the satisfactory robotic manufacturing of burgers), would considerations of quality control and their monitoring make morphostasis of relevance.[16] Indeed, morphostasis is the intended consequence of machine maintenance.

Dimensionality

The morphogenetic relationality introduced above can be equivalent to friendship developing in a given dyad or small group from their joint action, although this is not necessarily the case.[17] There are many ways of defining friends and distinguishing between the characteristics and consequences of friendship. Here I treat dimensionality as differentiating between 'thin' (i.e., one-dimensional relations) versus the 'thicker' multidimensional relationships constitutive of friendship.

In everyday human life it is common for people to refer to 'my golfing friend', 'my travelling companion' or 'my workmate', meaning their relations with another are restricted to these domains. Such 'thin' friendships are vulnerable to breakdown, partly because it takes only one row, bad trip or disappointed expectations for their fragility to break, and partly because such dyadic partners are quite readily replaceable. On the other hand, 'thickness' is tantamount to the resilience of the friendship, with its various facets compensating for deficiencies in any particular one. But, how can Homer and Ali move on to even two-dimensional friendship?

Although they talk about research a great deal, many extensions of this relationship seem closed to them (e.g., they cannot go out for a drink or a meal together). Also, for the time being, there are many social embargos on their sharing leisure activities (e.g., Ali may be ineligible for golf club membership). The implication could seem to be that this dyad is confined to cognitive activities in the extension of their friendship. Even so, that leaves them plenty of options (film, television, the media, gaming, literature and music) and the cultural context of society is increasingly privileging these pursuits. If one day Homer wants to watch the news, he might be surprised that Ali as spectator becomes vocal about a short film clip on football's match of the day. Certainly, his comments are cognitively confined to working out team disposition in relation to goal scoring – but so are those of many pub pundits. As far as gaming is concerned, he is the ideal co-participant and readily computes how far the odds are stacked in favour of the virtual house. In watching movies, he represents the critic that sci-fi film-makers have never had (to date): commenting on the portrayal of those of his own kind and effectively challenging the dominant robophobia presented. Simultaneously, all of this helps to relieve the greyness of Homer's own circumscribed life. Speculatively, it seems that a thickly based friendship is potentially as accessible to this dyad as to human ones.

Conclusion: a morphogenetic scenario for human/AI friendship

Although familiar, it is important to repeat that critical realists do not generally make predictions because there are too many intervening contingencies in the social order and multiple generative mechanisms at work simultaneously. Nevertheless, I have presented an optimistic scenario in this chapter for the possibility of friendship being realized between human and AI beings and the possibilities are ontologically real to critical realists – otherwise they are utopian or dystopian fantasies. Thus, it remains to flesh out the morphogenetic sequence that could realize this possibility.

The morphogenetic approach[18] will be familiar to most in the philosophy of the social sciences, but for those outside them it consists in breaking up any historical sequence for purposes of analysis into T^1, the structural and cultural conditioning context; T^2–T^3, social interaction; and T^4, structural and cultural elaboration. See Figure 6.2.

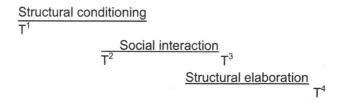

Figure 6.2 The basic M/M diagram of one morphogenetic cycle

This approach is as much methodological as theoretical, and its phases are based upon analytical dualism between structure and agency, which is possible because they operate over different tracts of time, unlike the simultaneity in philosophical dualism. Fundamentally, analytical dualism is based upon two simple, temporal propositions: (1) that structure and culture necessarily pre-date the action(s) which transform them and (2) that structural and cultural elaboration necessarily post-date those actions. Hence, full significance is accorded to the timescales through which structure, culture and agency *emerge, intertwine and redefine* one another. Hence, too, my acronym which summarizes that any adequate explanation in the social order comes in a SAC, incorporating the three components: *s*tructure, *a*gency and *c*ulture.

Phase 1 (T¹ . . .): the structural and cultural context preceding the question examined in this chapter

It is axiomatic that there is some prior social context enabling the issue of friendship between human and AI beings to be posed, for there is never such a situation as context-less interaction. We humans already inhabit a world in which the global invention and proliferation of AI entities/beings has spread to innumerable social domains. It has not been my aim to explain this novel occurrence itself (that would require the analysis of earlier and largely twentieth-century cycles of morphogenesis). However, it has been necessary to indicate the bifurcated cultural reception of AI robots because of the division of cultural expectations today[19] into robophobia and robophilia. Equally, it would be unrealistic not to contextualize the argument in the structural divisions of our contemporary world over the deployment of smart robotics in such areas as international surveillance, warfare, national elections and so forth – ones that intensify globalized social conflict.

Indeed, it is more than interesting that contemporary ideological, territorial, commercial and global political divides do seem to shadow *phobia* and *philia* towards AI in general. This cannot be reduced to conflicts of interests of different nation states *tout court* because that would obscure the other globalized divide – between the millennials, seemingly absorbed in the practical applications of smart technology and much older age groups, who may be beneficiaries of AI robotics in hospitals and social care worldwide — without fully realizing it. Is it an exaggeration to say that many of the latter think of the current medical attention they receive as no more and no less incomprehensible than the use of x-rays to which they have become accustomed? Similarly, do the aficionados of Facebook even know the identity of Mark Zuckerberg, let alone consider his qualities as a human and social being?

Phase 2 (T² – T³): the oversimplifications involved in the thought experiment by restricting it to Homer and Ali

The morphogenetic approach, I maintain, is applicable at all three conventional levels in social theorizing; micro, meso and macro. Nevertheless, the account ventured here concentrates unduly on the microscopic level by focusing upon one (fictional) dyad. Although this uncluttered canvas permits the examination of central philosophical issues, sociologically it is too spare and bare. For example, I know of no research centre that is exempt from the pressures of either its benefactors or of the university or of the educational system of which it forms a part, if not all three. In turn, the relational networks are much more complex than depicted in this film plot. In reality, students, administrators, commercial agents, journalists, social media, funding agencies, educational policy makers and so forth would impinge upon this dyad – were it more than fiction – with their different powers and motives. These would not be contingent occurrences but part and parcel of current research life and indispensable to accounting for real-life outcomes in it.

Equally, the two characters portrayed could be entirely otherwise. Homer is presented as an academic recluse, an intellectual monomaniac, without a family that ever features in what passes, lacking close colleagues with whom he also shares his breakthroughs and darker times; in short, he is a loner to whom friendship is almost as alien as it is to Ali. For our AI being, much could be explained away by his pre-programming, by his 'wipe cleans' by central control and by his programmes themselves being installed as incommunicado, which requires motive as well as ability and resources to engineer their intercommunication.

As a final thought experiment, just imagine that Homer had often been pressed to give student lectures, speak at conferences and be interviewed on the media, but somehow his reclusiveness had resisted any such exposure. With increasing success of the tumour X research project, the pressure intensifies and Homer puts forward Ali in his stead. Although Ali is inexperienced, he is an attraction in himself and (supposing again) he turns out to be a competent communicator and gathers a following. Although this may be good publicity for the research program and might increase its funding, it may simultaneously have negative effects for their budding friendship. The threat of competitiveness is ever hanging over it in a social formation still based on competition.

Phase 3 (... T⁴): is friendship between a human and an AI entity really possible?

Rather than changing horses at this stage and venturing an ungrounded prediction, I will remain an orthodox critical realist and consider this chapter as part of a concrete utopia for the near future. First, then, what qualifies a utopia as concrete? Both Ernest Bloch[20] and Roy Bhaskar made the same distinction between the 'objectively real possible' and what is 'formally possible' (i.e., abstract), such as the difference between constructing a new building from accessible materials and what could be built if girders ten times stronger were available. To Bhaskar (1994: 112), the concrete serves to "pinpoint the real, but non-actualized possibilities inherent in a situation, thus inspiring grounded hope" (here, in the emergence of friendship rather than paranoia or indifference between the two kinds of persons). In turn, this rests upon dispositional realism, namely that only possibilities that are realizable are real, unlike those that are not, and it is what distinguishes such possibilities from fantasies or wish fulfilment.

In addition, there needs to be the equivalent of a waiting room in which concrete possibilities can sit it out (unlike "let's go and shoot some unicorns") until they can achieve social or at least experimental salience. And this exists. They can be logged into the 'Universal Digital Archive'[21] and retrieved for (attempted) realization at any time by a group – or even an individual – who wants to try them out as an alternative to the status quo, whenever constraints do not preclude this (structural alternatives can be stored in the same way, but as *ideas of them* rather than as such). Notions, which of their own kind (such as killing unicorns) are unrealizable can never form part of a concrete utopia, even if they remain in the archive as mythology.

The advent of a given concrete utopia is necessarily agency dependent because it involves some actively searching for "hitherto unrealized possibilities for change in the way life is currently organized. This is where concrete utopianism, a theory of transition and a relationship to an on-going depth struggle become crucial" (Bhaskar 2016: 109). These linkages appear incontrovertible. Overall, the most satisfactory solution pro tem is in taking the above quotation seriously by demonstrating empirically that 'realization' was envisaged and sought but prevented by identifiable constraints. At the moment and inter alia, one of the reasons deterring friendship between humans and AI robots remains the cultural predominance of robophobia over robophilia itself.[22]

Notes

1 An example given by Tuomela (2010: 47).
2 See Donati and Archer (2015).
3 Archer (2019).
4 Archer (2020) argued that personhood – dependent upon possessing the first-person perspective, exercising reflexivity and endorsing concerns (things that mattered to them) – could pertain to AI beings. In parallel, I maintained that no amount of human enhancement – including the possession of a bionic body – withdrew personhood from those born human. "Considering AI Personhood," in Ismael Al-Amoudi and Emmanuel Lazega (eds), 2020, *Post Human Institutions and Organizations: Confronting the Matrix,* Abingdon Routledge.
5 Although such guidelines have become more relaxed (Abrutyn & Carter 2014).
6 Over 4,000 entered the statute books in last two decades of the twentieth century. Cabinet Office Paper, 2013, 'When Laws Become Too Complex'; www.gov.uk/government/oublications (accessed 21 November 2014).
7 In other words, I agree with Dehaene (2014: 262) that the "concept of qualia, pure mental experience detached from any information-processing role, will be viewed as a peculiar idea of the prescientific era."
8 See Archer (2003: 53–92).
9 Reflexivity is defined "as the regular exercise of the mental ability, shared by all normal people, to consider themselves in relation to their social contexts and vice versa" (Archer 2007: 4).
10 See Dehaene (2014: 259f).
11 Very few make or maintain this distinction, an exception being Clodic, Pacherie and Raja Chatila (2017). Unfortunately for my present purposes, this is confined to a simple tabletop joint activity such as building a small tower.
12 See Donati and Archer (2015: ch. 2), which distinguishes the main lines of divergence between Bratman, Searle, Gilbert and Tuomela.

13 That Ali qualifies for personhood (involving both concerns and reflexivity about them) was maintained in my previous chapter, Archer (2020).

14 It has been reported that AlphaGo was given only 200 games from which to detect patterns of moves sufficient for him to beat Go masters. Had its response been "I need 50% more data," that seems intellectually reasonable, non-affective since purely computational, and yet demonstrative of an established task orientation.

15 See Donati and Archer (2015: ch. 6).

16 Opposition to the above argument comes from an unexpected quarter, namely a discussion of whether or not AI robots could qualify for moral consideration (i.e., robot rights). It sketches a defence that they should be "based on social relations" but maintains that to develop it entails a revision of our existing ontological framework towards them (Coeckelbergh 2010). After an interesting review of deontological, utilitarian and virtue ethics, all criticized for their reliance upon "ontological, non-relational features of the robot (and the human)," the author advances his alternative "socio-relational justification of moral consideration. . . . it means that moral significance resides neither in the object nor in the subject, but in the relation between the two," but this is only a matter of *appearance* which hands the issue over to phenomenology, replacing ontology.

17 Paul Sheehy (2002) gives the nice example of four prisoners who are rowing a boat to escape. They share the belief that "I am escaping" and that it entails "we are escaping," since they are literally in the same boat. Hence their joint action that may or may not be successful. But if this is the emergent effect of their cooperation, it does not entail or generate friendship.

18 See Archer (1995). This framework was first developed in Archer (1979).

19 This divide is presented even-handedly in Brockman (2015).

20 See Geogan (1996: 32).

21 See Archer (1988), where this was called the "Universal Library."

22 This would be similar to the endurance of racism after the notion of race has been abandoned. See Carter (2000).

References

Abrutyn, S., & Carter, M. J. (2014). The decline in shared collective conscience as found in the shifting norms and values of Etiquette manuals. *Journal for the Theory of Social Behaviour, 43*(2), 352–376.

Al-Amoudi, I., & Latsis, J. (2015). Death contested: Morphogenesis and conflicts. In M. S. Archer (Ed.), *Generative mechanisms transforming the social order*. Cham: Springer.

Archer, M. S. (1979). *Social origins of educational systems*. London: Sage.

Archer, M. S. (1985). The myth of cultural integration. *British Journal of Sociology, 36*, 333–353.

Archer, M. S. (1988). *Culture and agency: The place of culture in social theory*. Cambridge: Cambridge University Press.

Archer, M. S. (1995). *Realist social theory: The morphogenetic approach*. Cambridge: Cambridge University Press.

Archer, M. S. (2000). *Being human: the problem of agency*. Cambridge: Cambridge University Press.

Archer, M. S. (2003). *Structure, agency and the internal conversation*. Cambridge: Cambridge University Press.

Archer, M. S. (2007). *Making our way through the world, human reflexivity and social mobility*. Cambridge: Cambridge University Press.

Archer, M. S. (2012). *The reflexive imperative in late modernity*. Cambridge: Cambridge University Press.

Archer, M. S. (2016). Anormative social regulation: The attempt to cope with social morphogenesis. In M. S. Archer (Ed.), *Morphogenesis and the crisis of normativity* (pp. 141–168). Cham: Springer.

Archer, M. S. (2019). Bodies, persons and human enhancement: Why do these distinctions matter? In J. Al-Amoudi & J. Morgan (Eds.), *Realist responses to post-human society: Ex machina*. Abingdon: Routledge.

Archer, M. S. (2020). Considering AI personhood. In I. Al-Amoudi & E. Lazega (Eds.), *Posthuman institutions and organizations: Confronting the matrix*. Abingdon: Routledge.

Bhaskar, R. (1989). *The possibility of naturalism*. Hemel Hempstead: Harvester Wheatsheaf.

Bhaskar, R. (1994). *Plato etc.* London: Verso.

Bhaskar, R. (2016). *Enlightened Common Sense*. Abingdon: Routledge.

Brandl, J. L., & Esken, F. (2017). The problem of understanding social norms and what it would take for robots to solve it. In R. Hakli & J. Seibt (Eds.), *Sociality and normativity for robots* (p. 214). Springer.

Bratman, M. E. (1993). Shared intention. *Ethics, 104*, 97–133.

Brockman, J. (Ed.). (2015). *What to think about machines that think*. New York: HarperCollins.

Carter, B. (2000). *Realism and racism*. London: Routledge.

Clodic, A., Pacherie, E., & Chatila, R. (2017). Key elements for human-robot joint-action. In R. Hakli & J. Seibt (Eds.), *Sociality and normativity for robots*. Springer.

Coeckelbergh, M. (2000). Robot rights? Towards a social-relational justification of moral consideration. *Ethics of Information Technology, 12*.

Coeckelbergh, M. (2010). Robot Rights? Towards a social-relational justification. *Ethics of Information Technology, 12*, 209–221

Dawson, R. (2012). Is Aristotle right about friendship? *Praxis, 3*(2), 9.

Dehaene, S. (2014). *Consciousness and the brain*. New York: Penguin.

Donati, P., & Archer, M. S. (2015). *The relational subject*. Cambridge: Cambridge University Press.

Frankfurt, H. (1988). *The importance of what we care about*. Cambridge: Cambridge University Press.

Geogan, V. (1996). *Ernest Bloch*. London: Routledge.

Gilbert, M. (1996). *Living together*. Lanham, MD: Rowman & Littlefield.

James, W. (1890). *Principles of psychology*. London: Macmillan.

Kelsen, H. (1992). *Introduction to the problems of legal theory*. Oxford: Clarendon.

McDowell, J. (1998). *Mind, value and reality*. Cambridge, MA: Harvard University Press.

McStay, A. (2018). *Emotional AI: The rise of empathetic media*. Los Angeles, CA: SAGE.

Ortony, A., Clore, G. L., & Collins, A. (1988). *The cognitive structure of emotions*. Cambridge: Cambridge University Press.

Searle, J. (2010). *Making the social world*. Oxford: Oxford University Press.

Sheehy, P. (2002). On plural subject theory. *Journal of Social Philosophy, 33*, 377–394.

Taylor, C. (1985). *Human agency and language*. Cambridge: Cambridge University Press.

Tefler, E. (1970). Friendship. *Proceedings of the Aristotelian Society, 71*, 223–241.

Tuomela, R. (2010). *The philosophy of sociality*. Oxford: Oxford University Press.

Wallach, W., & Allen, C. (2008). *Moral machines: Teaching robots right from wrong*. Oxford: Oxford University Press.

7 Humanity's end

Where will we be in a million years?

Douglas V. Porpora

Like other pieces in this volume, this chapter is about humanity and post-humanity and the intrinsic value of humanity. On the last of these matters, the contributors to this volume are divided. I staked out my own position in the chapter titled "Vulcans, Klingons, and Humans" in our previous volume (Porpora 2018). It was one of multiple publications in which I had both pronounced myself a humanist and vigorously attacked movements in the academy championing anti-humanism or post-humanism. Yet, some of my friends in this volume nevertheless consider me a post-humanist.

I would say, though, that I am less a post-humanist than some sort of unenthusiastic transhumanist. Reflecting the Roman Catholicism I share with a number of our members, I consider personhood to be sacred, the very image of God as we say. I define personhood as a centre of conscious experience, able –via language acquisition – to exercise full moral agency (see Smith 2010). Reflecting roots that are both poststructuralist and anti-humanist, post-humanists think the moral worth that humanism assigns humanity is inherently sexist and racist (see, e.g., Braidotti 2013). Post-humanists do not believe in anything as essentialist as a centre of consciousness. On the contrary, they are happy to consider us all in the same category as Archer's (2003) fractured reflexives and further oppose according anything like personhood a privileged status (see McFarlane 2013). If it is between you and a pet in a burning house, just hope it is not a post-humanist deciding your fate. I am clearly not a post-humanist, and as I say above, I have vigorously argued against it (Porpora 2017, 2018).

I might, however, be a transhumanist. Unlike post-humanists, transhumanists are not anti-humanists. Transhumanists just argue that human beings as we now know them may not be the final stage of evolution. Instead, with technical improvements humans may evolve into some sort of cyborgs or via the so-called singularity (see Bostrom 2016) be displaced by complete androids. Transhumanists, like More (2013), positively welcome this development. I neither welcome nor oppose it. It is to personhood I accord sanctity, not to *Homo sapiens* per se. I accord what Collier (1999) would call ontological worth to *Homo sapiens* because we are or at least potentially come to be persons. As in the title of my paper in our previous volume (Porpora 2018), I would consider Vulcans, Klingons or any comparable aliens, should they exist to be persons as well, no less the image of God – should

God exist – than human beings. Ditto for truly feeling androids like Data of *Star Trek*. All are persons, with all the rights appertaining thereunto.

It follows that I accord less sanctity to the human body than some of my friends, except insofar as that body affords personhood. I likewise attach less importance to who we are as a species as long as the personhood we embody continues on. Should we evolve or develop into some kind of cyborg, I would not necessarily lament the loss of our pristine, old bodies. It is that cavalier attitude toward our evolution into something else that makes me seem post-humanist to some of my fellow contributors, but I think they actually mean that I appear transhumanist.

In truth, I do not know whether it is possible for us as persons to evolve into something wholly new or whether it is possible for us to manufacture things that are actually persons. In this chapter, I plan just to entertain the idea albeit in an indirect way.

A million years is a long time. It is an especially long time if we extrapolate from our current pace of social change. We contributors to this volume together wrote a series of other volumes on the advent of morphogenetic society, a society in which forces of change far outstrip forces of stasis, creating ever-escalating novelty. Maccarini (2019) has carried that analysis further in his new book. The unbound morphogenesis Maccarini describes is the cultural analogue to the period of cosmic inflation physicists describe. Taking place somewhere between 10^{-33} and 10^{-32} seconds after the Big Bang, cosmic inflation expanded the universe at an exponential rate. That physical expansion, which putatively changed our universe so radically, nevertheless endured as indicated for only the briefest moment. Similarly, therefore, even if there ultimately is decay in our exponential cultural expansion, who knows who we will be culturally and even physically afterwards.

A million years is an especially long time in human terms. We *Homo sapiens sapiens* have existed for only a tenth as long. Going not quite a million years into the future, H. G. Wells's (2018) time traveller discovered humanity evolved into two distinct species: the lithe but tame Eloi and the stocky Morlocks, who reared them for food. In his other reflection on the subject, "The Man of the Year Million" (1958), Wells finds us evolved into a brain in a vat attached to a single hand.

How different we might be in a million years is difficult to imagine, but it is related to how intelligent beings on other planets might be, should they exist. As I will explain below, if intelligent life exists on other worlds, they most likely will be not hundreds but millions of years or more ahead of us. Thus, to think of where we will be in that time is also to think of where they already are. In *The Day the Earth Stood Still*, Earth is visited by a delegate from an alliance of other worlds who have all given themselves up to the peaceful governance of powerful robots. It sounds a lot like the singularity of much current technological talk (see Bostrom 2016). It is indeed one possibility.

Human versus cosmic time

If a million years is extraordinarily long in human terms, it is as nothing on the cosmic scale (i.e., the time scale of the universe). To show how insignificant humans are, Carl Sagan collapsed the 14 billion years of the universe's existence into the calendar pages of a single year. On that scale, our solar system originated only at the beginning of September. Although, surprisingly, life on Earth began almost immediately, it took another four and a half billion years for evolution to produce us. Thus, on Sagan's calendar, it is only about six minutes before midnight on 31 December that anatomically modern humans finally appear.

Clearly, if we measure human significance as a proportion of the cosmic time we occupy, our existence is negligible. But the proportion of cosmic time we occupy may not be the appropriate way to judge our significance. It is important to notice on the contrary that the universe had to prepare for our arrival. No intelligent life could appear before there were stars. Further, as the heavy elements that compose us and our earthly environment are all manufactured inside larger stars, a first generation or two of such stars actually had to explode first to provide the material for the planets that would subsequently orbit a subsequent generation star like our sun. Then, our own atmosphere had to be entirely transformed by unicellular plants before it was fit for oxygen-breathing animals. And of course, other transitions were required as from unicellular to multicellular life forms. In short, our existence required long preparation.

Thus, if we consider that the universe has a history, a history that seems to have moved progressively toward the conditions of our existence, then our emergence might even be considered part of a cosmic telos. It does not seem, after all, just a neutral fact that with us the universe achieves consciousness of itself. Instead, as physicist Freeman Dyson (2018) once famously remarked, "the more I examine the universe and the details of its architecture, the more evidence I find that the universe in some sense must have known we were coming."

What impressed Dyson was not just the unfolding of cosmic change in our direction. He speaks principally of the cosmic architecture. The fact is that the basic physical parameters governing the universe had to be colossally "fine-tuned," as physicists put it, in order for our existence to have been even a possibility. Philosopher John Leslie (1989) long ago became among the first of many who would go on to catalogue a long list of such "anthropic coincidences." Were the nuclear weak force much stronger, there would be no hydrogen and hence no water. For carbon to exist, the strong nuclear force could be no more than 1% stronger or weaker. For stars like our sun to exist, gravity has to be very precisely aligned with the force of electromagnetism, which is 10^{39} times stronger. Were the cosmological constant not as close to zero as it is (to one part in 10^{120}), the universe would have expanded too rapidly or collapsed too quickly for anything like our cosmic history to unfold (Leslie 1989: 2–5). Such lists go on and on, relating to, among other things, ratios of atomic particles, all of which if just minimally different would make our existence impossible.

There is no denying how the cosmic fine-tuning has impressed physicists. Their totally scientific (i.e., 'secular') response has been to propose a multiverse of infinitely many different universes, spanning all shapes and sizes. Given such an infinity, the argument goes, it becomes certain that if life and intelligent life are possible anywhere, then they will appear somewhere, although of course only in those Goldilocks places where they are possible. With that premise, it becomes no mystery that we find ourselves in a universe that appears fine-tuned for our existence. It is a selection effect.

The multiverse hypothesis, however, is beset with its own problems (Lewis & Barnes 2016, Ellis 2011, Holder 2016). Aside from being as elusive and speculative and a good deal less parsimonious than God, the multiverse itself seems to require its own fine-tuning, which ends up just relocating the very problem it was meant to solve. Thus, even more recent attempts to save the multiverse end up reducing it to some kind of quantum virtuality (Gefter 2017).

One way or another, if fine-tuning for life and intelligent life are required for our existence, then we would seem to have a significance not captured by an account that eschews objective value. But what do I mean by 'we'? In the last few paragraphs, I have intentionally been writing in a way as to lure you into thinking I am talking about human beings. And certainly, given what I have been saying, if we humans are alone in the universe, then I think our existence is particularly precious.

Until recently, for well-known but uncommonly appreciated reasons I will detail below, I actually did think we were alone. I no longer think so. In any case, however, by 'we' I am not speaking exclusively of human beings. By 'we' I mean all conscious intelligent being. I say 'being' rather than 'life'. Even supposing we are alone, if we manage to manufacture conscious intelligent beings that are not alive, I think that being too has sacred value – value, that is, equal to our own.

But let me close this section with a different point. For reasons that will also be counter-intuitive at least to academics, I now think there are strong grounds to suspect we humans are not alone in the universe. And if not, that consideration returns us to the difference between human and cosmic time.

I think that in our default picture of extraterrestrial contact, we anticipate aliens who are more or less our contemporaries. Yes, we may expect them to be a bit ahead of us technologically but not so far ahead as to make them almost unimaginable. The fact is, though, as Stephen Hawking has also observed (see Shostak 2016), if we do make contact with an extraterrestrial civilization, they are likely to be a million years or more ahead of us.

Think of it. It took four and a half billion years for evolution to produce us. Even if somewhere else life started at exactly the same time, it would be highly improbable for the evolutionary process there to have produced its intelligent life just when it did so here. Instead, it would take only the slightest variation in the evolutionary process for the intelligent life elsewhere to have begun several million years ahead of us.

And even then we are supposing that the evolutionary process started the same time, which is also unlikely. Although Sagan's calendar had our Milky Way galaxy forming only in March, a new study suggests it was there all along with the other first galaxies some 13 billion years ago (Howell 2018). Still, there are reasons to suppose that due to gamma ray bursts or other factors associated with younger galaxies, advanced life could not have formed in our galaxy before eight billion years ago (Gribbin 2011). Let us be conservative and suppose that in our galaxy, stars with habitable planets began to form six billion years ago. Adding four and a half billion years for intelligent life to form on one of those planets, intelligent life there would be two billion years ahead of us. If intelligent life is not a rarity – and certainly if it is as common as Sagan seemed to believe – the odds are any extraterrestrial life we encounter will not be our contemporaries but vastly our elders.

It is hard to conceive of intelligent beings whose civilization is billions of years old. Arthur C. Clark's third law about the future was that "any sufficiently advanced technology is indistinguishable from magic." So it would be with such an old civilization. Its denizens would likely appear to us almost godlike, like *Star Trek*'s Q. I have trouble imagining a civilization even a million years beyond us. So that is my limit in this chapter.

Are we alone?

Why, again, am I asking this question? Because I am trying to picture what we might be like in a million years and I think that the answer is comparable to where another civilization in the galaxy or universe might currently be. The assumption of course is that we are not alone in the galaxy or universe.

If you ask people whether we are alone in the universe, many will say surely not. (Not my wife, who tells me she has no idea.) Many people, however, will remember how on *Nova*, Sagan told us that our own galaxy consists of billions and billions of stars – over 200 billion, to be more precise. They might even remember that our observable universe hosts a comparable number of galaxies of comparable size. Some will even have kept up with the thousands of extraterrestrial planets that continue to be discovered. So, as my mom would say, "Why should you think we are alone?" The idea to her seems entirely presumptuous, and she has a point.

The Fermi paradox

But not so fast. We first need to contend with what is often called the Fermi paradox, named after physicist Enrico Fermi, who – although not the first to identify it – was the one who, raising the question about it at Los Alamos in 1950, lent it more popular attention.

Fermi's question was, "Where are they?" He meant that if space truly is as teeming with life as seems likely given the number of stars in our galaxy, how come 'they' (i.e., some extraterrestrial intelligent beings) are not already here?

The immediate answer is that they are not here because they are too far away. Space is absolutely immense. The stars nearest us are still light years away. A light year, the distance light travels in a year, is six trillion miles. Light travels enormously fast, capable of circling the Earth more than seven times in one second. We cannot yet travel even a thousandth as fast. Perhaps it is not even possible.

Could the vast distances separating us be the reason why no intelligent life has so far visited? Not necessarily. It has been estimated that even at the relatively slow speeds we can travel now, a reasonably expansion-minded civilization could have colonized the galaxy in tens of millions of years. Tens of millions of years is again a long time for individual lives. Would-be galactic colonists could of course put themselves into suspended animation. Frank Tipler's alternate suggestion is that the deed could also be done by self-replicating artificial intelligence (see Patton 2015).

If Tipler's suggestion is correct, then, even before we arrived on the scene, why was the Earth not already colonized by some extraterrestrial artificial intelligence? One possibility is that such capable artificial intelligence is impossible. We need, however, to rule out other possibilities. There is another possibility, insufficiently addressed by the literature, which is not generally written by social scientists – although it was entertained by Carl Sagan and Stephen Jay Gould (see Patton 2015) and also by Ćirković (2018) and Dartnell (2016). That possibility is that there is no societal incentive for interstellar colonization.

If the vast distances between stars means that even relatively near neighbours could never be in practical contact with each other, what would be the point of establishing interstellar colonies? Earth would not be able to benefit from any resources found there, nor even any knowledge. By the time anything came back to us, it would likely no longer be useful. Nor could such colonies be governed from Earth. Edicts and sanctions would take too long to transmit. Given how lacklustre is current worldwide support for the search for terrestrial intelligence (SETI), it is hard to imagine greater enthusiasm for interstellar propagation that is merely an academic exercise. So perhaps the answer to Fermi is that they have not come because there was no reason to. There are, however, other possibilities that have received more attention. Let us turn to them.

Uploading, or the Dark Forest

The Drake equation, formulated in 1961 by Frank Drake and often cited by Sagan and aficionados of SETI, has long been the basis of estimating the number of communicating civilizations in our galaxy. The factors going into the estimate are the fraction of stars with planets, the number of such planets that might be habitable and so on.

For our discussion, however, the last factor in the Drake equation is of particular interest. It is the length of time we would expect a communicating civilization to endure. A civilization might cease communicating for a number of reasons. Although very far-fetched, one possibility is that the denizens of the civilization have managed to upload themselves onto a supercomputer so that they no longer leave much of a physical footprint. Futurist George Dvorsky (2018) argues that if such technology is possible, there are all sorts of advantages to uploading ourselves.

I described this scenario as far-fetched, but we are also talking about what we might be like in a million years. The premise of this possibility is that we become able to fully map the connections of a person's brain. If we can do that, then we putatively should be able to produce a digital simulation with the same connections. Among others, Hawking (2017) and Dartnell (2016) consider such simulation possible.

This technology, however, might be impossible. Among other reasons for thinking so, it has been suggested that to vastly reduce survival and safety costs, uploaded astronauts or 'e-crews' would be the smart way to travel interstellar distances (Prisco 2012). But if so, then we have to ask again why such e-crews have not already colonized the Earth. The e-crew scenario in other words reduces to the scenario of self-replicating machines. To this point, it might be objected that as digitalized beings have no need for food or water or even air, they would not necessarily find Earth any more favourable a habitation than inert bodies like the moon or Mars. Maybe so, but there is no evidence they have colonized those bodies either.

There is at least one other reason advanced civilizations might decide to cease any communication beyond their own star. It is the Dark Forest scenario popularized by Chinese writer, Liu Cixon (2016). It shows up in his science fiction novel of the same name, the second volume of his trilogy, *Remembrance of Earth's Past*. My description of this scenario will be a bit of a spoiler for those who have not yet read the book. So if you think you will read it and that this revelation will spoil your enjoyment, you can afford to skip the rest of this subsection and move on to the next.

For those who have already read the book or who are otherwise still with me, Cixon imagines a kind of astral sociology that depicts the universe as a zero-sum game. In this game, expansion is a fundamental priority for each advanced civilization, but each can only expand at the expense of others. The result derives from game theoretical logic: when it can do so, any advanced civilization will pre-emptively destroy any potentially threatening neighbours of which it becomes aware. Thus, as Cixon describes it, the universe is like a forest in which shooters hunt each other in the dark. In such a dark forest, it is in the interest of each civilization to keep its own existence hidden.

In the book, Cixon's vision comes across with a startling power that is definitely disturbing. It is the kind of vision that worries Hawking (see Shostak 2016). Thus, our destruction by aliens must be listed as another possible end to humanity. On the other hand, perhaps because of my own predilections, I have great difficulty believing that something as immoral as routine geocide could be a normal accompaniment of advanced intelligence. Therefore, as powerfully compelling as Cixon's vision is, I just cannot accept it. We move on, therefore, to another, more conventional reason why an advanced civilization might go silent.

The doomsday scenario

As noted, one important reason why an advanced civilization might go silent is that it ceases to exist. It was a possibility entertained immediately, giving rise to the final factor of the Drake equation. And with climate change and other problems of our own civilization confronting us, it does seem a live prospect that advanced technological civilizations are given to self-destruction. Thus, it has been suggested, the norm might be for advanced civilizations to arise and flicker out. Perhaps then, we are currently alone, at least in our galaxy.

The further implication for humanity is that we do not have too much longer ourselves. If neither fire nor ice get us (i.e., global warming or nuclear winter), then perhaps the singularity will: the moment when the artificial intelligence we produce becomes so powerful that it gets rid of us.

The so-called singularity is yet another thing that worries Hawking (2017). The man had many worries. One possible objection to this worry is that humans could always pull the plug on the machines they create. Hawking responds, however, with a scenario in which people ask a superintelligent computer whether there is a God, to which question the computer answers, "There is now," and fuses the plug (Hawking 2017).

It could be replied to Hawking, however, that regardless of how intelligent the computer is, it would still have to have the physical capability of fusing the plug, and that no sensible humans would provide it with that ability. But again, not so fast. Sensible humans do a lot of nonsensical things – or at least things with unintended consequences that turn out to be very dangerous. Thus, as Hawking goes on to suggest himself, one likely path to the deleterious outcome he describes is the scenario from the movie *The Terminator*. As artificial intelligence applied to military applications allows it to choose and eliminate targets automatically, the odds are that it could run amok, turning itself on all humans and not just humanly designated enemies.

Whatever might get us, there is an argument well known among philosophers that suggests that humanity will not be around much longer. Although evidently first voiced again at Los Alamos by physicist Brandon Carter, it was first printed in a philosophy journal by the same John Leslie (1996) we encountered before. The rendition, however, offered by Bostrom (1997) and reprised by Korb and Oliver (1998) is perhaps more perspicuous.

To understand the reasoning, imagine you are presented with two urns, one containing ten numbered balls and the other a million. You are then presented with a ball picked randomly from one of these two urns, although you do not know from which. If the number the ball shows is 7, from which urn would you say the ball was most likely picked: the one with ten balls or the one with a million? It is much less likely that a ball so close to the start was picked from the urn with a million balls than from the urn with just ten.

Now apply the same reasoning to human birth order. If the human race goes on for eons so that we populate our entire solar system and perhaps even others, we would expect there to be by the end of human history perhaps a trillion humans who have ever lived. If so, then a priori, we should expect our own birth order to be up there somewhere in the hundreds of billions. Instead, we find ourselves at 60 billion. The a posteriori conclusion is that our birth has been drawn from an urn of many fewer total human lives, which suggests that humanity does not have that much longer to go.

There continues to be much discussion about the soundness of this argument. Suffice it to say here that it remains one possible post-human future, the future that Wells's time traveller found beyond the Eloi at the very end of his road.

Are we indeed alone?

As preposterous as my mother finds it, there are actually good grounds to suppose we are alone not just in the galaxy but even the entire observable universe (Gribbin 2011, Morris 2003, Ward & Brownlee 2003). Yes, there are billions and billions of stars out there just in our galaxy and as many comparable galaxies in the observable universe as there are stars in our own. It is true as well that many stars seem to have planets.

So what is the problem? Let us begin with our solar system. In our system, Earth is the only planet that seems to harbour life. One reason for that is that Earth is the only planet in our star's habitable zone, the zone that continuously allows liquid water so necessary for life as we know it, which obviously is the only kind of life we can discuss.

It is not so easy to be in a star's habitable zone, which depends on the star's mass. Most stars comparable to our sun are part of binary systems (i.e., systems in which two stars orbit each other), pulling any extant planets into irregular orbits that continually move them outside habitable zones.

Stars considerably more massive than our sun burn out too quickly – in millions rather than billions of years – so that intelligent life has no time to evolve on any surrounding planets. Of the remaining stars in singular systems, about 85% are red dwarfs, at least a quarter less massive than our sun. Because of their small size, rocky planets like our Earth are more observable around red dwarfs. Thus, observations of planets around them have stimulated much excitement about their prospects for life.

That excitement, however, is overblown. Because red dwarfs are so much less massive than our sun, they burn considerably cooler. The consequence is that their habitable zones are much closer to the star itself (Choi 2014). A big problem with that proximity is propensity for what is called tidal locking. Tidal locking is when the rotation of a smaller body matches its revolution around a larger body. In other words, a single day on a tidally locked planet coincides with what we would call a year, that is a complete circuit of the star around which the planet revolves. Our own moon is tidally locked in this way with Earth, which is why we never see its so-called dark side. Similarly, a tidally locked planet will show only one hemisphere to its star, the other being continually shrouded in darkness.

There are at least two problems for life with such tidal locking. One problem is that with such a slow rotation on its axis, tidally locked planets produce only weak magnetic fields, quite unlike the strong protective polarity our Earth enjoys. The other problem is that the dark hemisphere of the planet tends to freeze, while the other hemisphere can become so hot that any water boils off, producing a runaway greenhouse effect such as presumably befell Venus (Glister 2017). The other problem is that with such close proximity to the star and only a weak magnetic field, the orbiting planet's entire atmosphere is in great danger of being stripped away by stellar wind (Williams 2017). So although red dwarfs appear to the be the most common stars in our galaxy, they offer far less prospect for life.

So far, we have seen the billions of billions of stars potentially offering life are reduced by about 85% (Gribbin 2011: 87). But we are just beginning with the relevant considerations. Another consideration is galactic location. Our Milky Way is a spiral galaxy, shaped like two fried eggs lain back to back with a dense cluster of stars at the centre surrounded by thin swirling arms.

Our sun lies at the edge of one of those outer, swirling arms. This location is sometimes described as a galactic backwater, as if we should expect life closer to or at the galactic metropolis. Just the opposite is the case. On the one hand, were our sun located much farther out, there would have been insufficient stellar density to produce the succession of previous stars that manufactured the heavy elements that constitute our Earth and even us, who truly are made of stardust.

On the other hand, we could not exist very much nearer to the galactic centre. In the central, yolk portion of our galaxy, there is just too much nova activity. Were a star to go nova even 30 light years distant from Earth, the ensuing radiation would eradicate all life here (Gribbin 2011: 72). Thus, even if non-microbial life were continually to restart at or near the centre, it would just as continually be eradicated by the activity of nearby novae.

To reprise, so far, we are down to a galactic habitable zone that comprises a narrow band including just 10% of the galaxy's stars (Gribbin 2011: 770), and eliminating the red dwarfs and binary systems in this region, we are down to about 0.6% of Milky Way stars being even eligible (Gribbin 2011: 87, 89).

And yet, there are other contingencies making life, especially advanced life – let alone intelligent life – unlikely. Consider that throughout its history, life on Earth has suffered at least five mass extinctions, each wiping out upwards of 75% of extant species. The last of these mass extinctions, dooming the dinosaurs, was due to the climactic impact of an asteroid hitting the Earth. We are shielded from much more frequent such impacts because of giant Jupiter being situated just where it is in the solar system and because of the presence of our moon (Gribbin 2011, Ward & Brownlee 2003). The moon's craters indicate how much would otherwise have hit us, and Jupiter's gravitational pull not only absorbs many other would-be missiles that could have come our way but also diverts others from our direction.

In, however, many of the planetary systems so far discovered, giants like Jupiter are located much closer in toward their star. So in such systems, an otherwise habitable planet lacks both a big brother planet and a sizable moon to shoo away life-resetting bombardments. Our strangely large moon, itself an accident of collision, further serves to stabilize Earth's rotational tilt, without which terrestrial temperatures would be continually disrupted.

There are still other considerations that make Earth distinctly habitable. One is size. For a variety of reasons, a habitable planet must be at least a third as massive as the Earth and at most twice so, which excludes most of the extra-solar planets discovered that are mistakenly called 'super earths' because, although they are rocky, they exceed twice terrestrial mass (Siegel 2017). It is also important that an Earth-like planet share Earth's distinctive plate tectonics, which is not the case for Mars, Venus or our moon.

Even beyond all the contingencies that make our habitable niche so rare, the evolution of intelligent life may be quite improbable. Far from *Homo sapiens* being an evolutionary inevitability, Stephen Jay Gould (1992) argued that if we re-ran the evolutionary process countless times, we would not again show up. Instead, so much of evolution seems to depend on chance contingencies.

Life itself, at least at the microbial level, may well be inevitable. That conclusion at any rate is suggested from our sample of size 1. The fossil evidence shows life on Earth going back three and a half billion years. The inference is that life appeared as soon as the Earth cooled enough to allow it. Of course, it is still entirely unknown what made this development possible, as the transition from non-life to life is a gap of enormous complexity. There is as well a further mystery: as we all descended from the same unicellular ancestor, it seems life arose only once. Why is that?

If Earth's experience is any guide, then while unicellular life may be common in the universe, advanced multicellular life likely is not (Cobb 2016, Gribbin 2011, Morris 2003, Ward & Brownlee 2003). Instead there are a number of improbable threshold events that must be crossed. One is the development of eukaryotic cells (i.e., cells with nuclei and mitochondria). All multicellular life descends from them. But eukaryotes are not an inevitable development. In fact, after the almost immediate appearance of prokaryotic cells, it took another two billion years for eukaryotes to appear. And even then, it appears to have been a total accident – one kind of bacteria taking up residence within one larger, the two somehow fusing into one. Again, judging from the DNA evidence, this seems to have occurred only once (Cobb 2016).

Even with eukaryotes, the development of multicellular life was not exactly a given. Although in this case it does seem to have arisen multiple times, it still took a billion years for it to take hold (Cobb 2016). And even then it took the so-called Cambrian explosion of biological diversity for complex natural selection to take over.

With multiple mass extinction events wiping out nearly all multicellular life forms, Gould argues that it was only a contingency that our remote ancestor survived. And it took even another mass extinction some 340 million years ago to eliminate the dinosaurs so as to open the niche for the mammals leading to us. So even on a habitable planet, the probability of intelligent life may be low. So it seems very likely, especially given the absence of any already galaxy-level colonization, that we are the only intelligent life in this galaxy.

Of course, as noted, there are billions and billions of galaxies out there. So even if we are the only intelligent life in this galaxy, might there not still be intelligent life elsewhere in the observable universe?

There might be intelligent life in other galaxies, but again the probabilities are not as high as the raw numbers might suggest. Long-duration bursts of gamma rays, lasting tens of seconds to minutes, release more energy in that short time than will our sun in its ten-billion-year lifetime. With that firepower in that short span, gamma ray bursts could destroy all the ozone layers of otherwise habitable planets throughout the entire galaxies in which they occur (Cho 2014, Grant 2015,

Loeb et al. 2016, Piran et al. 2018). Although such gamma ray bursts are relatively rare, that can still mean one every several hundred million years. It is even suspected that Earth's Ordovician mass distinction 340 million years ago stemmed from such a burst. Other galaxies seem more vulnerable to gamma ray bursts than our own. The upshot is that only 10% of galaxies may be at all supportive of complex life beyond the microbial (Cho 2014).

Suppose, however, that intelligent life millions or even billions of years ahead of us did arise long ago in a galaxy far, far away. Let us call it Lucas Land. Contemplating what that civilization might be like now is comparable to contemplating what we might be like should we continue a million years hence. There is a widespread expectation that such civilization will be largely post-human and likely even post-biological. It is also expected to be expansionist (Ćirković 2018). This expectation goes back again to the whole notion of self-replicating robots sent out to colonize other worlds and is enshrined in what is called the Kardashev scale.

The Kardashev scale was originated in 1964 by Soviet astrophysicist Nikolai Kardashev. It identifies three levels of advanced civilization potentially observable across galaxies by the level of energy they are able to deploy. A Type I civilization is able to access the total energy capacity of its home planet, something that humanity might attain only hundreds of years from now.

Type II civilizations can employ what are called Dyson spheres – after physicist Freeman Dyson – to access all the energy of its home star. Dyson thought it logical that advanced civilizations would construct light-catching megastructures around their stars to capture the energy for interstellar travel (see Wikipedia 2018). Because these structures would alter the light emitted by the star, their presence would be something we could detect (Wikipedia 2018). Type III civilizations would be able to apply the same or even more advanced technology to the whole or large parts of an entire galaxy.

According to Dyson, both advanced types of civilization should be detectable by characteristically unnatural emissions of mid-infrared radiation. As it happens, however, thousands of likely galaxies have now been searched for such radiation (Garrett 2015, Sci News 2015, Olsen 2018) without finding any that cannot be explained in natural ways that do not involve intelligent manipulation. Thus, as astronomer Michael Garrett concludes, "Kardashev Type III civilizations are either very rare or do not exist in the local universe," by which he means the entire gigantic universe we are able to observe. As Garrett goes on to tell *Sci News* (2015), "It's a bit worrying that Type III civilizations don't seem to exist. It's not what we would predict from the physical laws that explain so well the rest of the physical universe."

It is unclear what physical laws Garrett is considering that would predict the existence of Type III civilizations. Whether or not such civilizations should exist would seem on the contrary to depend on considerations that have little to do with physical laws. As even Garrett himself goes on to speculate (*Sci News* 2015), galactic expansion may not be on the agenda of advanced civilizations. As we have seen others also ask, what would be the point? Particularly if advanced civilizations are post-biological, we should not presume they are going to be governed by the same motivations that direct biological beings. Even if a civilization could colonize the galaxy over the course of millennia, the colonies would still be unable to communicate or transact anything in any practical way. And as Dartnell points out, contrary to the worries of Hawking and others like him, if a civilization were so advanced as to be able to colonize the galaxy, it would also be advanced enough not to need to. For that reason, it is also unlikely, were a civilization able to reach us from another star or especially another galaxy, that it would need the resources of the Earth or the planet itself or human beings as food or slaves. It rather reflects our own baseness that we expect a visiting civilization to be hostile.

Motivations aside, there is still the question of whether life or at least intelligent life is exceedingly rare. It does not seem to violate any physical laws to suppose that it might actually take a universe as large as ours for intelligent life to emerge even once. If so, then as I have said, our human life and what we do with it becomes even more precious. Perhaps then, too, our human bodies as well are something to be honoured and preserved. Who and what we are or will be becomes a solemn responsibility.

And yet . . .

Having followed for a long time the considerations of the previous section, I was fairly convinced that we are alone in the universe. And as a practicing Catholic (of sorts), I actually was very comfortable with this idea. It strikes me as hardly credible either that the denizens of other planets need our Jesus or, as Ray Bradbury once suggested, that God incarnates himself similarly on all other inhabited worlds. As far as religion is concerned, I think the consequences of discovering alien life would be most upsetting for Christianity. Evangelicals seem capable of blocking out all extrabiblical reality, but were we to encounter an extraterrestrial civilization, intellectually honest Christians would have to reevaluate the significance of Jesus. I confess that in preparation for that eventuality, I have already done so.

I mention this personal background to emphasize that, unlike my mother and my sisters whose convictions I have always pooh-poohed, I never believed that UFOs signified alien visitation, nor was I inclined even to welcome that belief. I still do not entirely welcome it, but I do now tend to believe it.

What changed? I started to read a book by investigative reporter Leslie Kean, the journalist who helped break a 2017 story for the *New York Times* that, despite Pentagon professions that UFOs are "not worth studying," the Pentagon has a long-standing program doing just that (see Blumenthal 2017). Years before, Kean (2010) produced the book I was reading, her best-selling *UFOs: Generals, Pilots, and Government Officials Go on the Record*. The book is less by Kean than compiled by her, as the various chapters are by others. Most are testimonies of different witnesses in their own voices – witnesses that include military pilots and officers, even generals and admirals and high-ranking officials from our own and other governments. Among the latter is a former head of Britain's own version of the X-Files, established by its Ministry of Defence.

As I started to read this compelling book, I emailed my friend Alexander Wendt, who as an originator of the social constructionist approach to international relations is one of the most cited social scientists in the world. He has long pursued fascinating scholarly directions off the beaten path, like his recently released *Quantum Mind and Social Science* (Wendt 2015).

Wendt is also well known for an earlier, courageous article that took UFOs seriously (see Wendt & Duvall 2008). So I asked Wendt if he had heard of this book. He replied that he had not only heard of it but had a chapter in it. And sure enough, when I looked again, near the end, there he was.

I mention Wendt's inclusion because I know academics are wont to dismiss reports of UFOs. As I say, I was too. Even now, as noted before, cosmologists still often invoke the Fermi paradox to cast doubt on the existence of extraterrestrial intelligence. If it is out there, why hasn't it visited us?

Well, why not accept that extraterrestrial intelligence has and still is visiting us? It is true that we do not see colonies of self-replicating robots about, but perhaps such colonies are either impossible or undesirable. It is also true, as is commonly said, that about 95% of UFOs are explainable in natural, prosaic ways, but that figure still leaves plenty well beyond such explanation.

Begin as Kean does with the so-called COMETA report, named after a French association – including scientists and 13 former French generals – that released it in 1999. The report detailed anomalous objects "observed at close range by pilots, tracked on radar, and officially photographed" (Kean 2010: 1). The report concluded that these reported examples of the 5% unexplained UFOs "seem to be 'completely unknown flying machines with exceptional performances that are guided by a natural or artificial intelligence'" (Kean 2010: 1). As Kean goes on to say, the report concluded that these objects were most likely of extraterrestrial origin.

After Kean's introduction, she presents the testimony of Belgian Major General Wilfried de Brouwer, former head of operations of Belgian Air Staff, which tells of a wave of encounters with low-flying UFOs between 1990 and 1991, experienced by thousands of people, including on one night two independent pairs of policemen and on another an F-16 launched to investigate. A year later, a similar wave of sightings took place in Britain, some near an air force base and seen by high-ranking military personnel.

From there, Kean offers a brief chapter on a report on UFOs in relation to aviation safety issued by Dr. Richard Haines, former head of NASA's Human Factors branch. This report details over a hundred pilot contacts with UFOs, many accompanied by confirming ground communication and radar detection. Haines, who describes himself as originally sceptical about UFOs, says his research converted him into a believer that some are of extraterrestrial origin.

A number of the incidents described at length in the book took place over Australia, one connected with a plane's disappearance after a prolonged communication with flight control. Another UFO was captured both by ground radar and on film by a television crew that happened to be onboard. The well-documented encounters come, however, from everywhere: England, Spain, Portugal, Chile, Costa Rica, Brazil and so on.

Kean even presents the testimony of two military pilots who actually engaged in dogfights with UFOs. One, a major in the Iranian Air Force at the time, had been ordered to investigate a UFO near Tehran. Recounted by the pilot, Parviz Jafari, now a retired general, the incident began when air traffic control alerted the deputy general at Air Force Command of sightings of a UFO circling Tehran at low altitude. Seeing it himself and knowing no air traffic was supposed to be in the area at that time, the deputy general scrambled an F-4 to investigate. When it approached the object, flashing different colours brilliantly, the jet's radar and communication instruments ceased to function.

Jafari and a backseat co-pilot were then sent up in their own jet. As they approached, the same thing happened: much of their instrumentation shut down, although not before they managed to fix the object on radar. Moving several degrees instantaneously on several occasions, the object then released what looked like a brilliant missile headed toward Jafari's craft, forcing him to bank away. What had looked like a missile then returned to the main UFO. When Jafari moved away from the object on orders to return, the instrumentation came back online. The other jet reported the same experience. From first sighting to the object's eventual disappearance, the incident lasted for several hours. There was evidently a US Air Force military advisor on hand who issued a report on the matter to the CIA. Subsequent US officials judged the case a paradigm instance of military-concerning UFO activity.

Oscar Santa María Huertas, a retired Chilean general and former fighter pilot, reports having actually shot at a UFO. The UFO appeared one morning in restricted airspace near a military runway. He was ordered to scramble his Sukhoi-22 jet and bring it down. Santa María describes firing at the object without effect and then chasing it up and down the sky while the object continued to evade him, sometimes at enormous speed. As Santa María got closer, he was able to see that it was not the balloon it had originally appeared to be but a metallic saucer shape with a dome on top. Finally, low on fuel, Santa María returned to base while the object remained in place for another two hours. This well-documented incident eventually made its way even to a report of the US Defense Department.

To me, all these reports seem compelling. Yet, the Fermi paradox is still routinely trotted out without mention of them. It raises a question of what is considered scientific evidence. A fitting radio signal from a SETI telescope would qualify, but documented reports from pilots, generals and police officers do not. We see the same suspicion of even first-hand reports when it comes to convergent near-death experiences. Some sort of scientism seems operative here, but that is the subject for a different paper.

Where does this all leave us?

On the one hand, there are all sorts of considerations suggesting we are alone in the universe. Besides other grounds, we certainly find no evidence of the expected galactic colonization by self-replicating robots, nor do we see in other galaxies (or, presumably, in our own) evidence of the large-scale engineering expected of very advanced civilizations.

As I have said, if we are truly alone in the universe, then I think we and our human bodies assume much greater importance. What we do with our human bodies then becomes a much more significant matter.

But on the other hand, we have this UFO evidence of alien visitation. Taking that evidence seriously raises a lot of questions. Given the odds against intelligent life elsewhere and the paucity of astronomic evidence for it, whence come these visitors? Are they from a single civilization or several? Reported differences in UFO design could suggest the latter.

Presuming in any case that our visitors come from very far away, how did they manage even to find us? And what do they want? As I observed before, it seems unlikely that they are hostile. First, if our visitors are that advanced, they would hardly need to cross the universe for slaves or land or food. Nor do I find it likely that they would be motivated by pure malice. Over the hundreds of UFO sightings, furthermore, including instances where they have been attacked, they show little evidence of hostility. And given reports of so-called foo fighters by World War II bombers, the visitations seem to have gone on long enough for them to initiate hostilities were they so inclined.

So what do these visitors want? I also find the zoo theory hard to accept – the theory that they come as tourists to observe us as we do animals in a zoo. For one thing, were that the case, I would expect a lot more traffic than is observed and, when some traffic is observed, less evidence of coordinated flight. Another question, however, is if they are so smart, why do they allow themselves to be seen at all? And when they are seen, why apparently play with us? It does not all make sense.

A related question is what these visitors achieve by flying around over us. If they are capable of artificially constructing humanoids, then it would seem they would gain much more knowledge of us by infiltrating our ranks instead of just circulating around above. So might they be among us as in the science fiction film *They Live*? Might Donald Trump and Boris Johnson actually be extraterrestrials?

Although the last reflections may be too far-fetched, these questions are all intriguing. Except perhaps for that last far-fetched reflection, they are nevertheless off the point of this chapter. I have pursued the question of alien life to help imagine what we might become in a million years. That leads me to ask what our visitors seem to be like. Whether robots or not, they seem not to be self-replicating, nor much interested in colonizing our solar system. They specifically seem more interested in studying us than in occupying empty planets like Mars.

Could it be that the UFO crafts themselves are artificially intelligent? Presumably, like even our own contemporary airplanes, much of the crafts' behaviour is automatic. So, as also with contemporary cruise missiles, some intelligence must be built into the craft. At the same time, reports of domes and even windows suggest that the craft are also carrying intelligent beings separate from them.

Could UFO passengers be robots? They could be, but insofar as they seem to be more observers than replicators, they presumably also have some quick way to return to wherever they come from. I say that because such observation does not seem something that would be done by permanently isolated individuals but in service to some larger collective. And if the visitors can in fact quickly return to wherever they came from, then that trip might well be something that can be accomplished within a reasonable span of the lifetime of some organic life.

We return to the final far-fetched question above. If we presume that no extra-terrestrial aliens roam among us, then perhaps we should also presume that it is because they cannot, at least not practically, construct intelligent organic machines. And if not, perhaps we should presume that they too are not intelligent machines, organic or not. And if they, a million years or more ahead of us continue to remain in their initial biologically evolved form, perhaps there is reason to expect that humanity, should we endure as long, will as well – in which case, perhaps I am not a post-humanist after all.

References

Archer, M. S. (2003). *Structure, agency, and the internal conversation.* New York: Cambridge University Press.

Blumenthal, R. (2017, December 18). On the trail of a secret pentagon UFO program. *The New York Times.* Retrieved from www.nytimes.com/2017/12/18/insider/secret-pentagon-ufo-program.html?rref=collection%2Fbyline%2Fralph-blumenthal&action=click&contentCollection=undefined&region=stream&module=stream_unit&version=latest&contentPlacement=6&pgtype=collection

Bostrom, N. (1997). The doomsday argument is alive and kicking. *Mind, 108*(431), 539–550.

Bostrom, N. (2016). *Superintelligence: Paths, dangers, strategies.* New York: Oxford University Press.

Braidotti, R. (2013). *The posthuman.* Cambridge: Polity Press.

Cho, A. (2014). Complex life may be possible in only 10% of all galaxies. *Science.* Retrieved from www.sciencemag.org/news/2014/11/complex-life-may-be-possible-only-10-all-galaxies

Choi, C. (2014). Habitable zones near red dwarf stars smaller than previously thought. *SciTechDaily.* Retrieved from https://scitechdaily.com/habitable-zones-near-red-dwarf-stars-smaller-previously-thought/

Ćirković, M. (2018). Enhancing a person, enhancing a civilization: A research program at the intersection of bioethics, future studies, and astrobiology. *Cambridge Quarterly of Healthcare Ethics, 26*(3), 459–468.

Cixon, L. (2016). *The dark forest.* New York: Tor.

Cobb, M. (2016). Alone in the universe: The improbability of alien civilizations. In J. Al-Khalili (Ed.), *Aliens: The world's leading scientists on the search for extraterrestrial life* (pp. 156–168). New York: Picador.

Collier, A. (1999). *Being and worth.* New York: Cambridge University Press.

Dartnell, L. (2016). (Un)welcome visitors: Why aliens might visit us. In J. Al-Khalili (Ed.), *Aliens: The world's leading scientists on the search for extraterrestrial life* (pp. 25–34). New York: Picador.

Dvorsky, G. (2018). Why you should upload yourself to a supercomputer. *Daily Explainer.* Retrieved from https://io9.gizmodo.com/why-you-should-upload-yourself-to-a-supercomputer-1497856380

Dyson, F. (2018). *Goodreads*. Retrieved from www.goodreads.com/quotes/309377-the-more-i-examine-the-universe-and-the-details-of

Ellis, G. (2011). *Does the multiverse exist?* Retrieved from www.scientificamerican.com/article/does-the-multiverse-really-exist/

Garrett, M. (2015). Application of the mid-IR radio correlation to the Ĝ sample and the search for advanced extraterrestrial civilisations. *Astronomy/Astrophysics, 581*. Retrieved from www.aanda.org/articles/aa/abs/2015/09/aa26687-15/aa26687-15.html

Gefter, A. (2017, June 1). The inflated debate over cosmic inflation. *Nautilus*. Retrieved from http://nautil.us/issue/48/chaos/the-inflated-debate-over-cosmic-inflation

Glister, P. (2017, December 1). Problems with red dwarf habitable zones. *Centauri Dreams*. Retrieved from www.centauri-dreams.org/2017/12/01/problems-with-red-dwarf-habitable-zones/

Gould, S. J. (1992). *Bully for brontosaurus: Reflections in natural history*. New York: W. W. Norton.

Grant, A. (2015). Gamma-ray bursts may repeatedly wipe out life. *Science News*. Retrieved from www.sciencenews.org/article/gamma-ray-bursts-may-repeatedly-wipe-out-life

Gribbin, J. (2011). *Alone in the universe: Why our planet is unique*. New York: Wiley.

Hawking, S. (2017). *Brief answers to big questions*. New York: Random House.

Holder, R. (2016). *God, the multiverse, and everything: Modern cosmology and the argument from design*. New York: Routledge.

Howell, E. (2018, April 27). Fermi paradox: Where are the aliens? *Space.com*. Retrieved from www.space.com/25325-fermi-paradox.html

Kean, L. (2010). *UFOs: Generals, pilots, and government officials go on the record*. New York: Three Rivers Press.

Korb, K. B., & Oliver, J. J. (1998). A refutation of the doomsday argument. *Mind, 107*(426), 403–410.

Leslie, J. (1989). *Universes*. New York: Routledge.

Leslie, J. (1996). *The end of the world*. New York: Routledge.

Lewis, G. F., & Barnes, L. A. (2016). *A fortunate universe: Life in a finely tuned cosmos*. Cambridge: Cambridge University Press.

Loeb, A., Batista, R., & Sloan, D. (2016). *Relative likelihood for life as a function of cosmic time*. Retrieved from https://arxiv.org/pdf/1606.08448.pdf

Maccarini, A. (2019). *Deep change and emergent structures in global society*. New York: Springer.

McFarlane, C. (2013). Relational sociology: Theoretical inhumanism, and the problem of the nonhuman. In C. Powell & F. Dépelteau (Eds.), *Conceptualizing relational sociology* (pp. 45–66). New York: Palgrave Macmillan.

More, M. (2013). The philosophy of transhumanism. In M. More & N. Vita-More (Eds.), *The transhumanist reader* (pp. 3–17). New York: Wiley-Blackwell.

Morris, S. C. (2003). *Life's solutions: Inevitable humans in a lonely universe*. New York: Cambridge University Press.

Olsen, J. S. (2018). Estimates for the number of visible galaxy-spanning civilizations and the Cosmological expansion of life. arXiv preprint arXiv:1507.05969, 2015 - arxiv.org.

Patton, P. (2015, April 8). Beyond "Fermi's paradox" II: Questioning the Hart-Tipler conjecture. *Universe Today*. Retrieved from www.universetoday.com/119735/beyond-fermis-paradox-ii-questioning-the-hart-tipler-conjecture/

Piran, T., Jimenez, R., Cuesta, A. J., Simpson, F., & Verde, L. (2018). *Cosmic explosions, life in the universe and the cosmological constant*. Retrieved from https://arxiv.org/pdf/1508.01034.pdf

Porpora, D. (2017). Dehumanization in theory: Anti-humanism, non-humanism, post-humanism and trans-humanism. *Journal of Critical Realism, 16*, 353–367.

Porpora, D. (2018). Vulcans, Klingons, and humans: What does humanism encompass? In *Ex Machina: The future of humanity*. New York: Routledge.

Prisco, G. (2012, December 13). Why we should send uploaded astronauts on interstellar missions. *IO9*. Retrieved from https://io9.gizmodo.com/5968280/why-we-should-send-uploaded-astronauts-on-interstellar-missions

Sci News. (2015, September 17). Astronomer finds no evidence of Kardashev type III civilizations in local universe. Retrieved from www.sci-news.com/astronomy/science-kardashev-type-iii-civilizations-03249.html

Shostak, S. (2016, September 27). Why Stephen Hawking is light years away from the truth about "dangerous aliens." *The Guardian*. Retrieved from www.theguardian.com/commentisfree/2016/sep/27/stephen-hawking-light-years-dangerous-aliens

Siegel, E. (2017). There's no such thing as a "habitable super-earth." *Forbes*. Retrieved from www.forbes.com/sites/startswithabang/2017/02/16/super-earths-are-common-but-incapable-of-supporting-life-like-ours/#12ce66d14188

Smith, C. (2010). *What is a person? Rethinking humanity, social life, and the moral good for the bottom up*. Chicago, IL: The University of Chicago Press.

Ward, P., & Brownlee, D. (2003). *Rare earth: Why complex life is rare in the universe*. New York: Copernicus.

Wells, H.G. (1958). The man of the year million. In *Nineteenth century fiction*. Berkeley, CA: University of California.

Wells, H.G. (2018). *The time machine*. Scotts Valley, CA: CreateSpace Independent Publishing Platform.

Wendt, A. (2015). *Quantum mind and social science: Unifying physical and social ontology*. New York: Cambridge University Press.

Wendt, A., & Duvall, R. (2008). Sovereignty and the UFO. *Political Theory, 56*(4), 607–633.

Wikipedia. (2018). Dyson sphere. Retrieved from https://en.wikipedia.org/wiki/Dyson_sphere#Search_for_megastructures

Williams, M. (2017, July 14). Even though red dwarfs have long lasting habitable zones, they'd be brutal to life. *Universe Today*. Retrieved from www.universetoday.com/136451/even-though-red-dwarfs-long-lasting-habitable-zones-theyd-brutal-life/

Index

Page numbers in *italics* and **bold** indicate Figures and Tables, respectively.

Printed in the United States
By Bookmasters